Treasures of the Tropics

Please join the Guild Members of
Hibiscus Children's Center in a celebration
of the finest recipes of Florida's Treasure Coast.

The Hibiscus Guilds of Martin and Indian River Counties are made up of women brought together by their commitment to making children's lives free from abuse and neglect through promoting awareness, hosting fundraisers and volunteering many long hours in the various programs offered by Hibiscus Children's Center. All proceeds from the sale of this cookbook will go directly to the Center.

Copyright Pending by HCC
The Hibiscus Children's Center
First Printing   March, 2001   10,000 copies
ISBN Number: 0-9704715-0-5
LCCCN: 00109643

Information on obtaining additional copies of
Treasures of the Tropics
may be found at the back of the cookbook or by contacting:

The Hibiscus Children's Center
P.O. Box 305
Jensen Beach, Florida 34958
(561) 334-9311 office
(561) 334-1991 fax

The cover of **Treasures of the Tropics** was generously donated by artist Margaret Gray. The Hibiscus Children's Center Guilds wish to thank her for so graciously illustrating our theme.

Printed in the USA by
WIMMER
The Wimmer Companies
Memphis
1-800-548-2537

Categories

Appetizers 7

Breads and Brunch
Breads 31
Coffee Cakes 37
Brunch Fare 38

Soup and Salad
Soups 45
Chowder and Chili 53
Side Salads 54
Main Course Salad 70
Dressings 80

Fish and Shellfish
Fish 83
Shellfish 99

Poultry, Meat and Meatless
Meatless 111
Chicken and Turkey 120
Beef 142
Veal 155
Pork 160
Lamb 166

Side Dishes
Vegetables 169
Rice and Pasta 187

Desserts
Cakes 193
Cheesecakes and Custards 207
Pies and Pastry 216
Cookies, Candy and Ice Cream 228
Dessert Sauces 242

Marinades, Sauces and Salsas
Marinades 245
Sauces and Spreads 247
Salsas 252

Cookbook Development Committee
Committees 255
Restaurant Contributors 257
About the Artists 258

Index 263

Reorder Coupon 287

Hibiscus Children's Center began fifteen years ago as La Vaughn Tilton's dream. Today, it proudly saves thousands of the Treasure Coast's most vulnerable children through the efforts of hundreds of people. The newest Hibiscus venture is **Treasures of the Tropics**. Our hope is that it will prove to be a valued addition to any kitchen and ultimately will provide continued financial assistance in our efforts to prevent and reduce child abuse on the Treasure Coast. Our mission is accomplished through the following programs:

HIBISCUS CHILDREN'S SHELTER is a fully licensed residential child caring facility that provides safe haven for abused and neglected children and newborns removed from their homes through a court order. Here, the children receive 24-hour "awake" supervision, as well as comprehensive medical, dental and psychological care. These emotionally fragile children are nurtured, encouraged and counseled by the caring staff with the hope of bringing normality to their lives- celebrating birthdays, helping with meals, doing their homework.

HIBISCUS CRISIS NURSERY is a voluntary, abuse prevention program providing family support and respite services to families in crisis. Our shelter maintains eight beds for kids needing respite care. Through this short-term program, options are available to reduce the stressful impact of poverty, unemployment, a medical emergency or other factors that may precipitate child abuse. The goal of the program is to keep the problem from escalating into abuse and neglect.

HIBISCUS FAMILY BUILDERS is an in-home counseling and support program for families referred to Hibiscus through the child protection system. By working with parents and children intensively, in their own environment, a family builders counselor helps resolve the crisis that has led to abuse- to keep them together as a family. By teaching coping skills, and a host or other strategies, the family builders model promotes parental autonomy and helps reduce dependency on the child welfare system.

These wonderful programs have helped keep children safe, remove the risk of further abuse of children and kept families free of abuse and neglect. Hibiscus Children's Center has a great legacy of care and service on the Treasure Coast, all made possible by the generous support of our community. Your purchase of this cookbook will play a role in the continuation of this legacy of service, care and support for children. Enjoy and Bon Appetit'...

Dear Friends,

Treasures of the Tropics is the culmination of a two- year labor of love on the part of the Hibiscus Martin and Indian River Guilds. It contains tried and true recipes submitted by a diverse group of people committed to the cause of fighting child abuse. Our hope is that you will love these dishes as much as the individuals who submitted them as their "favorites."

Hibiscus Children's Center has always been blessed by a tremendous amount of community support. Hibiscus would never have become a reality if it were not for the creativity and energy of a group of concerned volunteers who saw a need to build a home of safety for abused children. You will find that same energy and creativity in the pages of this book. It is one more example of the ongoing dedication and commitment provided by Treasure Coast communities in fighting child abuse.

Our hope is that you will share this creation with your friends and loved ones and will continue the legacy of support for Hibiscus Children's Center that this community began in 1985 with the building of the shelter. Our deepest appreciation goes out to the many volunteers who made this publication a reality and to all who purchase it in support of Hibiscus Children's Center.

"Tastefully" yours,

Jill Borowicz, CEO
Hibiscus Children's Center

HIBISCUS CHILDREN'S CENTER DONATION FORM

Enclosed is my gift of $ _____

Name: _____

Address: _____

City: _____

State: _____ Zip: _____

Phone (home) _____

    (work) _____

Make all checks payable to:
Hibiscus Children's Center.

Hibiscus Children's Center
P.O. Box 305
Jensen Beach, Florida 34958
(561) 334-9311
(561) 334-1991 FAX

American. Express/MasterCard/Visa Account #:

_____ Exp. Date _____

Your signature: _____

Please contact me with more information concerning:
❑ Hibiscus Children's Center Programs
❑ Wills, bequests, estate planning
❑ Hibiscus Children's Center Guild
   and Social Events
❑ Other _____
This gift is given in
❑ Memory of   ❑ Honor of

_____

Hibiscus appreciates your gift in any amount. Donations provide assistance to the emotionally fragile children that we serve.

Appetizers

MEG WINTER CARELL
Tropical Daydreams
Watercolor, 1999

Appetizers

Old English Cheese
  Hors d'oeuvres 7
Baked Nuts 7
Salted Pecans 8
New Year's Day Caviar 8
Cheese Wafers 9
Temptation Appetizers 9
Jalapeño Cheese Squares 9
Trio Pesto Goat Cheese Cake 10
Pesto and Sun-Dried
  Tomato Torte 11
Brie with Sun-Dried Tomatoes 12
Marinated Goat Cheese..................... 12
Boursin-Style Herb Cheese 13
Warm Spinach Dip 13
Parmesan Spinach Balls 14
Olive Spread on Crostini 14
Mushrooms in Patty Shells 15
Mushrooms à la Russe 15
Hot Pecan Spread 16
Cocktail Meatballs 16
Mini Beef Wellingtons 17
Pat's Pâté 17
Empanadas (Little Meat Pies) 18
Hot Chili Dip 18

Spicy Chicken Quesadillas 19
Miami Chicken Wings 19
Mont Blanc Chicken Spread.............. 20
Marinated Grilled Shrimp 20
Grilled Texas Shrimp........................ 21
Pickled Shrimp 21
Pickled Shrimp
  and Mushrooms 22
Shrimp Snacks 22
Shrimp Mould 23
Shrimp Bread 23
Shrimp Pesto Canapés 24
Shrimp Spread 24
Bay Scallop Ceviche 24
Conch Fritter 25
Party Salmon Ball 25
Clams Oreganatta 26
Crab Dip.. 26
Crabmeat Quarters 27
King Crab Puffs 27
Baked Crock of Artichoke,
  Brie and Lump Crab...................... 28
Hot Crab and Artichoke Dip.............. 29
Artichoke Crab Spread 29
Thai Pot Stickers 30

Old English
Cheese Hors d'oeuvres

2 cups margarine, softened	1 teaspoon onion powder
4 (5 ounce) jars Kraft Old English cheese spread	2 tablespoons dill weed
1½ teaspoons Worcestershire sauce	3 loaves Pepperidge Farm sandwich bread, crusts removed
1 teaspoon Tabasco sauce	

Combine all ingredients except bread; blend well. Spread 3 slices of bread with cheese mixture and stack. Cut stack into quarters. Ice top and sides of quarters with mixture and place on a baking sheet. Repeat with remaining cheese mixture and bread.

Freeze quarters on baking sheet, then transfer to zip-top bags and store in freezer until ready to use. To serve, preheat oven to 350 degrees. Place frozen quarters on a baking sheet and bake 15 minutes.

Baked Nuts

2 cups pecans	2 egg whites
1½ cups walnuts	1 cup sugar
½ cup margarine	Dash of salt

Preheat oven to 300 degrees. Combine pecans, walnuts and margarine in a shallow glass dish. Place in oven until margarine melts. Beat egg whites until stiff. Fold sugar and salt into whites.

Using a slotted spoon to reserve margarine in dish, remove nuts from dish and fold into meringue. Spread nut/meringue mixture over margarine in dish. Bake 30 minutes, stirring every 10 minutes.

Salted Pecans

"A staple at any New Orleans cocktail party."

2   cups pecans
4   tablespoons butter, melted
1   tablespoon Worcestershire
      sauce
10   drops Tabasco sauce
      Salt to taste

Preheat oven to 350 degrees. Combine all ingredients except salt and place in a deep baking pan.

Bake 10 minutes, stirring frequently. Remove from oven and drain on paper towels. While still warm, season to taste with salt.

New Year's Day Caviar

**Black-eyed peas are considered good luck
and served on New Year's Day.**

3   (16 ounce) cans black-eyed
      peas, drained
½   cup minced green bell pepper
½   cup minced red bell pepper
¾   cup minced hot pepper
¾   cup minced onion
¼   cup drained and minced
      pimento
1   clove garlic, chopped
⅓   cup red wine vinegar
⅔   cup olive oil
1   tablespoon Dijon mustard
      Salt to taste
      Tabasco sauce to taste
      Tortilla chips

Combine peas, peppers, onion, pimiento and garlic in a large mixing bowl. In a separate bowl, whisk together vinegar, oil and mustard. Pour over pea mixture and mix well. Season with salt and Tabasco sauce.

Using a wood spoon or potato masher, mash mixture slightly. Refrigerate until ready to serve. To serve, drain mixture well. Serve with tortilla chips.

Yield: 10 to 12 servings

Caviar can be refrigerated up to 5 days. Recipe doubles easily for large parties.

Cheese Wafers

"Everyone loves these!"

1 (10 ounce) stick sharp
  cheddar cheese, shredded
½ cup butter (not margarine)
1 cup flour

Dash of salt
½ teaspoon cayenne pepper or
  to taste

Combine all ingredients with a spoon or your hands. Shape mixture into walnut-size balls. Place on a baking sheet and freeze. When frozen, transfer to zip-top bags and store in freezer until ready to use.

To serve, preheat oven to 450 degrees. Place desired number of balls on a baking sheet and bake 15 minutes.

Temptation Appetizers

1 (8 ounce) package shredded
  cheddar cheese
1 (3 ounce) jar capers, drained
4 green onions, chopped

2 tablespoons mayonnaise, or
  enough to moisten
English muffins

Preheat broiler. Combine all ingredients except muffins. Spread mixture over muffins. Broil until bubbly. Cut into quarters and serve.

Jalapeño Cheese Squares

1 (7 ounce) can or jar jalapeño
  peppers, diced
8 ounces cheddar cheese,
  shredded

8 ounces Monterey Jack
  cheese, shredded
6 eggs, beaten

Preheat oven to 325 degrees. Line the bottom of a greased small square pan or dish with jalapeño peppers. Cover jalapeño peppers with cheeses. Pour eggs over the top. Bake 30 minutes.

For a milder version, substitute 1 can green chiles for the jalapeño peppers.

Trio Pesto Goat Cheese Cake

1 pound goat cheese
2 ounces Boursin cheese
12 ounces Parmesan cheese, grated
18 ounces pine nuts, toasted
3 ounces garlic, chopped
4 ounces arugula, washed and dried

4 ounces sun-dried tomatoes, rehydrated
4 ounces kalamata olives, pitted
10 ounces extra virgin olive oil, divided
Cracked black pepper to taste

Lightly blend goat and Boursin cheeses; do not over mix. Chill mixture. Combine Parmesan cheese, pine nuts and garlic in a food processor and puree. Divide mixture into three separate bowls. Puree one batch of garlic mixture with arugula in food processor. Puree another batch with tomatoes. Puree remaining batch with olives. As you finish each mixture, pour 3 ounces olive oil to each mixture and blend well. Separate the different pestos into the three bowls again.

Grease two 10 inch springform cake pans with olive oil. Press one-fourth of chilled goat cheese mixture into the bottom of one of the pans, being sure to cover the bottom evenly. Add a one-fourth inch thick layer of the olive pesto over the cheese layer. Press another one-fourth cheese layer into the other pan. Pop open the sides of the pan and carefully flip the cheese layer onto the olive pesto layer in the first pan. Repeat the steps until you have layers of goat cheese, olive pesto, goat cheese, arugula pesto, goat cheese, sun-dried tomato pesto and a final layer of goat cheese on top. Chill entire cake overnight.

Open sides of pan and flip the cake upside down onto a chilled plate. Remove pan. Drizzle remaining 1 ounce of olive oil over cake and sprinkle with black pepper. Serve with butter knives and breads or crackers.

Disney's Vero Beach Resort
9250 Island Grove Terrace
Vero Beach Florida

Pesto and Sun-Dried Tomato Torte

1 (8 ounce) package cream cheese, softened	½ cup Parmesan cheese
½ cup feta cheese, crumbled	2 cloves garlic, minced
1 tablespoon milk	¼ cup pine nuts
2 cloves garlic, minced	3 tablespoons olive oil
1 cup firmly packed basil leaves	2 tablespoons pine nuts, toasted
1 cup firmly packed parsley leaves	½ cup oil-packed sun-dried tomatoes, drained and diced

To make a filling, combine cream cheese, feta, milk and 2 cloves garlic in a food processor. Process until smooth. Set aside.

For the pesto, combine basil, parsley, Parmesan cheese, 2 cloves garlic, ¼ cup pine nuts and olive oil in a food processor. Pulse until almost smooth, stopping machine several times and scraping sides. Set aside.

To assemble, line a 3½ to 4 cup mold with plastic wrap. Sprinkle toasted pine nuts over bottom of mold. Spread one-fourth of filling evenly over the nuts. Carefully spread half the pesto on top. Add another fourth of filling. Sprinkle with tomatoes. Add remaining layer of filling, followed by a layer of remaining pesto. Cover and chill at least 4 hours or overnight. To serve, unmold onto a serving platter. Serve with toasted French bread slices or crackers.

Brie with Sun-Dried Tomatoes

1   (1 ounce) package fresh basil
2-3 cloves garlic
1   (8½ ounce) jar sun-dried
        tomatoes in oil, drained

⅓   cup pine nuts
2   (14 ounce) rounds Brie
        cheese

Preheat oven to 325 degrees. Combine basil and garlic in a food processor. Chop and transfer to a mixing bowl. Place tomatoes in food processor and chop. Add tomatoes to mixing bowl. Stir pine nuts into mixture.

Place cheese rounds in an ovenproof serving dish. Cover each round with basil mixture. Bake 10 to 15 minutes, watching closely to be sure cheese doesn't start to run. Serve with sliced French baguette or crackers.

Marinated Goat Cheese

4   (4 ounce) packages goat
        cheese
¾   cup extra virgin olive oil
4   bay leaves
1   tablespoon mixed green,
        black and white
        peppercorns

1½   tablespoons dried thyme
3   large cloves garlic, cut into
        slivers
3   tablespoons slivered fresh
        basil
1   tablespoon dried pink
        peppercorns

Place cheese on a flat baking dish or an ovenproof plate large enough so cheeses do not touch. Heat oil, bay leaves, mixed peppercorns and thyme in a small saucepan over medium-high heat until mixture sizzles and pops. Immediately remove from heat and pour over cheeses.

Scatter garlic in oil marinade. Sprinkle basil and pink peppercorns on top. Marinate in refrigerator overnight. Bring to room temperature when ready to serve. Serve with thin slices of toasted French bread.

Boursin-Style Herb Cheese

1½ (8 ounce) packages cream
    cheese
1 large clove garlic, finely
    minced
2 tablespoons white vermouth
1 tablespoon finely minced
    fresh parsley
½ teaspoon salt
1½ teaspoons finely minced
    fresh basil

1 teaspoon finely minced
    fresh tarragon
¾ teaspoon finely minced
    chives
1¼ teaspoons dried thyme
¾ teaspoon finely minced
    fresh sage
4 tablespoons unsalted butter

Combine all ingredients until smooth. Place in a crock or serving bowl and chill until ready to serve. Flavor improves with age; will keep about 10 days in refrigerator.

If only dried herbs are available, use one-third the amount of fresh.

Warm Spinach Dip

1 (10 ounce) can Rotel diced
    tomatoes and green chiles
1 (10 ounce) package frozen
    chopped spinach, thawed
    and squeezed dry
2½ cups shredded Monterey
    Jack cheese

1 (8 ounce) package cream
    cheese
1 cup half-and-half
1½ tablespoons red wine
    vinegar
½ teaspoon salt
⅛ teaspoon black pepper
    Paprika

Preheat oven to 400 degrees. Combine tomatoes and chiles, spinach, Monterey Jack cheese, cream cheese, half-and-half, vinegar, salt and pepper in a large bowl. Stir well.

Pour into a 10 inch round baking dish sprayed with cooking spray. Sprinkle with paprika. Bake 20 to 25 minutes or until hot and bubbly. Serve with tortilla chips.

Parmesan Spinach Balls

1	(10 ounce) package frozen chopped spinach	2	cups cornbread stuffing mix
2	large onions, chopped	5	eggs, beaten
¾	cup butter	½	cup Parmesan cheese
		1	tablespoon garlic salt

Preheat oven to 400 degrees. Cook and drain spinach. Sauté onion in butter until transparent. Combine spinach, onion mixture, stuffing mix, eggs, cheese and garlic salt.

Roll into walnut-size balls and place on a baking sheet. Bake 15 to 20 minutes.

Balls can be frozen on baking sheet before baking. Transfer frozen balls to a zip-top bag and store in freezer until ready to use.

Olive Spread on Crostini

1	(4½ ounce) can chopped black olives	3	cloves garlic
1	(8 ounce) jar pimiento-stuffed green olives, chopped	¾	cup shredded Monterey Jack cheese
½	cup shredded Parmesan cheese	¼	cup minced fresh Italian parsley
		1	loaf French baguette

Preheat broiler. In a medium bowl, combine black and green olives, Parmesan cheese and garlic. Stir in Monterey Jack cheese and parsley.

Cut baguette into ¼ inch slices. Spread olive mixture over slices and place on a baking sheet. Broil 3 minutes or until mixture is bubbly and crust is brown.

Mushrooms in Patty Shells

1	tablespoon butter	1	tablespoon Worcestershire
2	cloves garlic, minced		sauce
1	pound mushrooms, thinly	¾	cup Parmesan cheese
	sliced	3	tablespoons sherry
½	cup chopped green onions	2	(1.5 ounce) boxes mini
1	(8 ounce) package cream		phyllo dough shells
	cheese		

Preheat oven to 350 degrees. Melt butter in a medium skillet. Add garlic and mushrooms and sauté over medium heat 3 to 4 minutes. Add green onions and sauté 2 minutes longer. Remove from heat.

In a large bowl, combine mushroom mixture, cream cheese, Worcestershire sauce, Parmesan cheese and sherry. Mix well. Spoon 1 tablespoon of mixture into each phyllo shell. Bake 7 to 10 minutes or until hot and bubbly.

Mushrooms à la Russe

8	ounces mushrooms	1	teaspoon Dijon mustard
⅓	cup minced onion		Salt and pepper to taste
2	tablespoons vegetable oil	1	loaf French or dark rye
1	tablespoon minced fresh dill		bread
2	teaspoons white wine vinegar		Butter, softened

Boil mushrooms in salted water for 5 to 10 minutes. Drain and chop fine. Combine chopped mushrooms, onion, oil, dill, vinegar and mustard. Mix well. Season with salt and pepper.

Cut bread into ½ inch slices. Brush slices with butter and toast in oven. Serve mushroom mixture on bread.

Yield: 4 servings

Hot Pecan Spread

2	(8 ounce) packages cream cheese, softened	2	tablespoons onion salt
4	teaspoons milk	2	teaspoons garlic salt
1	(5 ounce) jar chipped beef, chopped	1	cup sour cream
½	cup chopped green bell pepper	½	cup chopped pecans
		2	tablespoons butter
		½	teaspoon salt

Preheat oven to 350 degrees. Blend cream cheese and milk in a mixing bowl. Mix in beef, bell pepper, onion salt, garlic salt and sour cream. Spread mixture in a quiche dish.

Sauté pecans in butter and salt. Sprinkle over cream cheese mixture. Bake 20 minutes. Serve with your favorite crackers.

Cocktail Meatballs

2	pounds ground beef	¼	cup cracker crumbs
1	(1 ounce) envelope Lipton onion soup mix	2	tablespoons butter
1	egg	10	ounces ketchup
2	teaspoons Accent	½	cup chili sauce
		5	ounces currant or apple jelly

Preheat oven to 350 degrees. Mix ground beef, soup mix, egg, Accent and crumbs. Form into balls, using 1 tablespoon of mixture for each ball. Heat butter in a skillet. Add meatballs in batches and brown on all sides. As they get done, transfer meatballs to a baking dish.

Combine ketchup, chili sauce and jelly in a saucepan. Heat until melted and smooth. Pour over meatballs. Bake 25 minutes.

Yield: 80 meatballs

Mini Beef Wellingtons

1 (17 ounce) package frozen puff pastry dough, preferably all butter, thawed
⅓ cup Boursin cheese, softened

8 ounces trimmed beef tenderloin, cut into ½ inch cubes
Salt and freshly ground black pepper to taste
1 egg, lightly beaten

Preheat oven to 400 degrees. On a lightly floured sheet of parchment paper, roll out dough to a 7½ x 15 inch rectangle, about ⅛ inch thick. Cut into 1½ inch squares. Spoon a scant ¼ teaspoon of cheese into the center of each pastry square. Season beef with salt and pepper. Set a beef cube on each pastry square. Fold pastry over the beef, neatly tucking in the corners.

Arrange the pastries, seam side down, on a large parchment paper-lined baking sheet. If making ahead, pastries can be frozen at this point for up to 1 week. Lightly brush pastries with egg. Bake 10 to 12 minutes, or until puffed and golden brown. Cool slightly, then transfer to a serving platter.

Yield: about 4 dozen pastries

Pat's Pâté

2 (10½ ounce) cans consommé
2 envelopes unflavored gelatin
1 pound liverwurst

2 (8 ounce) packages cream cheese
6 dashes Worcestershire sauce

Heat consommé in a saucepan. Stir in gelatin until dissolved; do not boil. Pour mixture into a greased loaf pan to ¼ inch deep; set aside remainder of mixture. Place loaf pan on the level in the freezer for 15 minutes or until gelled.

Blend liverwurst, cream cheese, Worcestershire sauce and remaining consommé mixture in a food processor. Carefully add liverwurst mixture to loaf pan. Cool in refrigerator 2 hours.

Yield: 24 servings

Empanadas (Little Meat Pies)

*This is a featured appetizer at "La Fiesta Mexicana" —
auctioned at the Hibiscus Children's Center's Fall Benefit.*

8   ounces chorizo
1¼ cups sour cream
1   (4½ ounce) can chopped
    green chiles

1   (15 ounce) package Pillsbury
    refrigerated pie crusts,
    room temperature

Freeze chorizo to easily peel off casing. Bring to room temperature once casing is removed. Preheat oven to 350 degrees. Finely chop chorizo in a food processor. Transfer to a skillet and sauté 3 to 4 minutes; drain. Combine chorizo, sour cream and chiles. Mix well.

Unfold pie crusts. Cut out 2½ inch circles with a cookie cutter or jar lid. Spoon 2 teaspoons of chorizo filling into the center of each circle and fold over. Pinch edges securely to form crescents. Place on a baking sheet. Bake about 20 minutes.

Hot Chili Dip

1   (8 ounce) container sour
    cream
½   (1¼ ounce) package taco
    seasoning
2   (9 ounce) cans Frito Lay
    bean dip
1   (4 ounce) can chopped green
    chiles

1   (2¼ ounce) can sliced black
    olives
2   tomatoes, diced
½   onion, chopped
1   (8 ounce) package shredded
    taco cheese

Combine sour cream and taco seasoning. Spread bean dip in a square glass pan. Layer sour cream mixture on top.

Add layers of chiles, olives, tomatoes and onion. Top with enough cheese to cover pan. Microwave on high for 5 to 10 minutes.

Spicy Chicken Quesadillas

This is featured as an appetizer at "La Fiesta Mexicana" — auctioned at the Hibiscus Children's Center's Fall Benefit.

Jane's Marinade (page 245)
8   ounces boneless, skinless chicken breasts, pounded thin
4   slices red onion
3   (6 inch) flour tortillas
¼   cup shredded Monterey Jack cheese
¼   cup shredded cheddar cheese
    Salt and pepper to taste
    Sour cream, guacamole and salsa for garnish

Combine marinade and chicken and marinate 1 hour. Grill chicken 3 to 4 minutes on each side or until done. Grill onion slices 2 minutes on each side. Slice chicken and set aside.

Preheat oven to 450 degrees. Place 2 tortillas on a baking sheet. Divide the chicken, onion and cheeses between the tortillas. Season with salt and pepper. Stack the 2 layers and cover with remaining tortilla. At this point, quesadilla can be refrigerated until ready to bake. Bake 8 to 12 minutes. Cut into quarters and serve with garnishes.

Miami Chicken Wings

1   cup Dat'l Do-It or Devil Drops hot sauce, or hot sauce of choice
½   cup fresh lime juice
½   cup soy sauce
    Freshly ground black pepper
2   pounds chicken wings

Combine hot sauce, lime juice and soy sauce in a large zip-top bag. Season generously with black pepper. Wash and blot dry chicken wings. Separate wings at the joints, discarding wing tips. Add chicken wings to zip-top bag. Seal and turn bag to coat.

Refrigerate at least 4 hours or overnight, turning several times. When ready to cook, preheat grill or broiler. Drain wings. Grill or broil 2 to 3 minutes per side or until golden brown and cooked throughout.

Mont Blanc Chicken Spread

2   (4¾ ounce) cans Underwood
    chicken spread
1   cup finely chopped toasted
    walnuts
½   cup chopped green onions
    or chives

1½ tablespoons soy sauce
1   tablespoon garlic or wine
    vinegar
⅓   cup mayonnaise
1   cup sour cream

Combine chicken spread, walnuts, onions, soy sauce and vinegar.
Form into a round ball and refrigerate until firm. Combine
mayonnaise and sour cream.

Place chicken spread ball on a serving plate and frost with
mayonnaise mixture. Serve with crackers.

Marinated Grilled Shrimp

2   tablespoons olive oil
¼   teaspoon paprika
¼   teaspoon black pepper
¼   teaspoon piri-piri or
    cayenne pepper
1   small red onion, halved and
    sliced
12 cloves garlic, chopped

1   jalapeño pepper, seeded and
    chopped
1   bunch cilantro, chopped
3-4 sprigs lemon thyme
2   pounds medium to large
    shrimp, peeled and
    deveined

Combine oil, paprika, pepper and piri-piri in a large bowl. Add onion,
garlic, jalapeño, cilantro, thyme and shrimp. Cover with plastic and
refrigerate at least 8 hours or overnight.

When ready to cook, preheat grill or broiler. Soak 6 inch bamboo
skewers in water 5 minutes. Skewer 3 or 4 shrimp each skewer. Grill
5 minutes, turning halfway through cooking. Serve as an appetizer or
on top mixed greens with an oil and vinegar dressing.

Grilled Texas Shrimp

Great as an appetizer or on top of the Goat Cheese Salad.

12 large or jumbo shrimp, peeled and deveined	12 (1 x ⅛ inch) slices Monterey Jack cheese
12 slices jalapeño pepper	6 slices bacon, halved Creole seasoning to taste

Preheat grill. Butterfly shrimp. Insert a pepper slice and a cheese slice into each shrimp. Close shrimp tightly and wrap each with a bacon piece. Secure each with a toothpick. Sprinkle with seasoning to taste. Grill shrimp 2 to 3 minutes on each side or until done.

Pickled Shrimp

Shrimp

3 pounds shrimp in shells	1 tablespoon salt
¾ cup chopped celery tops	2½ cups sliced onion
½ cup mixed pickling spices	10 bay leaves

Marinade

4 cups salad oil	1 tablespoon celery seed
1 cup white vinegar	2 teaspoons salt
¼ cup capers, undrained	Few drops Tabasco sauce

Add shrimp to boiling water in a large pot. Stir in celery, pickling spices and salt. Cover and simmer 5 minutes. Drain shrimp. Peel and devein under cold water. Layer shrimp, onion and bay leaves in a glass baking dish.

To prepare marinade, combine all ingredients and mix well. Pour over shrimp mixture in dish. Cover and chill at least 24 hours, spooning marinade over shrimp occasionally.

Pickled Shrimp
and Mushrooms

3	cloves garlic, chopped		½	cup vegetable oil
2	onions, chopped		3-4	jalapeño peppers, seeded
¼	cup oil			and slivered
1	teaspoon salt		2	pounds cooked shrimp
½	teaspoon black pepper		4	(10 ounce) jars Green Giant
½	cup vinegar			mushroom caps, drained
¾	teaspoon dry mustard			

Sauté garlic and onions in oil in a skillet for 10 minutes. In a bowl, combine salt, pepper, vinegar, mustard, oil and jalapeño. Mix well. Add sautéed vegetables, shrimp and mushrooms to bowl. Marinate overnight.

Shrimp Snacks

2¼	cups water		2	tablespoons minced onion
¾	pound medium shrimp		2	tablespoons mayonnaise
18	(¼ to ½ inch thick) slices		2	tablespoons chopped fresh
	baguette bread			dill
½	cup shredded cheddar		⅛	teaspoon salt
	cheese			Dash black pepper
2	tablespoons minced celery			Fresh dill sprigs for garnish

Preheat oven to 350 degrees. Bring 2¼ cups water to a boil. Add shrimp and cook 3 minutes or until shrimp turn pink. Drain and rinse with cold water. Peel and devein shrimp. Cut 9 shrimp in half lengthwise and set aside. Dice remaining shrimp.

Bake bread slices on a baking sheet 5 to 10 minutes or until toasted. Combine diced shrimp, cheese, celery, onion, mayonnaise, dill, salt and pepper. Spread mixture over bread slices. Bake 5 minutes or until lightly browned. Top each slice with a shrimp half and garnish with a dill sprig.

Yield: 18 snacks

Shrimp Mould

1	envelope unflavored gelatin
⅓	cup cold water
1	cup undiluted canned tomato soup
1	(8 ounce) package cream cheese, softened
1	cup Miracle Whip
2	(4¼ ounce) cans small shrimp, mashed
½	cup chopped onion
½	cup chopped celery

Dissolve gelatin in cold water. Bring soup to a boil in a saucepan. Add gelatin mixture. Remove from heat and stir. Beat in cream cheese until smooth. Stir in Miracle Whip. Add shrimp, onion and celery.

Pour mixture into a mold and chill until firm. Serve with crackers of choice.

Shrimp Bread

1	loaf French bread
½	cup minced fresh parsley
3	cloves garlic, minced
2	tablespoons chopped shallots
2	tablespoons almonds
½	cup dry white wine
1	tablespoon Pernod apéritif
1½	teaspoons salt
1	teaspoon black pepper
1	cup unsalted butter, softened
1	(6 ounce) package cooked small shrimp

Preheat oven to 400 degrees. Cut off top of bread. Hollow out loaf, creating a bread shell. Use hollowed out bread to make bread crumbs in a food processor. Set aside shell and crumbs.

Combine parsley, garlic, shallots and almonds in food processor. Blend until minced. Mix together parsley mixture, wine, Pernod, salt, pepper, butter and shrimp. Stuff mixture into bread shell. Sprinkle bread crumbs on top. Bake 25 minutes. Cut into 2 inch slices and serve as a first course or as an appetizer.

Shrimp Pesto Canapés

½ (7 ounce) container store-
   bought pesto
½ cup mayonnaise

½ cup chopped uncooked
   shrimp
36 (¼ inch thick) slices
   baguette bread

Preheat broiler. Drain as much oil from pesto as possible. Blend in mayonnaise and shrimp. Spread mixture over bread slices. Broil 3 to 4 minutes.

Yield: 36 canapés

Shrimp Spread

2 (8 ounce) packages cream
   cheese
1 large spoonful mayonnaise

1 cup green onions, white and
   green parts
½-¾ cup minced celery
5-6 (4¼ ounce) cans small shrimp

Combine all ingredients except shrimp by hand or with an electric mixer. Stir in shrimp. Refrigerate at least 24 hours. Serve with Triscuit crackers.

Bay Scallop Ceviche

1 pound bay scallops
1 cup fresh lime or lemon juice
1 jalapeño pepper, minced, or
   to taste
¼ cup chopped green or red
   onion

½ cup chopped yellow bell
   pepper
Salt and pepper to taste
Cilantro or Italian parsley
   for garnish

Combine all ingredients except garnish in a large glass bowl; mix well. Cover and refrigerate at least 30 minutes or until scallops turn opaque.

To serve, drain off marinade and return scallops and vegetables to bowl. Garnish with cilantro.

Yield: 8 servings

Conch Fritter

Conch fritters are a part of every Bahamian meal.

Meat of 6 conch
1 medium onion
1 stalk celery
3 tablespoons Worcestershire sauce
1 heaping tablespoon tomato paste
1 heaping teaspoon baking powder
1 cup flour
1 egg
Salt and pepper to taste
1 tablespoon Tabasco sauce
Vegetable oil for frying

Combine conch, onion and celery in a food processor. Pulse until finely chopped. Combine conch mixture with Worcestershire sauce, tomato paste, baking powder, flour, egg, salt, pepper and Tabasco sauce. Add water, a small amount at a time, if batter is too stiff.

Heat oil in a pan or a deep fryer. Drop batter by teaspoons, a few at a time, into hot oil. Cook until golden. Drain on paper towel and serve.

Party Salmon Ball

1 (1 pound) can salmon
1 (8 ounce) package cream cheese, softened
1 tablespoon lemon juice
2 teaspoons grated onion
1 teaspoon prepared horseradish
Salt to taste
¼ teaspoon liquid smoke
½ cup chopped pecans
3 tablespoons snipped fresh parsley

Drain and flake salmon, removing skin and bones. Combine salmon, cream cheese, lemon juice, onion, horseradish, salt and liquid smoke. Mix thoroughly. Chill several hours.

Combine pecans and parsley. Shape salmon mixture into a ball. Roll ball in pecan mixture. Chill well. Serve with assorted crackers or bagel chips.

Clams Oreganatta

2	(6½ ounce) cans minced clams	1	tablespoon Parmesan cheese
¾	cup Italian-flavored bread crumbs	1	tomato, finely chopped
⅓	cup olive oil	2	dashes Tabasco sauce
1	teaspoon dried oregano	4	ounces provolone cheese, shredded
⅛	teaspoon salt	6-7	slices bacon, partially cooked

Preheat broiler. Combine clams, crumbs, oil, oregano, salt, cheese, tomato and Tabasco sauce. Mix well.

Divide mixture among ceramic seashells. Top with cheese and bacon. Broil until cheese is melted and bacon is cooked.

Ceramic seafood dishes are sold at local fish markets and grocery stores.

Crab Dip

2	(8 ounce) packages cream cheese, softened	3	shakes garlic salt
1	(8 ounce) container sour cream	3-5	dashes Tabasco sauce
¼	cup Italian salad dressing	2	tablespoons white wine
1	teaspoon lemon juice	1	pound lump crabmeat, picked over
1	teaspoon mustard		Old Bay seasoning

Preheat oven to 325 degrees. Beat cream cheese. Mix in sour cream, salad dressing, lemon juice, mustard, garlic salt, Tabasco sauce and wine. Stir in crab.

Divide mixture between 2 ceramic dishes sprayed with cooking spray. Sprinkle with Old Bay seasoning. Bake 30 minutes. Serve hot with crackers. Can freeze before cooking.

Crabmeat Quarters

6	English muffins, split	2	tablespoons mayonnaise
1	(5 ounce) jar Kraft Old English cheese spread	½	cup or less butter or margarine, softened
½	teaspoon garlic powder Dash of Tabasco sauce, or to taste	1	(6 ounce) can crabmeat, drained

Lightly toast muffins; set aside. Mix cheese spread, garlic powder, Tabasco sauce, mayonnaise and butter until blended. Gently fold in crabmeat. Spread mixture on muffins. Cut each muffin into quarters.

Place quarters on a baking sheet and freeze. When frozen, transfer to zip-top bags until ready to use. To serve, preheat oven to 425 degrees. Bake 10 minutes.

King Crab Puffs

1	(6 ounce) can white crabmeat, drained	¼	teaspoon dry mustard
¼	cup chopped green onion	1	cup water
½	cup Parmesan cheese	½	cup butter
½	teaspoon Worcestershire sauce	½	teaspoon salt
		1	cup flour
		4	eggs

Preheat oven to 400 degrees. Combine crabmeat, onion, cheese, Worcestershire sauce and mustard; set aside.

In a saucepan, combine water, butter and salt and bring to a boil. Add flour all at once, beating until mixture forms a ball and leaves sides of pan. Add eggs, one at a time, beating after each addition. Blend in crab mixture.

Drop by spoonfuls onto an ungreased baking sheet. Bake 20 minutes. Reduce heat to 350 degrees and bake 10 minutes longer. Serve hot.

Baked Crock of Artichoke, Brie and Lump Crab

1	leek, chopped	1	bunch mixed fresh tarragon, parsley and dill, chopped
1	ounce minced garlic		
1	Vidalia onion, diced	8	ounces Brie cheese, cut into cubes
2	tablespoons olive oil		
½	cup chopped spinach	1	pound fresh jumbo lump crabmeat
½	cup chopped artichoke hearts		
		¼	cup Grey Poupon mustard
¼	cup Riesling wine	2	tablespoons Tabasco sauce
⅔	cup heavy cream		Salt and pepper to taste

Preheat oven to 425 degrees. Sauté leeks, garlic and onion in oil in a large skillet until light brown. Add spinach and artichokes to skillet. Deglaze with wine and cook until spinach is soft. Add cream, tarragon, parsley and dill. Bring to a slight simmer. Stir in cheese until blended. Remove from heat and pour into a mixing bowl; cool.

In a separate bowl, combine crabmeat, mustard and Tabasco sauce. Season with salt and pepper. Add to cheese mixture. Transfer mixture to a large casserole dish or individual ramekins. Bake 10 minutes or until slightly browned.

Yield: 6 to 8 servings

Tangos
925 Bougainvillea Lane
Vero Beach, Florida

Hot Crab and Artichoke Dip

1	large green bell pepper, chopped
1	tablespoon vegetable oil
2	(14 ounce) cans artichoke hearts, drained and chopped
2	cups mayonnaise
½	cup chopped green onion
½	cup drained and chopped roasted red pepper
1	cup Parmesan cheese
1½	tablespoons fresh lemon juice
4	teaspoons Worcestershire sauce
3	pickled jalapeño peppers, minced
1	teaspoon celery salt
1	pound crabmeat
⅓	cup sliced almonds, toasted

Preheat oven to 375 degrees. Sauté bell pepper in oil until softened; cool.

In a large bowl, combine sautéed pepper, artichoke, mayonnaise, green onion, red pepper, cheese, lemon juice, Worcestershire sauce, jalapeño and celery salt. Mix well. Gently stir in crabmeat. Transfer mixture to a baking dish and top with almonds. If making ahead, dish can be refrigerated up to 1 day at this point.

Bake 25 to 30 minutes or until top is golden and crisp and dip is bubbly. Serve with pita triangles or crackers.

Artichoke Crab Spread

1	(6 ounce) can crabmeat
1	(8 ounce) package cream cheese
1	cup mayonnaise
⅓	cup chopped onion
1	(13¾ ounce) can artichokes
¾	cup shredded Parmesan cheese

Preheat oven to 375 degrees. Combine all ingredients and place in a baking dish. Bake 15 to 18 minutes.

Thai Pot Stickers

Pot Stickers

2   small green onions, minced
1   tablespoon very finely minced ginger
1   pound ground veal, pork or chicken
1   tablespoon oyster sauce

2   teaspoons Chinese rice wine or dry sherry
½   teaspoon Asian chile sauce
40 thin won ton skins
¼   cup cornstarch
3   tablespoons vegetable oil

Sauce

1   tablespoon minced fresh basil leaves
1   tablespoon chopped fresh cilantro
1   small green onion, minced
½   cup unsweetened coconut milk

¼   cup Chinese rice wine or dry sherry
1   tablespoon oyster sauce
1   teaspoon Asian chile sauce
½   teaspoon curry powder
½   teaspoon sugar

To make pot stickers, combine green onion, ginger, ground meat, oyster sauce, wine and chile sauce. Mix thoroughly. If using square won tons, trim off corners. Place 2 teaspoons of meat filling in the center of a skin. Fold and seal edges together. Squeeze the index finger and thumb of one hand around center of dumpling while using the index finger and thumb of other hand to press on the top and bottom of the dumpling. Line a baking sheet with parchment paper. Dust paper heavily with cornstarch. Place dumplings on baking sheet, cover and refrigerate up to 8 hours.

To make sauce, combine all ingredients and mix well. Set aside up to 8 hours.

When ready to cook, heat a 12 inch non-stick skillet over high heat. Add 3 tablespoons vegetable oil and immediately add dumplings, bottom-side down. Fry 2 minutes or until dark golden brown. Pour in sauce and immediately cover pan. Reduce heat to medium and steam dumplings 2 minutes or until firm. Shake pan to turn dumplings. Turn dumplings out onto a heated serving platter or 4 heated dinner plates. Serve immediately.

Yield: 6 to 10 appetizer servings

Breads and Brunch

LINDA COBURN
Tea By The Sea
Oil, 1999

Breads and Brunch

Breads

Robert Frost Popovers 31
Jordan Pond House Popovers 31
Jalapeño Cornbread 32
Best Ever Cornbread 32
Raisin Bread 33
Peppery Cheese Bread 33
Best Banana Bread Ever..................... 34
Banana Nut Bread 34
Zucchini Pineapple Bread 35
Oatmeal Sunflower
    Seed Bread 35
Key Lime Bread
    with Blueberries 36
Beer Bread 36

Coffee Cakes

Easy Living Coffee Cake 37
Sour Cream Coffee Cake 38
Granola 38
Pumpkin Coffee Cake 39

Brunch Fare

Eggs Hussarde.................................. 39
Pumpkin Ring 40
Southern Cheese Grits 40
Mexican Breakfast Casserole 41
Scrambled Egg Casserole 41
Overnight Egg
    and Sausage Casserole 42
Dixie's "Leekless" Quiche 43
Crustless Spinach Quiche 44

Robert Frost Popovers

1	cup all-purpose flour	3	eggs
⅛	teaspoon salt	1	cup milk

Preheat oven to 450 degrees. Using two 12 cup muffin pans, grease and flour 5 alternating cups of one pan and 4 cups of the second pan.

Combine flour and salt in a bowl. In a separate bowl, mix eggs and milk. Whisk into dry ingredients until just blended.

Pour batter into greased and floured cups, filling two-thirds full. Fill empty cups two-thirds full with water. Bake 15 minutes. Reduce heat to 350 degrees and bake 15 minutes longer or until golden brown. Do not open oven door while baking; do not underbake.

Yield: 9 popovers

Jordan Pond House Popovers

Recipe adapted from a recipe from
Jordan Pond House, Acadia National Park, Maine.

1	cup all-purpose flour	2	large eggs
½	teaspoon salt	1	cup whole milk
⅛	teaspoon baking soda		

Preheat oven to 425 degrees. Grease custard cups or muffin or popover pans and place in oven. Mix flour, salt and baking soda with a fork or whisk. Beat eggs slightly in a bowl. Beat in milk. Add dry ingredients and beat vigorously with an electric mixer or by hand for 2 minutes.

Remove hot pans from oven and pour batter into cups, filling two-thirds full. Bake about 40 minutes or until dark golden. Do not open oven door while baking. Remove pans from oven and turn off heat. Prick the top or side of each popover and return pan to warm oven for 5 minutes to dry the inside. Remove from oven and serve immediately. Serve with strawberry jam.

Jalapeño Cornbread

2½ cups cornmeal
1   cup flour
2   tablespoons sugar
4   teaspoons baking powder
1   teaspoon salt
3   eggs
1½ cups milk

½   cup vegetable oil
6-8 jalapeño peppers, chopped
1   (14¾ ounce) can creamed
       corn
2   cups shredded sharp
       cheddar cheese
1   large onion, minced

Preheat oven to 450 degrees. Combine cornmeal, flour, sugar, baking powder and salt in a bowl.

In a separate bowl, beat eggs, milk and oil. Stir into dry ingredients. Add jalapeño, corn, cheese and onion. Mix well and pour into 2 well-greased 9x11 inch baking pans. Bake 25 minutes or until done.

Best Ever Cornbread

1   cup butter or margarine
⅓   cup sugar
4   eggs
1   teaspoon salt

1   teaspoon baking soda
2   cups flour
2   cups buttermilk
2   cups yellow cornmeal

Preheat oven to 375 degrees. Melt butter in oven in a 9x13 inch baking pan. Remove from heat and stir in sugar, eggs and salt. Mix well.

Add baking soda, flour, buttermilk and cornmeal. Stir until blended. Bake 30 minutes.

Raisin Bread

1	cup raisins	½	teaspoon salt	
2	cups flour	1	teaspoon butter, melted	
½	cup sugar	1	egg	
½	teaspoon baking soda	⅔	cup buttermilk	
1½	teaspoons baking powder			

Preheat oven to 325 degrees. Soak raisins in hot water for 5 minutes. Drain. Combine drained raisins and remaining ingredients in a bowl. Mix thoroughly.

Transfer batter to a loaf pan. Bake 30 to 35 minutes.

Yield: 1 loaf, or 5 mini loaves

If buttermilk is not available, substitute 1 teaspoon lemon juice plus enough milk to measure ⅔ cup. Let stand 5 minutes before using.

For an extra taste, add ½ teaspoon nutmeg and 1½ cups applesauce.

Peppery Cheese Bread

2½	cups all-purpose flour	1	(8 ounce) container plain yogurt	
1	tablespoon sugar			
1½-2	teaspoons cracked black pepper	½	cup vegetable oil	
		¼	cup milk	
1	teaspoon baking powder	1	tablespoon spicy brown mustard	
¾	teaspoon salt			
½	teaspoon baking soda	1	cup shredded cheddar cheese	
2	eggs, beaten			
		¼	cup sliced green onion	

Preheat oven to 350 degrees. Combine flour, sugar, pepper, baking powder, salt and baking soda in a large bowl.

In a medium bowl, combine eggs, yogurt, oil, milk and mustard. Stir liquid ingredients into dry ingredients along with cheese and onion. Transfer batter to a loaf pan sprayed with cooking spray. Bake 45 to 50 minutes.

Best Banana Bread Ever

3	ripe bananas	½	teaspoon salt
2	eggs	1	teaspoon baking soda
½	cup butter, softened	1	cup sugar
1¼	cups flour		Nuts (optional)

Preheat oven to 350 degrees. Mash together bananas, eggs and butter in a mixing bowl. In a separate bowl, sift together flour, salt and baking soda. Stir into banana mixture. Mix in sugar. Add nuts.

Pour batter into 1 medium loaf pan or 2 small loaf pans. Bake about 45 minutes; do not overbake.

Banana Nut Bread

3	cups sugar	½	teaspoon salt
3	cups vegetable shortening	1	cup milk
4	eggs	5-6	ripe bananas, mashed
2	teaspoons vanilla	1	cup chopped pecans
3	cups flour		(optional)
2	teaspoons baking soda		

Preheat oven to 325 degrees. Cream sugar and shortening in a mixing bowl. Beat in eggs and vanilla. Add flour, baking soda, salt and milk. Stir until mixed. Fold in banana and nuts. Pour batter into 3 greased and floured loaf pans.

Bake 45 to 60 minutes or until a toothpick inserted in the center comes out clean. Remove from pans when cooled.

Yield: 3 loaves

Zucchini Pineapple Bread

3	cups flour
2	teaspoons baking soda
¼	teaspoon baking powder
1	teaspoon salt
2	cups sugar
1¼	teaspoons cinnamon
¾	teaspoon nutmeg

3	eggs, lightly beaten
⅔	cup vegetable oil
2	teaspoons vanilla
2	cups shredded zucchini
1	cup chopped pecans
1	(8¼ ounce) can crushed pineapple, well drained

Preheat oven to 350 degrees. Combine flour, baking soda, baking powder, salt, sugar, cinnamon and nutmeg in a large bowl. Make a well in the center.

In a separate bowl, mix eggs, oil and vanilla. Pour into well in dry ingredients and stir until just moistened. Stir in zucchini, pecans and pineapple.

Spoon batter into 2 greased 9x5 inch loaf pans. Bake 55 minutes or until a toothpick inserted in the center comes out clean.

Yield: 2 loaves

Oatmeal Sunflower Seed Bread

4	cups boiling water
3	cups dry rolled oats
¼	cup vegetable oil
¼	cup molasses
¼	cup honey

2	tablespoons dry yeast
7	cups all-purpose flour
1½	tablespoons salt
½	cup hulled sunflower seeds
½	cup sesame seeds

Combine boiling water and oats in a mixing bowl. Allow to cool to lukewarm.

Mix together oil, molasses and honey. Add to lukewarm oats mixture. Add yeast, flour and salt to mixture. Mix with an electric mixer on low for 3 to 4 minutes. Stir in sunflower seeds and sesame seeds. Transfer to a greased bowl and allow to rise for 1 hour.

Divide dough into 3 greased loaf pans. Allow to rise to top of pans. Preheat oven to 350 degrees. Bake 15 to 20 minute or until done.

Key Lime Bread
with Blueberries

Bread

6	tablespoons butter, softened	1	teaspoon baking powder
1	cup sugar	½	teaspoon salt
2	eggs		Juice of 2 limes
½	cup milk		Zest of 1 lime
1½	cups flour	1	cup blueberries

Glaze

	Juice of 1 lime	½	cup sugar

Preheat oven to 350 degrees. Cream butter and sugar in a mixing bowl until light. Beat in eggs. Add milk and mix well.

In a separate bowl, sift together flour, baking powder and salt. Add dry ingredients to creamed mixture and blend well. Mix in lime juice. Stir in zest and blueberries. Pour batter into a greased loaf pan. Bake 1 hour or until a toothpick inserted in the center comes out clean.

To make glaze, mix lime juice and sugar. Spoon over hot bread before removing from pan. Cool and cut with a sharp knife.

Yield: 1 loaf

Raspberries can be substituted for the blueberries.

Beer Bread

3	cups self-rising flour	1	(12 ounce) can beer
2	tablespoons sugar		Sesame seeds
1	teaspoon dill weed		

Preheat oven to 350 degrees. Combine flour, sugar and dill weed in a bowl. Add beer and stir until a soft dough forms.

Divide mixture between two greased 7½x3½ inch loaf pans. Sprinkle sesame seeds on top. Let stand 15 minutes. Bake 30 minutes or until brown on top and bread springs back when lightly touched.

Easy Living Coffee Cake

Batter

½	cup butter, softened	1	teaspoon baking powder
1	cup sugar	½	teaspoon salt
2	eggs	1	cup buttermilk
2	cups flour	1	teaspoon vanilla
1	teaspoon baking soda		

Topping

⅓	cup dark brown sugar	½	cup chopped walnuts or
¼	cup sugar		pecans
1	teaspoon cinnamon		

Preheat oven to 350 degrees. Beat all cake ingredients together in a large mixing bowl until smooth and fluffy.

Prepare topping by mixing together all ingredients.

Pour half the cake batter into a greased 9x13 inch pan. Sprinkle half the topping over batter. Pour remaining batter into pan and top with remaining topping. Bake 30 minutes.

Sour Cream Coffee Cake

Batter

2	cups sugar
¾	cup butter, softened
3	eggs
1	tablespoon milk
1	teaspoon vanilla

2	cups flour
1	(8 ounce) container sour cream
¼	teaspoon salt
1	teaspoon baking powder

Topping

½	cup brown sugar
1	teaspoon cinnamon

1	cup chopped pecans

Preheat oven to 350 degrees. Cream sugar and butter in a mixing bowl. Mix in eggs, milk and vanilla. Add flour, sour cream, salt and baking powder. Mix well.

Combine all topping ingredients in a separate bowl.

Pour half the cake batter into a greased 9x13 inch baking pan. Sprinkle half the topping over batter. Pour remaining batter into pan and top with remaining topping. Bake 45 minutes. Cut into squares when cool.

Granola

4	cups dry rolled oats
1½	cups shredded coconut
1	cup wheat germ
1	cup nuts
½	cup sunflower seeds
¾	cup sesame seeds

½	cup vegetable oil
½	cup honey
½	tablespoon vanilla
	Dried fruit of choice, such as raisins, chopped dates or chopped apricots

Preheat oven to 300 degrees. Combine oats, coconut, wheat germ, nuts, sunflower seeds and sesame seeds on a cookie sheet. Mix well. Blend oil, honey and vanilla and pour over dry ingredients. Mix until dry ingredients are well-coated.

Bake, turning with a spoon as edges of mixture brown, until mixture is evenly golden brown and somewhat dried. Remove from pan and cool. Add dried fruit. Store in the refrigerator in an airtight container.

Pumpkin Coffee Cake

Batter

½ cup butter	2 cups flour
¾ cup sugar	1 teaspoon baking soda
1 teaspoon vanilla	1 teaspoon baking powder
3 eggs	1 cup sour cream

Filling

1 (16 ounce) can pumpkin	1 egg, lightly beaten
⅓ cup sugar	1 teaspoon pumpkin pie spice

Strudel

⅓ cup butter	¾ cup chopped pecans
1 cup brown sugar	2 teaspoons cinnamon

Preheat oven to 325 degrees. To make batter, cream butter, sugar and vanilla. Beat in eggs. Combine flour, baking soda, baking powder and add to creamed mixture. Blend in sour cream.

In a separate bowl, combine all filling ingredients. Mix well.

Prepare strudel by cutting butter into sugar. Add pecans and cinnamon.

Spoon half the batter into a greased 9x13 inch pan. Sprinkle half the strudel over batter. Add all of the filling. Pour remaining batter over filling and top with remaining strudel. Bake 40 minutes or until a toothpick inserted in the center comes out clean.

Eggs Hussarde

A specialty at Brennan's in New Orleans.

2 English muffins, halved	4 slices tomato, grilled
4 thin slices ham	4 eggs, soft poached
½ cup Marchands de Vin sauce (page 251)	½ cup hollandaise sauce Paprika

Toast muffin halves. Lay a ham slice on each muffin half. Cover ham with Marchands de Vin sauce. Add a tomato slice to each muffin and place a poached egg on top of each tomato slice. Spoon hollandaise sauce over eggs and sprinkle with paprika.

Pumpkin Ring

Batter

3	cups Bisquick baking mix	4	eggs
1	cup granulated sugar	1	(16 ounce) can pumpkin
1	cup brown sugar	2½	teaspoons pumpkin pie
4	tablespoons margarine or		spice
	butter, softened	¼	cup milk

Glaze

1	cup powdered sugar	½	teaspoon vanilla
1	tablespoon milk		

Preheat oven to 350 degrees. Combine all batter ingredients on low speed of an electric mixer, scraping bowl constantly. Increase speed to medium and beat 3 minutes, scraping bowl occasionally. Spread batter in a greased and floured 12 cup Bundt pan or 10 inch angel food pan.

Bake about 50 minutes or until a toothpick inserted in the center comes out clean. Cool 10 minutes before removing from pan. Cool completely before adding glaze.

To make glaze, beat together sugar, milk and vanilla. Drizzle over cooled cake.

Southern Cheese Grits

6	cups water	1	teaspoon seasoning salt
1½	cups grits	2-6	dashes Tabasco sauce
2	teaspoons salt	3	eggs, well beaten
½	cup butter		Garlic salt to taste (optional)
1	pound Velveeta cheese, shredded		

Preheat oven to 350 degrees. Cook water, grits and salt as directed on grits package. Stir in butter, cheese, seasoning salt and Tabasco sauce. Cool.

When cool, add eggs and garlic salt. Pour into a 9x13 inch baking pan. Bake 35 to 40 minutes.

Mexican Breakfast Casserole

5	corn tortillas, cut into quarters	1	cup shredded colby-Jack cheese
9	eggs	1	cup chopped ham, or cooked bulk sausage
1	cup buttermilk	1	jalapeño pepper, chopped (optional)
¼	cup chopped onion		

Preheat oven to 350 degrees. Line the bottom of a greased 8x12 inch baking dish with tortillas.

Beat eggs in a bowl. Add buttermilk and beat again. Mix in onion, cheese, ham and jalapeño. Pour over tortillas. Bake 35 to 40 minutes or until firm. Cut into squares and serve with salsa.

Yield: 6 to 8 servings

Scrambled Egg Casserole

This is great for brunch.
Make a day before — even children like it!

2	cups soft bread cubes	8	ounces Swiss cheese, sliced
1	cup milk	1	cup bread cubes
8	eggs, beaten	2	tablespoons butter
2	tablespoons butter	8	slices bacon, cooked and crumbled
	Salt and pepper to taste		
½	teaspoon seasoning salt		

Preheat oven to 400 degrees. Soak 2 cups bread cubes in milk. Set aside. Cook eggs in 2 tablespoons butter until just set. Add soaked bread cubes and mix well. Season with salt and pepper. Transfer mixture to a greased 1½ quart flat baking dish. Sprinkle seasoning salt over eggs. Top with cheese.

Sauté 1 cup bread cubes in 2 tablespoons butter until brown. Sprinkle sautéed cubes and bacon over casserole. Bake 15 minutes.

Yield: 6 servings

Overnight Egg and Sausage Casserole

12	slices bread, cubed	4	cups milk
2	cups shredded cheddar cheese	8	eggs, or egg substitute equivalent
½	pound ground sausage, cooked and drained	1	teaspoon salt
½	pound bacon, cooked, drained and crumbled	1	teaspoon dry mustard Dash of Worcestershire sauce

Place half of bread cubes in a greased 11x14 inch baking pan. Top with 1 cup of cheese. Combine sausage and bacon and add to pan. Add remaining bread cubes and top with remaining cheese. Beat together eggs, salt, mustard and Worcestershire sauce. Pour over casserole and cover. Refrigerate overnight.

When ready to bake, preheat oven to 325 degrees. Bake 45 to 60 minutes or until top is dry and slightly browned. Cut into squares and serve.

Yield: 8 servings

Substitute turkey sausage, if desired. Also, any combination of sausage and bacon can be used.

Dixie's "Leekless" Quiche

This was originally a recipe for a "leek" quiche.

¾	cup chopped onion or mushrooms	¼	teaspoon nutmeg
2	tablespoons butter or margarine	1½	cups light cream or evaporated milk, warmed
3	eggs	½	cup Parmesan cheese
1	teaspoon mustard	1	tablespoon chives
½	teaspoon herbed salt	1	frozen deep-dish pie crust

Preheat oven to 350 degrees. Sauté onion in butter. Set aside and cool. Mix eggs, mustard, herbed salt, nutmeg, cream, cheese and chives in a blender.

Place sautéed onion in the bottom of the pie crust. Pour egg mixture over onion. Bake 35 to 40 minutes or until a knife inserted near the center comes out clean.

Crustless Spinach Quiche

1 (10 ounce) package frozen
   chopped spinach
1 tablespoon vegetable oil
4 ounces mushrooms, sliced
1 cup chopped onion
½ clove garlic, minced
½ cup plain low-fat yogurt

1 tablespoon all-purpose flour
3 eggs, beaten
5 ounces Gruyère cheese,
   shredded
½ teaspoon salt
   Dash of black pepper
   Dash of nutmeg

Preheat oven to 375 degrees. Cook spinach according to package instructions; drain thoroughly.

Heat oil in a medium skillet. Add mushrooms and sauté until golden; remove and set aside. Add onion and garlic to skillet and cook until soft but not brown.

Combine yogurt and flour in a medium bowl. Add spinach, sautéed mushrooms, onion and garlic. Mix in eggs, cheese, salt, pepper and nutmeg. Pour into an 8 inch pie pan, square pan or quiche pan. Bake about 40 minutes or until a toothpick inserted in the center comes out clean.

Soup and Salad

TERRY MADDEN
Magnolia and Teacup
Watercolor, 1999

Soups

Cheesy Broccoli Bisque 45
Hot or Cold Spinach Soup 45
Baby Carrot Soup 46
Minted Pea Soup 46
Black Bean Soup 47
So Easy Tomato Soup 48
Tomato Basil Soup 48
Creamy Five Onion Soup 49
Strawberry Soup 49
Chilled Mint-Cucumber
    Yogurt Soup 50
Cold Cucumber Soup 50
California Gazpacho 51
Fresh Mushroom Chicken Soup 51
Fiesta Tortilla Soup 52
Hearty Tortilla Soup 53

Chowder and Chili

Grouper Chowder 53
Conch Chowder 54
Texas Five Alarm Chili 55

Side Salads

Walnut and Goat Cheese Salad
    with Raspberry Dressing 54
Hearts of Palm Salad 55
St. Bart's Salad 56
Chilled Artichoke Hearts and Peas 56
Goat Cheese Salad
    with Warm Dressing 57
Spinach-Strawberry Salad 57
Spinach Salad
    with Mimosa Dressing 58
Warm Spinach-Orange Salad 58
Orange Salad Bowl 59
Moroccan Orange Salad 59
Mandarin Orange Salad 60
Summer Salad 60
Fruit and Almond Salad
    with Curry Vinaigrette Dressing 61
Texas Potato Salad 61
Potato Salad 62
Sauerkraut Salad 62

Strawberry Salad 63
Sissy's Orange-Cream Fruit Salad 63
Fresh Asparagus Salad 64
Green Bean and
    Mozzarella Salad 64
Marinated Cucumber Salad 65
Cucumber Salad 65
Parslied Cherry Tomatoes
    with Garlic 66
Layered Greek Salad 66
Broccoli Salad 67
Portobello Mushroom Salad 67
Ribbon Jello Mold 68
Cranberry Salad 68
Napa Salad 69
Emerald Salad 69

Main Course Salads

Bow Tie Pasta Salad 70
Bayou Pasta Salad 70
Dolphin Safe Pasta 71
Martha's Vineyard Salad 71
Steak Salad 72
Sonoma Salad 73
Paella Salad 74
Dill Chicken Salad 75
Chinese Chicken Salad
    with Noodles 75
Pam's Oriental Chicken Salad 76
Chicken Salad 77
Chutney Chicken Salad 78
Easy Chinese Chicken Salad 79
Smoked Turkey Salad 79
Susie's Scrumptious Gingery
    Grilled Salmon Salad 80
Grilled Shrimp Salad
    with Balsamic Vinaigrette
    and Corn Salsa 81

Dressings

Jane's Balsamic Vinaigrette 80
Emily's Italian Salad Dressing 81
Blue Cheese Dressing 82
Poppy Seed Dressing 82

Cheesy Broccoli Bisque

Tasty soup for soup and salad dinner.

1 cup sliced leeks	1 cup broccoli florets
1 cup sliced mushrooms	1 cup light cream or
3 tablespoons butter	half-and-half
3 tablespoons flour	1 cup shredded cheddar
3 cups chicken broth	cheese

Sauté leeks and mushrooms in butter in a large saucepan until tender; do not brown. Add flour and cook and stir until bubbly. Remove from heat and gradually blend in broth. Return to heat and cook and stir until thickened and smooth.

Add broccoli. Reduce heat and simmer 10 to 20 minutes; do not overcook broccoli. Blend in cream and cheese. Simmer until cheese melts and bisque is heated through.

Yield: 4 entrée servings or 8 side dish servings

If thicker soup is desired, add a mixture of equal amounts of cornstarch and water. Simmer 1 to 2 minutes after adding.

Hot or Cold Spinach Soup

1 (12 ounce) package Stouffer's spinach soufflé	½ (8 ounce) container sour cream
1 (10¾ ounce) can condensed cream of potato soup	½ cup diced onion
1½ cups low-fat milk	1 teaspoon lemon juice
	¼ teaspoon dried thyme
	Salt and pepper to taste

Blend all ingredients in a blender or food processor. Transfer to a saucepan and simmer 15 minutes. Serve hot or cold.

Baby Carrot Soup

1 (1 pound) package baby carrots
2 sweet onions, such as Vidalia or Spanish
4 tablespoons butter
1 teaspoon ground ginger
1 tablespoon orange zest
5 cups chicken broth
½ cup milk
½ cup half-and-half
Salt and pepper to taste
½ cup Parmesan cheese for garnish
½ cup chopped fresh parsley for garnish

Chop carrots and onions in a food processor. Combine chopped vegetables with butter in a saucepan and cook 15 minutes over medium-low heat. Add ginger, zest and half of broth. Simmer 30 minutes.

Puree carrot mixture in food processor and return to saucepan. Add remaining broth, milk, half-and-half, salt and pepper. Cook until heated through. Garnish individual servings with cheese and parsley on top.

Minted Pea Soup

Served at the Greenhouse Spa in Texas.

1 teaspoon margarine
¼ cup minced onion
1½ cups low-sodium chicken broth
1 (10 ounce) box frozen peas
2 leaves Romaine or Iceberg lettuce
¼ cup parsley sprigs
3-4 fresh mint leaves, or to taste
1 cup skim milk
Dash of Tabasco sauce
Dash of Worcestershire sauce
Chopped chives for garnish

Melt margarine in a saucepan. Add onions and broth. Cook over medium heat until onions are soft. Add peas, lettuce, parsley and mint. Cover and bring to a boil. Cook 2 minutes. Cool.

Puree mixture in a blender or food processor until smooth. Add milk. Chill. Season with Tabasco and Worcestershire sauces. Garnish with chives.

Black Bean Soup

1	pound dry black beans (2 cups)	½	cup diced green bell pepper
2	ounces tasso, or 2 ounces smoked ham plus ⅛ teaspoon cayenne pepper	½	cup diced celery
		1	large jalapeño pepper, seeded and minced
4	ounces andouille sausage, diced, or any other hot, spicy smoked sausage	1	teaspoon minced garlic
		½	bay leaf
		⅛	teaspoon dried thyme
2	strips bacon	10	cups chicken broth
½	cup diced onion	4	cups water
⅓	cup diced carrot	1	teaspoon salt or to taste
		½	cup port wine

Wash beans and remove any stones. Soak beans in enough water to cover for at least one hour, preferably overnight.

Sauté tasso, sausage and bacon in a large pot until brown. Add onion, carrot, bell pepper, celery and jalapeño and cook 5 minutes. Stir in garlic and cook 10 minutes longer. Add bay leaf and thyme and cook 5 minutes more.

Drain beans. Add beans, broth, 4 cups water and salt to pot. Bring to a boil. Reduce heat and simmer about 1 hour or until beans are softened. Add more broth or water while cooking, if needed. Remove soup from heat and skim off fat. Stir in wine. Serve with salsa and sour cream on the side.

So Easy Tomato Soup

Mix it all together and tell everyone how hard it was to make!

1 (10¾ ounce) can tomato soup	½ cup dry sherry
1 (10½ ounce) can beef consommé	¼ cup minced onion
	½ teaspoon celery salt
½ (8 ounce) container sour cream	½ teaspoon black pepper

Combine all ingredients in a saucepan. Cook until heated through.

Tomato Basil Soup

¼ cup extra virgin olive oil	1 large bunch basil, stemmed
1 medium onion, coarsely chopped	10 plum tomatoes, coarsely chopped
8 cloves garlic, coarsely chopped	2 (16 ounce) cans peeled plum tomatoes, undrained
2 tablespoons fresh oregano, stemmed	2 (16 ounce) cans tomato juice
¼ cup fresh parsley, stemmed	Salt and pepper to taste

Heat an 8 quart heavy pot over medium-high heat. When hot, add oil.
Add onion and sauté until golden brown. Add garlic and sauté until
aromatic. Add oregano, parsley and three-fourths of basil. Cook about
3 to 5 minutes. Add fresh tomatoes and cook 3 to 5 minutes longer,
stirring so not to burn. Add canned tomatoes and tomato juice. Reduce
heat to low and simmer 1 hour, stirring about every 10 minutes.

Puree mixture with a blender until no large pieces or chunks remain.
Season with salt and pepper. Add water as needed to thin. Chiffonade
or chop remaining basil as a garnish for on top of individual servings.

Yield: 1 gallon

Orchid Island Golf and Beach Club
One Beachside Drive
Vero Beach, Florida

Creamy Five Onion Soup

2	Spanish onions, diced
2	red onions, diced
2	leeks, white part only, cleaned and diced
4	shallots, minced
4	tablespoons clarified butter
1	cup red burgundy wine
4	cups beef broth
4	cups chicken broth

1	cup butter
1	cup flour
1	tablespoon chopped fresh sage
4	cups heavy cream
1	teaspoon dried thyme
	Salt and pepper to taste
½	ounce chopped fresh chives for garnish

Sauté Spanish onions, red onions, leeks and shallots in clarified butter in a saucepan until lightly caramelized. Deglaze pan with wine and cook until almost all liquid evaporates. Add beef and chicken broth to saucepan. Simmer 15 minutes.

Meanwhile, prepare a roux by combining butter and flour in a small saucepan. Cook 15 minutes. Whisk into broth mixture. Simmer 20 minutes. Add sage, cream and thyme. Season with salt and pepper. Garnish individual servings with chives.

Yield: 15 servings

Disney's Vero Beach Resort
9250 Island Grove Terrace
Vero Beach, Florida

Strawberry Soup

1	quart fresh strawberries
2	(8 ounce) containers strawberry yogurt

2	tablespoons lemon juice

Wash and hull strawberries. Set aside a few large berries for garnish. Combine all ingredients except garnish in a blender; puree. Refrigerate until chilled. Serve in a chilled bowl. Slice reserved berries and float a few slices on each serving as garnish.

Chilled Mint-Cucumber Yogurt Soup

2 cucumbers
½ small onion, cut into chunks
1 clove garlic
2 cups nonfat or low-fat yogurt
3 tablespoons thinly sliced fresh mint leaves

½ teaspoon salt
⅛ teaspoon freshly ground black pepper
Pinch of cayenne pepper
4 thin slices cucumber for garnish (optional)

Peel cucumber and halve lengthwise. Scoop out seeds and discard seeds. Cut cucumber into chunks. Combine cucumber chunks, onion and garlic in a food processor; blend until smooth. Add half the yogurt and process until smooth. Stir in remaining yogurt, mint, salt, black pepper and cayenne pepper. Cover and chill at least 2 hours. To serve, ladle into individual serving bowls and garnish each with a cucumber slice.

Yield: 4 servings

Cold Cucumber Soup

1 cup chicken broth
¼ cup minced onion
1 teaspoon salt
½ teaspoon dried dill weed
Dash of garlic powder
1 teaspoon lemon zest
3 tablespoons fresh lemon juice

1 cup plain yogurt
1 cup sour cream
3 cucumbers, peeled, seeded and chopped
Lemon zest, lemon slices and cucumber slices for garnish

Combine broth, onion, salt, dill, garlic powder, lemon zest and lemon juice in a blender or food processor. Blend until smooth.

Combine yogurt and sour cream and add to mixture in blender. Process until mixed. Add cucumber to blender and pulse to grate but not liquefy. Chill 1 hour. Adjust seasonings as needed. Serve in wine goblets or glass bowls. Garnish as desired.

Yield: 4 to 6 servings

California Gazpacho

½   Spanish onion
1   large tomato, peeled
½   cucumber
1   large stalk celery
½   green bell pepper
1   teaspoon minced fresh chives
1   teaspoon minced fresh
      parsley
1   clove garlic, minced
2   cups V-8 juice
2-3 tablespoons red wine vinegar

2   tablespoons olive oil
1   teaspoon sugar
1   tablespoon lemon juice
1   teaspoon salt
¼   teaspoon black pepper
½   teaspoon Worcestershire
      sauce
⅛   teaspoon Tabasco sauce
½   ripe avocado
2   cups sour cream

Finely chop onion, tomato, cucumber, celery and bell pepper in a food processor. Add chives, parsley, garlic, V-8 juice, vinegar, oil, sugar, lemon juice, salt, black pepper, Worcestershire sauce and Tabasco sauce. Chill several hours.

Just before serving, dice avocado by hand. Top individual servings with avocado and a dollop of sour cream.

Fresh Mushroom Chicken Soup

4   cups water
1   (14 ounce) can chicken
      broth
1½ tablespoons soy sauce
3   boneless, skinless chicken
      breast halves, cut into
      1 inch chunks

½   cup thinly sliced carrot
½   cup thinly sliced celery
8   ounces mushrooms, sliced
⅓   cup sliced green onions
2   ounces dry egg noodles
¼-½ teaspoon dried thyme
      Salt and pepper to taste

Combine water, broth and soy sauce in a 3 to 4 quart saucepan. Bring to a boil. Add chicken, carrot and celery. Simmer 10 minutes. Skim top. Add mushrooms, onions, noodles and thyme. Simmer about 10 minutes or until noodles are cooked. Season with salt and pepper.

Yield: 4 to 6 entrée servings

Fiesta Tortilla Soup

**Served at the second course at "La Fiesta Mexicana" —
auctioned at the Hibiscus Children's Center Fall Benefit.**

2 tablespoons olive oil
4 medium tomatoes, peeled and chopped
1 medium onion, chopped
4 corn tortillas, cut into quarters
1 jalapeño pepper, diced
2 tablespoons chopped fresh cilantro

6 cups chicken broth
½ teaspoon ground cumin
½ teaspoon salt
White pepper to taste
Avocado slices for garnish
Shredded Monterey Jack cheese for garnish
Fried corn tortilla strips for garnish

Heat oil in a heavy saucepan. Add tomatoes, onion, tortilla quarters, jalapeño and cilantro. Cook until tortillas and tomatoes are very soft. Add broth, cumin, salt and white pepper. Bring to a boil. Reduce heat to a simmer and cook 20 minutes.

Puree soup in small batches in a blender or food processor. Garnish as desired with avocado slices, cheese and tortilla strips.

This soup is quite fiery hot. For a milder flavor, remove jalapeño seeds or use half of a jalapeño. For even hotter soup, substitute 2 cans of Rotel diced tomatoes and chiles for the tomatoes and jalapeño.

To make fried corn tortilla strips, cut 2 corn tortillas into thin strips. Let them sit out for 1 hour to dry. Fry lightly in vegetable oil; drain on paper towels.

Yield: 6 servings

Hearty Tortilla Soup

½ cup chopped onion
1 clove garlic, crushed
1 tablespoon vegetable oil
3 medium zucchini, sliced
4 cups chicken or vegetable broth
1 (14½ ounce) can stewed tomatoes, undrained

1 (16 ounce) can corn, undrained
1 teaspoon ground cumin
½ teaspoon hot sauce
½ cup dry pasta, cooked
½ cup kidney beans
Shredded cheddar cheese

Sauté onion and garlic in oil. Add zucchini, broth, tomatoes, corn, cumin and hot sauce. Bring to a boil. Reduce heat to a simmer, cover and cook 15 to 20 minutes.

Add pasta and beans and cook until heated through. Adjust seasonings as needed. Top individual servings with cheese. Serve with tortilla chips.

Grouper Chowder

2 carrots, diced
3 celery sticks, diced
1 large white onion, diced
2 tablespoons butter
12 ounces grouper, cut into small cubes
3 quarts heavy cream
2 cups milk

4 bay leaves
3 baking potatoes, diced
Salt and pepper to taste
3 tablespoons cornstarch mixed with 3 tablespoons water (optional)
Fresh chopped dill for garnish

Sauté carrots, celery and onion in butter in a large pot. When cooked about halfway, add grouper and cook about 5 minutes. Add cream, milk and bay leaves. Bring to a boil. Reduce heat to a simmer. Add potatoes and simmer until potatoes are tender. Season to taste with salt and pepper.

If thicker chowder is desired, stir in cornstarch and water mixture. Continue to simmer about 10 minutes. Garnish with fresh dill.

Orchid Island Golf and Beach Club
One Beachside Drive
Vero Beach, Florida

Conch Chowder

Serve with Marinated Mahi Mahi and
Bahamian Peas and Rice.

2	cups ground conch	2	tablespoons Worcestershire sauce
1	large onion, diced	¼	teaspoon dried thyme
⅓	cup diced green bell pepper	1	teaspoon ground cumin
½	cup diced celery	½	teaspoon cayenne pepper
2	tablespoons vegetable oil	1	(10 ounce) can Rotel diced tomatoes and chiles
1	(14½ ounce) can tomatoes, crushed	3-4	dashes Tabasco sauce
2	ounces bacon, diced		Salt and pepper to taste
2	cups diced potato	2	quarts water
½	cup diced carrot		
1	(6 ounce) can tomato paste		

Sauté conch, onion, bell pepper and celery in oil in a large pot until vegetables are tender. Add tomatoes, bacon, potato, carrot, tomato paste, Worcestershire sauce, thyme, cumin, cayenne pepper, tomatoes and chiles, Tabasco sauce, salt, pepper and 2 quarts water. Cook until all vegetables are tender. Adjust consistency, as desired, with extra tomatoes or tomato paste.

Walnut and Goat Cheese Salad with Raspberry Dressing

1	pound mesclun (combo of baby leaf greens)	½	(4 ounce) package goat cheese, crumbled
½	cup walnuts, toasted		Marzetti's Wild Raspberry Dressing to taste
1	apple, unpeeled and chopped		

Toss together mesclun, walnuts, apple and cheese in a large salad bowl. Pour dressing over salad and toss.

Yield: 4 servings

Texas Five Alarm Chili

**Serve with the rest of the six-pack,
a green salad and hot cornbread.**

4	pounds lean ground meat	1	teaspoon black pepper
1	large onion, chopped	1	(28 ounce) can crushed
3	fresh jalapeño peppers,		tomatoes
	seeded and chopped	1	(12 ounce) can beer
1	large clove garlic, minced		Chopped green onion and
2	tablespoons ground cumin		shredded cheddar cheese
2	tablespoons chili powder		for garnish
2	teaspoons salt		

Brown meat and onion in a saucepan; drain fat and return meat to saucepan. Add jalapeños, garlic, cumin, chili powder, salt and black pepper. Mix well. Add tomatoes and beer.

Bring to a boil. Reduce heat to a simmer and cook 2½ to 3 hours. Add water as needed while cooking. Serve with green onion and cheese for garnish.

Hearts of Palm Salad

½	cup olive oil	¼	teaspoon black pepper
⅓	cup tarragon vinegar	3	(14 ounce) cans hearts of
4	teaspoons capers		palm, drained, cut into
1	tablespoon snipped fresh		1 inch pieces
	chives		Bibb lettuce
¼	teaspoon dried chervil,	1	large avocado
	crushed		Pimento slices
½	teaspoon salt		

To make a dressing, combine oil, vinegar, capers, chives, chervil, salt and pepper. Cover and shake well. In a mixing bowl, combine hearts of palm and dressing mixture. Chill several hours.

To serve, transfer hearts of palm to a lettuce-lined serving plate, reserving dressing. Slice avocado and arrange on serving plate. Add extra dressing, as desired, and pimento slices.

Yield: 8 to 10 servings

St. Bart's Salad

¼   cup pecan or walnut pieces
1   tablespoon balsamic vinegar
    Salt and pepper to taste
3-4 tablespoons extra virgin
    olive oil

1   (10 ounce) package spring
    or herb salad mix greens
12 niçoise olives
¼   cup crumbled blue cheese

Preheat oven to 350 degrees. Toast pecans in oven for 6 to 7 minutes. Set aside to cool.

Whisk together vinegar, salt and pepper in a large salad bowl. Whisk in oil, a little at a time. Add greens, olives, cheese and pecans. Toss and serve.

Chilled Artichoke Hearts and Peas

1   (9 ounce) package frozen
    artichoke hearts
1   (10 ounce) package frozen
    peas
1   cup diagonally sliced celery
½   cup pitted green olives
1   cup garbanzo beans (chick
    peas)

½   cup vegetable oil
¼   cup cider vinegar
1   teaspoon salt
¼   teaspoon black pepper
½   teaspoon sugar
    Croutons
    Romaine lettuce leaves

Cook artichoke hearts and peas according to package instructions; drain well. Combine artichokes, peas, celery, olives, garbanzo beans, oil, vinegar, salt, pepper and sugar in a bowl. Cover and refrigerate about 1 hour or until chilled, stirring occasionally.

Add croutons just before serving. Spoon mixture into individual serving dishes lined with lettuce leaves.

Also good with a small amount of chopped sweet or red onion mixed in before chilling.

Yield: 6 servings

Goat Cheese Salad with Warm Dressing

Can also top each serving with Grilled Texas Shrimp.

5	ounces bacon, chopped	1	(5½ ounce) log goat cheese with 4-pepper crust
2	shallots, minced		
1	large clove garlic, minced	1	(10 ounce) package Italian blend salad greens
⅓	cup olive oil		
¼	cup red wine vinegar	1	heart of romaine lettuce, sliced
2	teaspoons sugar		
½	cup port wine	½	cup pine nuts, toasted

Preheat oven to 350 degrees. Sauté bacon in a heavy skillet over medium-low heat for 8 minutes or until crisp. Add shallots and garlic and cook 2 minutes. Add oil, vinegar and sugar to skillet. Cook and stir until sugar dissolves. Stir in wine. Keep warm.

Cut goat cheese into ½ inch thick slices. Place slices on a foil-lined baking sheet. Bake cheese 8 to 10 minutes or until warm.

In a salad bowl, combine greens, romaine lettuce and pine nuts. Pour bacon dressing over salad and toss. Divide salad among individual salad plates. Top each serving with goat cheese.

Yield: 6 servings

Spinach-Strawberry Salad

½	cup sugar	2	tablespoons sesame seeds
1½	teaspoons minced onion	1	tablespoon poppy seeds
¼	teaspoon Worcestershire sauce	1	quart fresh strawberries, hulled and chilled
¼	teaspoon paprika	1	(1 pound) package fresh spinach, stemmed and chilled
¼	cup cider vinegar		
½	cup vegetable oil		

To make a dressing, combine sugar, onion, Worcestershire sauce, paprika, vinegar, oil, sesame seeds and poppy seeds in a jar. Shake until well mixed. Chill.

To serve, cut strawberries into thin slices. Toss strawberries with spinach and dressing.

Spinach Salad
with Mimosa Dressing

Salad

1 (10 ounce) package fresh spinach, washed and torn

Sliced fresh mushrooms, (optional)

3 hard-cooked eggs, sliced

8 ounces bacon, chopped and cooked

1 (8 ounce) can sliced water chestnuts, drained

4-5 green onions, chopped

Salt and pepper to taste

Dressing

1 cup oil

¾ cup sugar

½ cup ketchup

¼ cup cider vinegar

Combine all salad ingredients in a large salad bowl.

To make dressing, combine all ingredients in a saucepan. Heat until sugar dissolves. Cool. Pour dressing over salad to taste. Toss. Refrigerate remaining dressing for a later use.

Warm Spinach-Orange Salad

½ (10 ounce) package fresh spinach, stemmed

1 orange, peeled and sectioned

¼ cup sliced almonds

2 tablespoons cider vinegar

1½ tablespoons orange juice

1½ tablespoons olive oil

1½ tablespoons honey

Combine spinach, orange sections and almonds in a large bowl.

In a small saucepan, bring vinegar, juice, oil and honey to a boil over medium heat. Pour immediately over salad. Toss and serve.

Orange Salad Bowl
"This is great with the Jambalaya!"

Salad

8 cups torn salad greens
1 (11 ounce) can Mandarin
   orange sections

1 small purple onion, sliced
   into rings
½ cup pecan pieces or
   sunflower seed kernels

Celery Seed Dressing

⅓ cup sugar
1 teaspoon salt
1 teaspoon dry mustard
⅓ cup cider vinegar

1 small onion, finely chopped
1 cup vegetable oil
1 tablespoon celery seeds

Combine all salad ingredients in a salad bowl.

To make dressing, combine all ingredients in a jar. Cover and shake well. Let stand at least 1 hour for flavors to blend. Pour dressing over salad and toss.

Moroccan Orange Salad

6 large oranges
1 tablespoon honey
½ teaspoon cinnamon
½ pound each spinach and
   romaine lettuce, torn into
   bite-size pieces

½ cup thinly sliced red onion
1 cup thinly sliced radish
1 cup walnuts, toasted
3 tablespoons olive oil
   Salt and pepper to taste

Use a serrated knife to cut away orange peel. Slice peeled oranges. Drizzle honey and cinnamon over orange slices and let stand 1 hour.

Combine greens, onion, radish and walnuts in a salad bowl; toss. Drizzle oil over salad and toss to mix. Season with salt and pepper. Just before serving, add orange slices and any orange liquid that has accumulated. Mix well and serve.

Mandarin Orange Salad

1	head lettuce, torn into bite-size pieces
1	avocado, peeled and sliced
2	green onions, chopped
1	(11 ounce) can Mandarin oranges, drained

½	cup sliced almonds, toasted
3	ounces Romano cheese, grated
1	(.75 ounce) package Good Seasons cheese and garlic dressing mix

Combine all ingredients except dressing in a salad bowl. Make dressing according to package. Pour dressing over salad and toss.

Summer Salad

Salad

1½	cups chopped Granny Smith apple, unpeeled
1½	cups chopped Golden Delicious apple, unpeeled
¾	cup chopped Red Delicious apple, unpeeled

1	cup thinly sliced celery
½	cup seedless red grapes, halved
½	cup golden raisins
¼	cup chopped pecans

Dressing

½	cup plain nonfat yogurt
2	tablespoons honey

1	tablespoon white wine vinegar
1½	teaspoons Dijon mustard

Combine all salad ingredients in a large bowl. Toss well.

To make dressing, mix all ingredients in a small bowl with a wire whisk. Pour dressing over salad. Toss gently. Cover and chill 30 minutes. Serve on a bed of lettuce.

Yield: six (1 cup) servings

Fruit and Almond Salad with Curry Vinaigrette Dressing

Salad

½ cup slivered almonds
1 head iceberg lettuce, torn into pieces
1 cup spinach, torn into pieces

1 (11 ounce) can Mandarin oranges, chilled and drained
1 cup seedless grapes, halved
1 avocado, peeled and diced

Dressing

½ cup vegetable oil
½ cup white vinegar
1 clove garlic, minced
2 tablespoons brown sugar

2 tablespoons minced fresh chives
1 tablespoon curry powder
1 teaspoon soy sauce

Toast almonds under a broiler until golden, watching carefully to prevent burning. Combine lettuce, spinach, oranges, grapes and avocado in a large salad bowl. Add almonds.

Prepare dressing by mixing all ingredients. Pour dressing over salad and toss gently.

Yield: 10 to 12 servings

Texas Potato Salad

Salad

1 (5 pound) bag red potatoes, boiled and sliced
3-4 hard-boiled eggs, sliced
1 red onion, chopped

Chopped dill pickle
8 ounces bacon, cooked and crumbled

Dressing

½-¾ cup mayonnaise
¼ cup sugar
¼ cup vinegar

3 tablespoons yellow mustard
3 tablespoons vegetable oil
Salt and pepper to taste

Combine all salad ingredients in a large bowl.

Mix together dressing ingredients and pour over salad. Mix gently and chill.

Potato Salad

Salad

12-13	red potatoes	1	tablespoon dill pickle relish
1	medium onion, chopped		
4-5	stalks celery hearts, chopped	3-4	hard-cooked eggs, chopped
	Salt and pepper		

Dressing

1	cup mayonnaise	1	tablespoon distilled vinegar
⅓	cup Dijon mustard		
1	teaspoon celery salt	1	teaspoon sugar
			Half-and-half

Cook potatoes in boiling water until tender but not mushy. Cut into bite-size cubes and place in a large mixing bowl over onion and celery while still hot. Season layers of potatoes with salt and pepper as they are put into bowl. Cover bowl with a plate and let stand until cooled.

Meanwhile, combine all dressing ingredients, using enough half-and-half to reach desired consistency. Taste dressing and adjust seasoning, adding more mustard if more "bite" is desired.

Add pickle relish to cooled potatoes and toss. Add dressing and toss. Add eggs and toss. Refrigerate until chilled.

Sauerkraut Salad

1	(16 ounce) can sauerkraut	½	cup minced carrot
½	cup sugar	½	cup minced green bell pepper
½	cup minced celery	¼	cup minced onion

Combine all ingredients. Chill at least 12 hours before serving.

Strawberry Salad

Salad

1	head Bibb lettuce

1   pint fresh strawberries, sliced

Dressing

⅓   cup vegetable oil

⅓   cup cider vinegar

½   cup sugar

1-2 tablespoons sesame seeds

1   tablespoon minced onion

½   teaspoon Worcestershire
     sauce

Dash of hot sauce

Open lettuce head on a serving plate. Place strawberries on lettuce in a decorative manner.

Combine all dressing ingredients. Drizzle dressing to taste over salad. Refrigerate any remaining dressing for a future use.

Sissy's Orange-Cream Fruit Salad

1   (20 ounce) can crushed
     pineapple, drained

2   (16 ounce) cans sliced
     peaches, drained and cut
     into bite-size pieces

1   (11 ounce) can Mandarin
     oranges, drained

3   medium bananas, sliced

1   medium red apple, unpeeled
     and chopped

1   medium green apple,
     unpeeled and chopped

1   (3½ ounce) package vanilla
     instant pudding mix

1½ cups milk

½   (6 ounce) container frozen
     orange juice concentrate
     (⅓ cup), thawed

1   (8 ounce) container sour
     cream

Combine pineapple, peaches, oranges, bananas and apples in a large bowl. Set aside. In a small bowl, combine pudding mix, milk and juice. Beat with a hand beater 1 to 2 minutes or until blended. Beat in sour cream. Fold pudding mixture into fruit. Cover and refrigerate several hours or overnight.

Granny Smith and Red Delicious apples work well for color. If desired, add red and green cherries for extra color.

Fresh Asparagus Salad

1	pound fresh asparagus		Salt and pepper to taste
⅓	cup water	1	roasted red bell pepper, chopped, or 2 tablespoons jarred
2	tablespoons balsamic vinegar		
½	teaspoon minced shallots	¼	cup pine nuts, toasted
½	teaspoon Dijon mustard	2	tablespoons capers, drained
¼	cup olive oil	2	ounces Parmesan cheese, shredded
1	teaspoon chopped Italian parsley		

Place asparagus in a microwave-safe baking dish. Add ⅓ cup water and cover. Microwave on high 5 to 7 minutes or until crisp-tender. Drain and rinse in cold water.

To make a dressing, mix together vinegar, shallots and mustard. Add oil, parsley, salt and pepper. Whisk until mixed.

Arrange asparagus on a serving plate. Top with bell pepper, pine nuts, capers and cheese. Drizzle with dressing and serve.

Green Bean and Mozzarella Salad

2	cups fresh green beans, cooked and drained	½	cup Italian dressing
8	ounces mozzarella cheese, cut into ½ inch cubes	6	fresh plum tomatoes, sliced
		⅓	cup chopped fresh basil
		⅛	teaspoon black pepper

Combine all ingredients in a large bowl. Cover and refrigerate 1 hour.

Yield: 4 servings

Marinated Cucumber Salad

Salad
3	cucumbers, peeled
½	medium red onion, thinly sliced

2	(4 ounce) cans sliced black olives, drained
2	ounces crumbled feta cheese

Dressing
⅓	cup white wine vinegar
1	tablespoon Dijon mustard
2	teaspoons vegetable oil
1	teaspoon soy sauce
1	clove garlic, crushed

¼	teaspoon dried basil
¼	teaspoon dried tarragon
¼	teaspoon dried thyme
¼	teaspoon black pepper

Halve cucumbers lengthwise. Scoop out seeds and cut cucumbers into ¼ inch thick slices. Combine cucumber slices, onion, olives and feta in a bowl.

To make dressing, combine all ingredients. Pour dressing over salad. Cover and refrigerate at least 2 hours, tossing twice while chilling.

Cucumber Salad

A perfect cool taste when serving a spicy entrée.

Salad
4	large cucumbers, thinly sliced
1½	teaspoons salt

¼	cup minced green onion
2	tablespoons chopped dill weed

Dressing
3	tablespoons tarragon vinegar
1	tablespoon olive oil
1	teaspoon Dijon mustard

2	teaspoons white pepper
½	teaspoon salt
2	teaspoons sugar

Sprinkle cucumber slices with salt. Refrigerate 30 minutes. Rinse, drain and pat dry. Combine cucumber slices with onion and dill in a bowl.

Combine all dressing ingredients and pour over salad.

Yield: 6 servings

Parslied Cherry Tomatoes with Garlic

1 pint cherry tomatoes, halved	2 tablespoons olive oil
2 cloves garlic, minced	2 teaspoons fresh lemon juice
¼ teaspoon salt	⅓ cup coarsely chopped fresh parsley

Toss tomatoes, garlic, salt, oil and lemon juice in a bowl. Stir in parsley just before serving.

Yield: 4 servings

Layered Greek Salad

Salad

1 (16 ounce) can wax beans, drained	1 (7 ounce) can mushrooms, drained
1 (16 ounce) can Le Sueur peas, drained	1 (14 ounce) can artichoke hearts, drained
1 (8 ounce) can bamboo shoots, drained	1 (4 ounce) can sliced black olives, drained
1 (8 ounce) can sliced water chestnuts, drained	

Dressing

½ cup vegetable oil	Seasoned salt to taste
½ cup vinegar	1½ tablespoons dill weed
½ cup sugar	

To make salad, layer all ingredients in a glass bowl.

Combine all dressing ingredients. Pour dressing over salad. Tip bowl to disperse dressing without mixing layers. Refrigerate several hours.

Broccoli Salad

Salad

1	large bunch broccoli, cut into bite-size pieces	½	medium-size red onion, chopped
8	ounces bacon, cooked crisp and crumbled	½	cup sunflower seeds
		½	cup golden raisins
		½	cup sliced fresh mushrooms

Dressing

1	cup mayonnaise	2	tablespoons cider vinegar
¼	cup sugar		

Combine all salad ingredients in a bowl.

To make dressing, mix all ingredients. Pour dressing over salad. Mix and refrigerate overnight.

Portobello Mushroom Salad

1	tablespoon balsamic vinegar	2	tablespoons minced shallots
3	tablespoons olive oil	4	portobello mushrooms
1	teaspoon salt		Baby lettuce greens
¼	teaspoon black pepper		

Combine vinegar, oil, salt, pepper and shallots. Add mushrooms and marinate for 1 hour.

Remove mushrooms from marinade, reserving marinade. Sauté mushrooms a few minutes or until soft. Slice mushrooms into strips. Place mushroom slices over a bed of baby lettuce. Drizzle salad with some of reserved marinade.

Ribbon Jello Mold

4 (3 ounce) packages gelatin; orange, lime, lemon and cherry	4 pints vanilla ice cream
	1 (16 ounce) container sour cream
4 cups hot water	

Mix 1 package of gelatin with 1 cup hot water. Stir to dissolve. Add 1 pint vanilla ice cream and stir until ice cream is melted and smooth. Pour mixture into a glass 9x13 inch baking dish. Chill 1 hour.

Spread a thin layer of sour cream, using about one-third of container, over gelled orange layer. Refrigerate while preparing remaining layers. Repeat process with remaining gelatin flavors, ice cream and sour cream, ending with a gelatin layer. Chill until firm.

Cranberry Salad

***This has been served with our turkey at
Thanksgiving and Christmas for four generations.***

2 (3 ounce) packages lemon gelatin	1 (12 ounce) package cranberries
1½ cups sugar	1 cup pecans
2 cups boiling water	1 tablespoon orange zest
	Juice of 2 oranges

Dissolve gelatin and sugar in boiling water. Cool. Grind cranberries, pecans and orange zest together. Stir cranberry mixture and orange juice into gelatin. Pour into an 8x12 inch pan. Chill until firm. Slice into squares.

Yield: 12 servings

Emerald Salad

1	(3 ounce) package lime gelatin	1	(8 ounce) container cream-style cottage cheese
¾	cup boiling water	1	cup mayonnaise
¾	cup shredded cucumber	⅓	cup slivered almonds
2	tablespoons grated onion		

Dissolve gelatin in boiling water. Chill mixture until thickened to the consistency of unbeaten egg white.

Squeeze dry cucumber and onion in paper towels. Combine vegetables with cottage cheese, mayonnaise and almonds. Stir mixture into gelatin until well mixed. Pour into a lightly greased 4 cup mold. Chill until firm.

Napa Salad

Salad

1	head napa cabbage, shredded	½	cup slivered almonds
3	green onions, chopped	2	tablespoons sesame seeds
2	(3 ounce) packages ramen noodles, crushed, seasoning packet discarded	6	tablespoons butter

Dressing

½	cup vegetable oil	2	teaspoons soy sauce
¾	cup sugar	½	cup cider vinegar

Combine cabbage and onions in a large bowl. Sauté noodles, almonds and sesame seeds in butter. Add to cabbage mixture.

Combine all dressing ingredients and shake well. Pour dressing over salad just before serving.

Bow Tie Pasta Salad

2   cups dry bow tie pasta,
      cooked and drained
3   avocados, peeled and cubed
2   cups sliced fresh
      mushrooms
2   cups cherry tomatoes, halved

¼   cup sliced green onions
½   cup cubed summer sausage
¾   cup spicy Italian salad
      dressing or Emily's Italian
      Dressing (page 81)

Combine all ingredients in a large bowl. Toss gently. Cover and chill.

Bayou Pasta Salad

Serves a very large crowd.

2   pounds dry tri-colored
      corkscrew pasta
1   medium red bell pepper,
      diced
1   medium green bell pepper,
      diced
1   medium yellow bell pepper,
      diced
1   large yellow onion, diced
2   bunches green onions,
      sliced diagonally
1   pound andouille sausage,
      diced

1   pound tasso ham, chopped
1   pound cooked crawfish tail
      meat, chopped
1   pound cooked blackfin lump
      crabmeat, chopped
3   cups mayonnaise
2   cups whole grain mustard
6   tablespoons hot sauce
1   tablespoon thyme
1   tablespoon cayenne pepper
    Salt and pepper to taste

Cook pasta al dente. Drain, cool with cold water and drain again.
Combine pasta, bell peppers, onions, sausage, ham, crawfish and
crabmeat in a bowl.

In a separate bowl, mix together mayonnaise, mustard, hot sauce,
thyme, cayenne pepper, salt and pepper. Add mayonnaise mixture to
salad and mix. Refrigerate until chilled.

Dolphin Safe Pasta

10	ounces dry pasta of choice, cooked and drained	1	(16 ounce) can garbanzo beans, drained
2	(6 ounce) cans tuna (dolphin safe)		Olives to taste
		1	cup sour cream
2	large tomatoes, diced	⅓	cup Parmesan cheese
½	cup chopped white or red onion	1	teaspoon dill weed
			Garlic powder to taste
1	(16 ounce) can niblet corn, drained		Red wine vinegar to taste
			Salt and pepper to taste

Combine all ingredients. Chill.

Martha's Vineyard Salad

Raspberry Vinegar
1   cup white wine vinegar
1   cup red wine vinegar

½   cup fresh or frozen raspberries

Raspberry-Maple Dressing
½   cup Raspberry Vinegar
½   cup olive oil
½   cup vegetable oil
½   cup maple syrup

2   tablespoons Dijon mustard
2   tablespoons dried tarragon, or ¼ cup fresh
Dash of salt

Salad
1   head Bibb lettuce, torn
½   head red leaf lettuce, torn
¼   cup crumbled blue cheese

12   (¼ inch thick) rings red onion
3   tablespoons pine nuts, toasted

To prepare raspberry vinegar, combine vinegars and raspberries in a glass container. Cover and let stand 48 hours. Strain vinegar and store at room temperature.

Whisk together all dressing ingredients.

Combine all salad ingredients in a large bowl. Add ¾ cup of dressing to salad and toss.

Yield: 6 servings

Commercial raspberry vinegar, available at specialty stores, can also be used.

Steak Salad

Salad

6	cups mixed field greens, chilled
1	medium tomato, cut into chunks
1	small red onion, sliced and separated into rings
3	tablespoons chopped fresh parsley
3	tablespoons chopped fresh chives
½	cup crumbled blue cheese
4	slices bacon, cooked and crumbled (optional)
½	cup fried onion rings, crumbled (optional)
4-6	ounces beef tenderloin tip, seared medium rare and thinly sliced
	Salt and pepper to taste

Lemon-Scented Vinaigrette

⅔	cup extra-virgin olive oil
1	teaspoon very finely minced garlic
1	teaspoon finely minced onion
1	tablespoon Italian herb blend
⅓	cup freshly squeezed lemon juice
1	teaspoon finely grated lemon zest
¼	teaspoon salt
¼	teaspoon black pepper

Divide greens among three large, chilled salad plates. Layer remaining salad ingredients on greens. Toss briefly.

To prepare vinaigrette, place all ingredients in a jar with a tight-fitting lid; shake well. Drizzle a few tablespoons of vinaigrette over each salad and serve immediately.

Yield: 3 salads, about 1 cup vinaigrette

Vinaigrette also makes a great marinade.

Ruth's Chris Steak House
661 US1
North Palm Beach, Florida

Sonoma Salad

4	boneless, skinless chicken breast halves	1	cup shredded carrot
½	cup Spiedie Sauce Marinade, or Jane's Balsamic Vinaigrette (page 80)	½	cup hazelnuts, halved, toasted and skin removed
½	cup dried sweetened cranberries	1	(16 ounce) package mixed Italian salad greens
1	Granny Smith apple, thinly sliced	1	heart of romaine lettuce head, chopped
1	cup shredded white New York cheddar cheese		Ken's Raspberry Walnut vinaigrette or Ken's Cranberry vinaigrette

Marinate chicken in Spiedie Sauce Marinade for about 30 minutes. Remove chicken from marinade and grill about 5 minutes on each side or until done. Cool, slice and set aside.

Combine cranberries, apple, cheese, carrot, hazelnuts, greens and lettuce in a salad bowl. Toss with Ken's vinaigrette. Divide salad among individual salad plates. Top with sliced chicken.

Yield: 8 servings

Paella Salad

Salad

4	cups chicken broth	¾	cup diced green bell pepper
¾	teaspoon curry powder	5	ounces green onions, chopped
½	teaspoon salt	2	stalks celery, diced
¼	teaspoon Tabasco sauce	1	(4 ounce) jar pimento-stuffed green olives, chopped
¼	teaspoon saffron		
2	cloves garlic		
6	tablespoons vegetable oil	8	ounces crabmeat
1	cup chopped onion	½	cup Curry Mayonnaise
1½	cups dry rice	1	tablespoon plain mayonnaise
1½	pounds boneless, skinless chicken breast, cooked and cut into 1 inch pieces	16-20	clams or mussels, washed
		1	head romaine lettuce
3	(6 ounce) jars marinated artichoke hearts, diced, liquid reserved	1	pound shrimp, cooked

Curry Mayonnaise

1	cup mayonnaise	1½	teaspoons curry powder
	Liquid from artichoke hearts		Salt and pepper to taste

Combine broth, curry, salt, Tabasco sauce, saffron and garlic in a saucepan. Bring to a boil. Meanwhile, heat oil in a skillet. Add onion and sauté. Add rice and cook and stir until brown. Slowly pour in hot broth mixture. Reduce heat and simmer 15 minutes or until liquid is absorbed. Cool. Stir chicken, artichoke, bell pepper, green onions, celery, olives and crabmeat into rice mixture. Add ½ cup Curry Mayonnaise to mixture. Use plain mayonnaise to grease an 8 cup fish mold. Pack rice mixture into mold and refrigerate overnight.

Two hours before serving, bring 1½ inches of water in a saucepan to a boil. Add clams and steam 6 to 10 minutes. Discard any clams that do not open. To serve, line a large platter with romaine lettuce leaves. Unmold rice salad onto platter. Arrange shrimp around rice mold. Dab a little Curry Mayonnaise onto each clam and add clams to platter.

To make Curry Mayonnaise, combine all ingredients. Refrigerate until ready to use.

Yield: 12 servings

Dill Chicken Salad

4   boneless, skinless chicken
        breast halves
¼   cup mayonnaise

2   tablespoons Dijon mustard
¼   cup chopped fresh dill
2   tablespoons sesame seeds

Cook chicken in microwave until no longer pink. Cool and cut into
½ inch cubes. Set aside. Mix mayonnaise, mustard, dill and sesame
seeds in a bowl. Add chicken and toss to coat. Chill until ready to
serve. Serve in whole wheat pitas with sliced cucumbers, lettuce and
tomatoes.

Chinese Chicken Salad
with Noodles

*"It is a delicious cold salad for picnics, etc.
and is a little out of the ordinary."*

Salad
2   (3 ounce) packages chicken-
        flavored ramen noodles
1   head napa cabbage, cut into
        bite-size chunks
1   pound chicken breast,
        cooked and cubed

1   (2 ounce) package slivered
        almonds, lightly toasted
1   cup sesame seeds, lightly
        toasted

Dressing
¾   cup vegetable oil
3   tablespoons sugar
7   tablespoons white vinegar

Seasoning packets from
    noodles

Cook noodles according to package directions, reserving seasoning
packets for dressing. Noodles can be broken before cooking, if
desired. Combine cooked noodles, cabbage, chicken, almonds and
sesame seeds.

In a small saucepan, combine all dressing ingredients. Bring to just
boiling. Stir and pour over salad. Toss salad to mix. Serve or
refrigerate until ready to serve.

Pam's Oriental Chicken Salad

"A Guild members' favorite! This is requested every time the meeting is at my house. A bit of trouble, but well worth it!"

Chicken

3 whole skinless chicken breasts
2 cups chicken broth
1 small onion, quartered
½ stalk celery, thickly sliced
1 bay leaf
3 peppercorns
2 sprigs fresh parsley

Marinade

3 tablespoons soy sauce
1 teaspoon sesame oil
½ teaspoon minced garlic
1 tablespoon rice wine vinegar
½ teaspoon minced fresh ginger
1 teaspoon salt
1½ teaspoons Chinese chili garlic paste
1 teaspoon sugar

Noodles

3 quarts water
1 tablespoon peanut oil
1 teaspoon salt
6 ounces Chinese egg noodles

Vegetables

1½ cups bean sprouts
½ pound snow peas
½ cup sliced green onions
3 red bell peppers, sliced into thin strips

Creamy Peanut Sauce

½ cup chunky peanut butter
⅓ cup reserved chicken broth
¼ cup soy sauce
3 tablespoons sesame oil
1 tablespoon minced garlic
1 tablespoon sugar
2 tablespoons red wine vinegar
2 teaspoons Chinese chili garlic paste
1 tablespoon minced fresh ginger
¼ cup heavy cream

Combine all ingredients for preparing chicken in a saucepan. Bring to a boil. Reduce heat to medium-low and simmer 5 minutes. Remove saucepan from heat and let stand 20 minutes. Remove chicken and strain broth through a sieve. Return ½ cup of broth to saucepan and cook until it reduces to ⅓ cup; set aside. Shred chicken by hand into bite-size pieces.

Combine all marinade ingredients and pour over cooked chicken. Mix well and refrigerate.

(Pam's Oriental Chicken Salad continued)

To make noodles, bring 3 quarts water, oil and salt to a boil. Add noodles and cook until al dente. Drain and rinse with cold water. Combine noodles with chicken and marinade.

Blanch bean sprouts and snow peas in boiling water for 30 seconds. Drain and rinse with cold water. Add bean sprouts, peas, onions and pepper strips to chicken mixture.

In a food processor, blend all peanut sauce ingredients except cream. With motor running, add cream in a steady stream until blended. Pour sauce over chicken mixture and toss. Serve in a large bowl or on individual serving plates over a bed of freshly fried rice noodles.

Chicken Salad

Salad

2 cups chicken, cut into large chunks	½ cup chopped celery
¼ cup sliced water chestnuts	½ cup slivered almonds, toasted
8 ounces seedless green grapes, halved	1 (8 ounce) can pineapple chunks, drained

Dressing

¾ cup mayonnaise	2 teaspoons soy sauce
1 teaspoon curry powder	2 teaspoons lemon juice

Combine salad ingredients in a bowl.

In a separate bowl, mix together dressing ingredients. Combine salad and dressing. Mix well and chill.

Chutney Chicken Salad

Salad

4   cups cooked and cubed chicken breast

1   cup diagonally sliced celery

4   green onions, sliced

1   (5 ounce) can sliced water chestnuts, drained

8   slices bacon, cooked and cut into bite-size pieces

    Lettuce if making individual servings

2   avocados, peeled and cut in wedges (optional)

½   cup slivered almonds, lightly toasted

Dressing

1   cup mayonnaise

¼   cup fresh lime juice

¼   cup chopped mango chutney

2   teaspoons lime zest

1   teaspoon curry powder

½   teaspoon salt

½   teaspoon black pepper

Place chicken in a saucepan and add enough water to just cover. Bring to a boil. Reduce heat and simmer over medium-low heat 5 minutes. Remove from heat and let stand 20 minutes. Drain, cool and cut into cubes. Combine cooked chicken, celery, onions, water chestnuts and bacon in a large bowl.

In a small bowl, combine all dressing ingredients. Whisk until well mixed. Pour dressing over salad and mix well.

To assemble, line individual serving plates with lettuce leaves. Spoon salad onto lettuce. Arrange avocados around salad and sprinkle with almonds. If serving in a buffet, omit avocados and lettuce and serve in a large bowl.

For extra flavor, add 1 stalk of celery, 1 small onion and 5 peppercorns to cooking liquid for chicken. Discard with liquid when done cooking.

Easy Chinese Chicken Salad

Makes a light lady's lunch

Salad

4	boneless, skinless chicken breasts
1	tablespoon sesame oil
½	cup water
	Salt and pepper to taste
¼	cup pine nuts or slivered almonds

1	teaspoon sugar
6	cups lettuce, torn into bite-size pieces
	Crushed tortilla chips or crispy Chinese chow mein noodles

Dressing

¼	cup rice wine vinegar
1	tablespoon sugar

¼	cup sesame oil

Sauté chicken in 1 tablespoon sesame oil in a skillet until lightly browned. Add ½ cup water and simmer until tender. Cool, drain and season with salt and pepper. Shred chicken into bite-size pieces. Place pine nuts on a baking sheet and sprinkle with 1 teaspoon sugar. Toast lightly in oven and cool. In a large bowl, toss lettuce, chicken and pine nuts.

Combine dressing ingredients in a jar and shake well. Pour over salad and toss. Top individual servings with crushed tortilla chips or noodles.

Smoked Turkey Salad

1½	pounds smoked turkey, ham or chicken, cut into 2 inch julienne strips
12	ounces Jarlsberg cheese, cut into 2 inch julienne strips
2	cups seedless green or red grapes

1	cup chopped celery
1½	cups Sherry Mayonnaise (page 250)
	Salt and pepper to taste
	Lettuce leaves
1-2	tablespoons water-packed green peppercorns, drained

Combine turkey, cheese, grapes and celery. Add mayonnaise and gently toss. Season with salt and pepper and refrigerate until ready to serve. To serve, arrange salad on a lettuce-lined salad plate. Top with peppercorns.

Susie's Scrumptious Gingery Grilled Salmon Salad

Salmon

¼	cup nonfat plain yogurt	1	tablespoon honey
2	tablespoons chopped ginger	1	tablespoon vegetable oil
2	cloves garlic, chopped		Salt and pepper to taste
2	tablespoons fresh lime juice	1½	pounds salmon fillet
1	tablespoon lime zest		

Watercress and Pickled Ginger Salad

1	clove garlic, crushed	4	green onions, chopped
1	tablespoon juice from ginger	⅓	cup drained pickled ginger
		1	tablespoon vegetable oil
1	tablespoon fresh lime juice	1	teaspoon honey
6	cups watercress		Salt to taste

Combine all salmon ingredients. Marinate about 1 hour.

Meanwhile, prepare salad by combining all ingredients. Toss. When ready to serve, remove fish from marinade and grill until done. Serve salmon over salad.

Jane's Balsamic Vinaigrette

3	tablespoons balsamic vinegar	½	teaspoon Dijon mustard
1	teaspoon salt	½	teaspoon lemon juice
½	teaspoon black pepper	2	cloves garlic, crushed
		⅔	cup olive oil

Combine vinegar, salt, pepper, mustard, lemon juice and garlic in a bowl. Whisk in olive oil. Store vinaigrette in a glass jar.

Grilled Shrimp Salad with Balsamic Vinaigrette and Corn Salsa

Served as a first course at "La Fiesta Mexicana" — auctioned at the Hibiscus Children's Center's Fall Benefit.

4	cloves garlic	16	large shrimp, peeled and deveined
1	teaspoon Dijon mustard		
½	teaspoon cayenne pepper	4	cups mixed greens
1	bunch cilantro	½	cup Jane's Balsamic Vinaigrette (page 80)
1	teaspoon coriander		
	Juice of 1 lemon	½	cup Jane's Corn Salsa (page 253)
	Salt and pepper to taste		
½	cup olive oil		

Combine garlic, mustard, cayenne pepper, cilantro, coriander, lemon juice, salt, pepper and oil in a food processor; blend to make a marinade. Marinate shrimp in marinade.

When ready to serve, remove shrimp from marinade and grill 2 to 3 minutes on each side. Set aside. Toss greens with about half the vinaigrette. Divide mixture among 4 salad plates. Top each with 3 to 4 shrimp and 2 tablespoons salsa. Drizzle with remaining vinaigrette.

Emily's Italian Salad Dressing

3-4	cloves garlic, or to taste	½	teaspoon Accent
1	teaspoon dry mustard	1	part red wine vinegar
	Salt and pepper to taste	3	parts olive or vegetable oil

Combine garlic, mustard, salt, pepper and Accent in a jar. Add vinegar and shake. Pour in oil and shake well.

Blue Cheese Dressing

1 (4 ounce) package blue
   cheese
1 (8 ounce) container sour
   cream
½-1 teaspoon dry mustard

2 dashes Worcestershire sauce
1 teaspoon sugar
1 teaspoon white wine vinegar
   Dash of garlic salt or to
   taste

Combine all ingredients.

Poppy Seed Dressing

1½ cups sugar
2 teaspoons mustard
2 teaspoons salt
¾ cup vinegar

3 tablespoons onion juice
2 cups vegetable oil
3 tablespoons poppy seeds

Combine sugar, mustard, salt and vinegar in a blender. Add onion
juice and mix. With blender running, slowly add oil until dressing is
thick. Add poppy seeds and blend again. Use as a dressing for fruit
salad. Store extra dressing in refrigerator.

Fish and Shellfish

BRIAN SYLVESTER
Yellowfins
Acrylic and Oil, 2000

Fish and Shellfish

Fish

Marinated Mahi Mahi 83
Mahi Mahi with
   Spicy Mango Cilantro Sauce 83
Dolphin Grand Cay 84
Fresh Grilled Grouper Topped
   with a Roma Tomato-Fresh
   Mint Salsa 85
Grouper Provolone 86
Pecan Grouper 86
Pan Seared Grouper,
   Blackening Rub 87
Bahamian Grouper 88
Caribbean Banana Snapper 88
Heavenly Fillets 89
Bacon, Tomato and Fish Casserole 89
Herb Crusted Snapper with Roasted
   Plum Tomato Vinaigrette 90
Snapper Martinique 91
Nutty Pompano,
   Orange-Passion Fruit Menuière 92
Baked Asian Fish Packets 93
White Fish Epicurean 93
Chilean Sea Bass over Portobella
   Mushroom with a Roasted
   Red Bell Pepper Sauce 94
Salmon Fillets Aloha 95
Basil Marinated Fish 95
Guilt Free Salmon 96
Grilled Salmon
   with Honey-Mustard Sauce 96

Grilled Tuna with Arugula
   Tomato Salad and Garlic Chips 97
Peppercorn Crusted Tuna
   with Orange BBQ Glaze
   with Sauté Jerked Shallots
   and Jicama Cake 98
Tuna Angel Hair Pasta 99

Shellfish

San Francisco Scampi 99
Shrimp Cristoforo 100
Shrimp Scampi 101
Shrimp and Lobster Linguine 102
Italian Scallops 102
Mom's Shrimp
   Casserole Au Gratin.................... 103
Frogmore Stew 104
Shrimp Victoria.............................. 104
Pan Seared Jumbo BBQ Shrimp,
   Country Style Grits and
   Pineapple Salsa 105
Minced Lobster.............................. 106
Angel Hair Commotion 106
Florida Lobster Pot Pie 107
Jake's Blackened Lobster Tails
   with Spinach Fettuccine with
   Tomato-Basil Cream Sauce 108
Baked Squid with
   Garlic Anchovy Pasta.................. 109
Twisted Crab Cakes 110
Maryland Jumbo Lump
   Crab Cakes 110

Marinated Mahi Mahi

**Serve with Bahamian Peas and Rice
and Pam's Black Bean and Mango Salsa.**

1	(1 pound) mahi mahi fillet	2	tablespoons minced fresh
½	cup soy sauce		ginger
½	cup pineapple juice	2	tablespoons sesame oil
	Juice of 1 lime		

Place fillet in a shallow dish. Combine soy sauce, pineapple juice, lime juice, ginger and oil. Pour over fillet. Cover and refrigerate 3 to 4 hours.

To grill, cut fillet into 4 pieces and cook over medium heat for 10 to 15 minutes, turning once and basting with marinade. To bake, preheat oven to 400 degrees. Bake 12 to 15 minutes.

Mahi Mahi with
Spicy Mango Cilantro Sauce

½	cup chopped dried mango	8	(¾ inch thick) mahi mahi
2	fresh serrano chiles, seeded and chopped		fillets
			Salt and pepper to taste
5	cloves garlic, chopped	1	tablespoon olive oil
½	white onion, chopped	½	cup skim milk
¾	cup dry white wine	2	tablespoons chopped
¼	cup orange juice		macadamia nuts
1	cup chopped fresh cilantro		

Combine mango, chiles, garlic, onion, wine and orange juice in a medium saucepan. Bring to a boil over medium heat. Cook 5 minutes. Reduce heat and simmer until ingredients are tender and liquid is reduced by about half. Add cilantro. Puree mixture in a blender. Set aside.

Season fillets with salt and pepper. In a large skillet, heat oil. Add fillets and cook 2 minutes on each side or until lightly browned. Turn off heat and cover.

Add milk to sauce and puree again. Reheat sauce. Place fillets on a serving platter. Pour sauce over top and sprinkle with nuts.

Yield: 8 servings

Dolphin Grand Cay

This recipe was invented aboard my 31 foot ketch "Sunrise"
by Chef/General Manager Pete Mudgett of Conchy Joe's.
We were sailing from Grand Cay (next to Walker's Cay)
to Green Turtle, and had caught the dolphin the day
before while crossing the Gulf Stream.

Flour
Salt and pepper
1 tablespoon vegetable oil
2 fresh dolphin fillets, cut
    into 4 servings
Egg wash
½ cup light rum

1 fresh pineapple, cut into
    1 inch chunks
1 cup Myers's dark rum
2 teaspoons sugar
3 tablespoons butter, chilled
1 lime, halved

Season flour with salt and pepper. Heat oil in a large skillet. Dredge fillets in seasoned flour and coat with egg wash. Brown on both sides in medium hot oil. Do not cook through. Add light rum and reduce heat to a simmer. Add pineapple chunks around fish and half the Myers's dark rum. Take a swig of Myers's rum.

Sprinkle sugar over pineapple and fillets. Gently stir and turn the fish. Take another swig of rum.

Sprinkle fish with salt and pepper to taste. Add butter. Take a final swig of rum and pour what is left over the pineapple. Squeeze lime halves over skillet. Gently stir. Serve fillets with pineapple and rum sauce spooned on top.

Yield: 4 servings

Conchy Joe's Seafood
3945 N.E. Indian River Drive
Jensen Beach, Florida

Fresh Grilled Grouper Topped with a Roma Tomato-Fresh Mint Salsa

Salsa

4	cups diced roma tomatoes (½ inch dice)		Kosher salt to taste
¼	cup minced fresh garlic		Freshly cracked black pepper to taste
½	cup diced red onion (¼ inch dice)	¼	cup fresh lemon juice
1	cup chopped fresh mint leaves	¾	cup extra virgin olive oil

Grouper

6-8 (8 to 10 ounce) fresh grouper fillets

Salt and pepper to taste

To make salsa, combine tomatoes, garlic, onion, mint, salt and pepper in a mixing bowl. Toss to blend. Add lemon juice and oil and mix well. Let stand 15 minutes to allow flavors to meld. Stir well before serving.

Preheat grill until hot. Just before placing fish on grill, lightly brush grill with oil to keep fish from sticking. Season fillets with salt and pepper. Grill 3 to 5 minutes on each side for a 1 inch thick fillet. Serve topped with a generous portion of salsa.

Yield: 6 to 8 servings

This salsa will go well with most grilled fish.

Grouper Provolone

1	(9 ounce) package frozen artichoke hearts	4	(4 ounce) grouper fillets
8	ounces mushrooms, sliced		Dash of white pepper
¼	cup Marsala wine	½	cup grated provolone cheese
¼	cup water	2	tablespoons grated Parmesan cheese
1	tablespoon lemon juice	2	tablespoons chopped fresh parsley
½	teaspoon chicken bouillon		

Preheat oven to 375 degrees. Cook artichoke hearts according to package directions, omitting salt. Drain and set aside. Sauté mushrooms in a skillet sprayed with cooking spray over medium heat for 3 minutes. Stir in wine, water, lemon juice and bouillon. Simmer 5 minutes. Add reserved artichoke hearts. Remove from heat.

Rinse fillets in cold water and pat dry. Season with white pepper and place in a greased 9x13 inch baking dish. Spoon mushroom mixture over fillets. Combine cheeses and sprinkle on top. Bake 15 to 25 minutes, depending on thickness of fillets, or until fish flakes easily with a fork. Sprinkle with fresh parsley.

Yield: 4 servings

Pecan Grouper

2	pounds grouper fillets	5	tablespoons butter
½	teaspoon salt	½	cup chopped pecans
¼	teaspoon black pepper	2	teaspoons fresh lemon juice
½	cup flour	¼	cup chopped fresh parsley
3	tablespoons butter		

Sprinkle grouper with salt and pepper. Dredge in flour. Melt 3 tablespoons butter in a large skillet over medium high heat. Add fillets and cook 6 minutes on each side or until fish flakes easily with a fork. Transfer to a serving platter and cover to keep warm.

Melt 5 tablespoons butter in same skillet over medium high heat. Add pecans and sauté 2 minutes or until butter begins to brown. Stir in lemon juice. Pour pecan mixture over fillets and sprinkle with parsley.

Pan Seared Grouper, Blackening Rub

A thick, juicy piece of pan blackened fresh grouper fillet provides the greatest taste sensation ever. Be sure to super heat the cast iron pan, being careful when you add the fish to avoid any oil splattering.

Blackening Rub

¼	cup bay salt	2	teaspoons dried thyme
2	tablespoons granulated garlic	1	teaspoon dried rosemary
1	tablespoon onion powder	1	teaspoon crushed black pepper
2	teaspoons annatto or paprika	1	teaspoon ground white pepper
1	tablespoon dried basil	½	teaspoon cayenne pepper or to taste
2	teaspoons dried oregano		

Grouper

4	(8 to 10 ounce) grouper fillets	2	tablespoons canola oil

Combine all ingredients for blackening rub in a bowl. Stir well with a wire whisk. Store extra in an airtight container.

To prepare grouper, preheat oven to 450 degrees. Place a cast iron skillet over high heat for 3 to 5 minutes. Meanwhile, rub fillets with blackening rub. Add oil to pan. Gently lay fillets in skillet and sear quickly on one side. Turn fillets and transfer skillet to oven. Bake 10 minutes per inch of fillet thickness.

Yield: 4 servings

To vary the degree of spiciness, try these tricks:

> *Mild — rub one side of fillet only*

> *Medium — rub both sides of fillet*

> *Hot 'n Spicy — rub both sides and add a sprinkle or two of extra cayenne pepper*

Fish Tales
5042 Southeast Federal Highway
Stuart, Florida

Bahamian Grouper

¼	cup extra virgin olive oil	1	bay leaf
1	medium onion, chopped	1	teaspoon salt
2	cloves garlic, chopped, or 1 teaspoon garlic powder	¼	teaspoon black pepper
2	tablespoons chopped fresh parsley	1	tablespoon Worcestershire sauce
1	(28 ounce) can crushed tomatoes	¼	teaspoon dried oregano
		1-2	pounds fresh grouper fillets

Heat oil in a large skillet. Add onion, garlic and parsley and simmer but do not brown. Add tomatoes, bay leaf, salt, pepper, Worcestershire sauce and oregano. Bring to a boil. Reduce heat, cover and simmer 30 minutes.

Add grouper and cover. Simmer 5 to 10 minutes. Remove from heat and let stand until fish is firm and white. Serve with your favorite rice dish and salad.

Caribbean Banana Snapper

4	(4 ounce) snapper fillets	2	bananas, sliced
¼	cup flour	4	small green onions, chopped
1¼	teaspoons Lysander's seasoning	¼	cup sweetened coconut milk
		¼	cup rum

Place a skillet coated with cooking spray over medium high heat until hot. Dredge fillets in flour and arrange in skillet. Sprinkle fillets with half of Lysander's seasoning and cook until light brown. Turn fillets and sprinkle with remaining seasoning. Cook until brown.

Place banana slices over fillets and sprinkle with onions. Add coconut milk and cook until fish flakes easily with a fork. Add rum to skillet, cover and let stand 5 minutes. Place fish on a serving platter. Pour a few spoonfuls of rum sauce over fillets and serve remaining sauce on the side.

Yield: 4 servings

Heavenly Fillets

and they really are!

¼ cup Parmesan cheese
2 tablespoons margarine, softened
2 tablespoons light mayonnaise
3 tablespoons chopped green onions
¼ teaspoon salt

Dash of hot pepper sauce
1½ pounds mild flavored fish fillets, such as grouper or snapper, cut into serving pieces
2 tablespoons lemon juice

Combine cheese, margarine, mayonnaise, onions, salt and pepper sauce in a bowl. Mix well.

Preheat broiler. Brush fillets with lemon juice. Broil 4 inches from heat source for 5 minutes. Spread cheese mixture over entire surface of each fillet. Broil 3 minutes longer or until fish is opaque.

Bacon, Tomato and Fish Casserole

8 slices bacon, diced
1 large onion, chopped
3-4 fish fillets, cut into bite-size pieces
Salt and pepper to taste
2 tomatoes, peeled, seeded and chopped

1 tablespoon fresh dill
1 teaspoon salt
1 cup shredded mild cheese
2 tablespoons buttered bread crumbs

Preheat oven to 350 degrees. Cook bacon in a skillet until crisp. Remove bacon, reserving fat in skillet. Sauté onion in bacon fat. Spread cooked bacon and onion in the bottom of a baking dish. Season fillets with salt and pepper to taste and place on bacon and onion. Combine tomatoes, dill and 1 teaspoon salt. Sprinkle over fillets.

Bake 20 to 25 minutes. Sprinkle with cheese and bread crumbs. Bake until bread crumbs are browned.

Herb Crusted Snapper with Roasted Plum Tomato Vinaigrette

Vinaigrette

2	pounds fresh Italian plum tomatoes	1	tablespoon kosher salt
¼	cup olive oil	1	tablespoon black pepper
½	cup chopped fresh basil	1	cup olive oil
2	tablespoons minced garlic	½-¾	cup rice wine vinegar

Snapper

1   tablespoon chopped fresh chives

2   tablespoons chopped fresh Italian parsley

2   tablespoons chopped fresh basil

1   teaspoon chopped fresh thyme

1   tablespoon minced garlic
   Zest of 1 large lemon

2½ cups Japanese bread crumbs

1   (6 to 8 ounce) red, yellowtail or lane snapper fillet per serving
   Olive oil

Preheat oven to 350 degrees. Score tomatoes with an "x" on the bottom and plunge into boiling salted water for 1 minute. Transfer immediately to a bowl of ice water until cool enough to handle. Remove skins and cut tomatoes in half lengthwise. Gently squeeze out seeds. Place tomatoes, cut-side down, on a nonstick baking sheet. Drizzle with ¼ cup olive oil, basil and garlic. Season with salt and pepper. Bake 30 to 45 minutes or until excess liquid has evaporated. Cool. Place cooled roasted tomatoes in a food processor or blender and puree 1 minute. With motor running, alternately add 1 cup olive oil and rice vinegar. Season as needed with salt and pepper. Set aside.

To prepare the snapper, combine chives, parsley, basil, thyme, garlic, zest and bread crumbs in a food processor. Pulse until thoroughly combined. Brush fillets with olive oil. Dredge in breadcrumb mixture, patting down breading to form an even coating.

Heat a nonstick skillet that has been coated with cooking spray or a small amount of olive oil. Add fillets, skin-side up, and sauté 3 minutes or until golden. Turn and cook 3 minutes longer or until done. If fillets are thick, it may be necessary to finish cooking them in the oven. Serve immediately. To serve, drizzle tomato vinaigrette

(Herbed Crusted Snapper continued)

on each serving plate. Place a fillet on each plate and drizzle vinaigrette over fish. Do not saturate fish with vinaigrette or breading will become soggy.

Japanese bread crumbs, or panko, can be found at Oriental food stores.

At the Flagler Grill, we serve this dish with roasted garlic mashed potatoes, but you can substitute rice or couscous.

Snapper Martinique

4	snapper fillets	½	fresh pineapple, cut into
	Flour for dusting		chunks, or one (16 ounce)
	Salt and pepper		can pineapple chunks
4	tablespoons butter	¼	cup coconut rum
2	bananas, sliced into 1 to	¼	cup chicken broth
	1½ inch chunks	¼	cup almonds, toasted

Preheat oven to 350 degrees. Lightly dust fillets in flour seasoned with salt and pepper. Cook fillets in butter in a hot skillet until both sides are lightly browned. Add banana, pineapple, rum and broth. Cook 2 minutes.

Transfer skillet to oven. Bake 5 minutes or until fish turns opaque throughout. Serve fillets with fruit sauce and sprinkled with almonds. Excellent with rice pilaf or yellow rice and black beans.

Yield: 4 servings

For variety, add ½ of a peeled and diced mango. For a little "kick", add 1 tablespoon minced fresh chile pepper.

Nutty Pompano, Orange-Passion Fruit Menuière

The mixture of nuts in this recipe enhances the flavor of the pompano and adds an exotic twist. Pompano cooks quickly so do all your preparation in advance and cook at the last moment.

¼ cup macadamia nuts	1 egg, beaten, or egg
¼ cup pistachio nuts	substitute equivalent
¼ cup pecan bits	½ cup milk
¼ cup pine nuts	1 cup all-purpose flour
½ cup fresh or frozen orange juice	1 teaspoon seasoning salt
2 tablespoons passion fruit juice	4 pompano fillets
½ cup dry white wine	2 tablespoons clarified butter or margarine

Place all nuts in a food processor and pulse until coarsely chopped. Combine orange juice, passion fruit juice and wine in a measuring cup. Mix egg and milk in a shallow pan for an egg wash. Combine flour and seasoning salt in another shallow pan. Dip fillets in egg wash, then in seasoned flour until evenly coated.

Heat two sauté pans over medium high heat. Add clarified butter to pans. Place fillets, skin side up, in pan and brown on one side. Turn and add juice mixture. Cook 3 to 4 minutes longer or until liquid reduces to a thickened sauce. Carefully transfer fillets to a serving platter. Sprinkle with nut mixture and pour sauce on top.

Yield: 4 servings

Fish Tales
5042 Southeast Federal Highway
Stuart, Florida

Baked Asian Fish Packets

1½	pounds fresh firm white fish fillets, such as sea bass, halibut or red snapper, or salmon fillets (4 fillets)	2	tablespoons orange juice
		1	tablespoon sesame oil
		½	teaspoon grated fresh ginger
3	tablespoons soy sauce	2-4	green onions, white and green parts, very thinly sliced
½	teaspoon orange zest		

Cut parchment paper into four (14 inch) squares and fold each square in half. Unfold and place one fillet in the center of each square. Combine soy sauce, zest, orange juice, sesame oil and ginger. Spoon mixture evenly over fillets. Sprinkle with onions. Fold paper over fish. Roll and crimp edges together tightly. Place packages on a large rimmed baking sheet and let stand 15 minutes.

Preheat oven to 450 degrees. Bake 10 minutes or until fish flakes easily with a fork. Transfer package to individual plates, slit open tops or unroll and pull back edges to serve.

Yield: 4 servings

White Fish Epicurean

Works best with light, flaky fish.

2	pounds fish fillets, such as sole, flounder or orange roughy	⅛	teaspoon paprika
		½	cup clarified butter
1½	teaspoons seasoning salt		Juice of 1 lemon
	White pepper	1	tablespoon tarragon

Preheat broiler. Place fish skin-side down on a broiler pan. Sprinkle with seasoning salt, pepper and paprika. Combine butter, lemon juice and tarragon in a saucepan. Simmer until golden brown. Brush half of mixture over fish. Broil 4 minutes or until fish flakes easily with a fork. Serve with remaining butter sauce.

Yield: 4 servings

Chilean Sea Bass over Portobello Mushroom with a Roasted Red Bell Pepper Sauce

Sea Bass and Mushroom

2	(4 to 6 inch diameter caps) portobello mushrooms		Butter (optional)
	Olive oil	6	ounces Phillip's jumbo lump blue crabmeat
	Salt and pepper to taste		Heavy cream
	Chopped garlic	2	(9 ounce) fillets Chilean sea bass
1	large red bell pepper		
3	tablespoons heavy cream		Flour

Preheat oven to 350 degrees. Lightly twist off mushroom stems and gently scrape away the black meat on the underside of the cap. Wash cap with water and place in a baking dish. Add olive oil, salt and garlic to cap and marinate at least 30 minutes. Bake mushrooms 10 minutes. Cool.

Season bell pepper with olive oil and salt, rubbing evenly over outside of pepper. Roast pepper about 15 minutes. Cover and cool. When cooled, remove skin, core and seeds of pepper. Puree pepper in a blender and strain into a saucepan. Add 3 tablespoons cream, salt, pepper and butter. Heat sauce just before ready to serve. Combine crabmeat with salt, pepper and enough cream to moisten mixture, being careful not to break up lumps. Stuff mixture into mushroom caps. Bake mushrooms until hot.

Season fillets with salt and pepper and lightly dust with flour. Heat a skillet coated with oil. Add fillets and cook on each side until golden brown. To serve, spoon heated sauce onto the bottom of two serving plates. Place a mushroom cap in the center of each plate. Top each cap with a fillet.

Yield: 2 servings

Dockside
131 SW Flagler Ave.
Stuart, Florida

Salmon Fillets Aloha

Fresh salmon fillets, cut into
  serving sizes
Lawry's Hawaiian marinade

Salt and pepper to taste
Pineapple, cut into small
  pieces

Marinate salmon in marinade for at least 30 minutes. Season with salt and pepper.

Steam fish in a steamer or wrapped in foil in a skillet for 10 to 15 minutes until it flakes easily with a fork. Add pineapple pieces and cook until heated through. Serve with rice pilaf and your favorite salad.

Basil Marinated Fish

4 fish steaks, such as tuna,
    wahoo or swordfish
¼ cup olive oil
¼ cup vegetable oil
1½ tablespoons Dijon mustard

1½ tablespoons fresh lemon
    juice
2 large cloves garlic, minced
¾ cup sliced fresh basil leaves
    Lemon slices and basil
    sprigs for garnish

Arrange fish in a single layer in a shallow dish. Combine oils, mustard, lemon juice, garlic and basil. Pour marinade mixture over fish. Cover and refrigerate 3 hours, turning occasionally.

When ready to serve, preheat grill. Remove fish from marinade and grill about 5 minutes per side. Garnish with lemon slices and basil sprigs.

Yield: 4 servings

Guilt Free Salmon

It's great for folks with high cholesterol.

1½ pounds salmon fillet	2 tablespoons Golden Dipt
3-4 tablespoons fat-free	fat-free lemon butter dill
mayonnaise	sauce
	Salt to taste (optional)

Preheat oven to 350 degrees. Place salmon on a broiling pan. Combine mayonnaise and dill sauce and spread generously over fillet. Season with salt. Bake 20 minutes.

Yield: 4 servings

Grilled Salmon
with Honey-Mustard Sauce

4 (4 ounce, ½ inch thick)	3 tablespoons honey
salmon steaks	2 tablespoons plain low-fat
1 tablespoon lemon juice	yogurt
¼ cup Dijon mustard	

Preheat grill. Spray hot grill with cooking spray. Brush salmon with lemon juice and place on grill. Cook, uncovered, for 5 to 6 minutes on each side or until fish flakes easily with a fork.

Combine mustard, honey and yogurt in a saucepan. Simmer on medium heat until warm. Spoon sauce over salmon.

Yield: 4 servings

Grilled Tuna with Arugula Tomato Salad and Garlic Chips

Garlic Chips

6-8 large cloves garlic, very thinly sliced

¼ cup virgin olive oil

1 tablespoon chopped fresh parsley

Salt and freshly ground black pepper to taste

Vinaigrette

2 tablespoons balsamic vinegar

3 tablespoons virgin olive oil

½ teaspoon chopped garlic

Salt and freshly ground black pepper to taste

Salad

4 ounces arugula, stemmed, or mixed greens

¼ cup thinly sliced red onion

8 plum tomatoes, quartered and seeded

Tuna

4 tuna steaks

¼ cup chopped fresh basil

1 teaspoon chopped garlic

1 tablespoon coarsely ground black pepper

Salt to taste

To make garlic chips, in a small pot of salted water, bring garlic slices to a strong boil. Strain and cool. When cool, fry slices in olive oil until lightly browned; if garlic becomes too brown, it will taste bitter. Add parsley, salt and pepper to garlic. Strain garlic, reserving oil to marinate fish. Set garlic chips aside.

Whisk together all vinaigrette ingredients in a small bowl. Set aside.

Toss together salad ingredients. Set aside.

Marinate fish 20 minutes with basil, garlic, pepper, salt and just enough of reserved olive oil from the garlic chips to coat the fish. Preheat grill. Grill fish 1½ minutes on each side or more, depending on thickness of steak and desired doneness.

To serve, toss salad with vinaigrette, reserving some vinaigrette to drizzle on fish. Serve tuna on plates with salad and garnished with garlic chips.

Yield: 4 servings

This is great served with mashed potatoes — complements the garlic.

Peppercorn Crusted Tuna with Orange BBQ Glaze with Sauté Jerked Shallots and Jicama Cake

Orange BBQ Glaze

1	cup orange juice	½	cup chutney of choice
½	cup BBQ sauce of choice		

Jerked Shallots

1¼	pounds shallots, peeled	1	papaya, finely diced
1	tablespoon olive oil	1	mango, finely diced
	Salt and pepper to taste	½	red onion, finely diced
1	ounce jerk seasoning		

Jicama Cakes

1¾	pounds jicama, peeled and grated	½	bunch green onions, thinly sliced
2	eggs	1½	teaspoons minced garlic
½	teaspoon cayenne pepper		Salt and pepper to taste
¼	teaspoon nutmeg	¼	cup olive oil

Tuna

1¾	pounds fresh tuna, cut into 3 to 4 ounce medallions	7	ounces fresh cracked peppercorns
			Coarse salt

To make glaze, mix all ingredients in a saucepan. Bring to a light simmer.

For Jerked Shallots, sauté shallots in hot oil in a skillet. Season with salt and pepper and jerk seasoning. When caramelized, bake in oven until tender. Toss with papaya, mango and red onion just before serving.

To make jicama cakes, place jicama in a bowl. Fold in eggs, cayenne pepper, nutmeg, onions, garlic, salt and pepper. Form into 3½ to 4 ounce portions. Sauté on both sides in olive oil until golden brown. Finish in oven for 5 to 6 minutes or until tender and crispy.

To make tuna, dredge tuna in peppercorns and season with coarse salt. Pan sear both sides of tuna for about 1 minute on each side. Brush both sides with glaze. Finish cooking in a 375 degree oven for 3 to 4 minutes for medium rare to medium doneness. Serve tuna with jerked shallots and jicama cakes on the side.

Yield: 6 servings

The Black Marlin
53 W. Osceola Street
Stuart, Florida

Tuna Angel Hair Pasta

4	tablespoons butter
½	teaspoon salt
½	teaspoon garlic powder
½	teaspoon dried rosemary
½	teaspoon dried basil
¼	teaspoon dry mustard
½	teaspoon black pepper
½	teaspoon onion powder
½	teaspoon dried dill
½	teaspoon dried parsley
	Dash of cayenne pepper
1½	cups milk
¼	cup flour
¼	cup dry sherry
2	(6 ounce) cans tuna, drained
1	cup shredded cheese
	Angel hair pasta, cooked and drained

Melt butter over low heat in a saucepan. Mix in salt, garlic powder, rosemary, basil, mustard, black pepper, onion powder, dill, parsley and cayenne pepper. Stir in milk, flour and sherry. Bring to a slow boil over medium high heat, stirring constantly. Add tuna and cheese. Remove from heat and let stand until cheese melts. Serve over pasta.

Yield: 4 servings

San Francisco Scampi

12	large shrimp, shelled and butterflied
1	cup milk
3	tablespoons flour
	Salt and pepper to taste
	Oil for frying
2	cups dry white wine
1	tablespoon minced shallots
½	teaspoon minced fresh garlic
2	teaspoons lemon juice
½	cup butter, softened
¼	cup chopped fresh parsley

Soak shrimp in milk for 15 minutes. Pour off milk and drain on a paper towel. Combine flour, salt and pepper and lightly dust mixture over shrimp. Fry shrimp in 1 inch deep hot oil in a skillet for 2 minutes. Drain on paper towels and keep warm.

Combine wine, shallots and garlic in a large saucepan. Bring to a boil and cook until reduced to 1 cup. Add shrimp and boil 1 minute. Remove from heat. Add lemon juice and butter and stir until blended. Sprinkle with parsley. Serve with toothpicks as an appetizer, or over rice or pasta as an entrée.

Shrimp Cristoforo

Basil Butter

2 ounces fresh basil leaves, washed and stemmed
1¼ cups butter, softened
1 teaspoon chopped fresh garlic

¼ teaspoon salt
⅛ teaspoon black pepper
3 tablespoons Parmesan cheese
1 tablespoon Romano cheese

Shrimp

1 pound fresh linguine or angel hair pasta
  Basil Butter

1 pound medium shrimp, shelled
  Freshly grated Parmesan cheese

Place basil leaves in a food processor. Process, in two batches if necessary, until finely chopped, to yield about ¾ cup. Place butter in a small mixing bowl. Whip butter with an electric mixer. Add garlic, salt, black pepper, cheeses and basil. Use immediately or store, covered, in the refrigerator for up to 4 days.

To make shrimp, cook pasta according to directions. Drain well and keep warm. Melt Basil Butter in a large skillet over medium heat. Add shrimp and sauté 2 to 3 minutes or until just done. Serve shrimp with Basil Butter over hot pasta. Pass Parmesan cheese on the side.

Yield: 4 to 6 servings

Shrimp Scampi

½ cup olive oil
16 (26/30 count) shrimp, butterflied, shelled with tail left on
Flour for dredging
2 (3 ounce) roma tomatoes, cut 1 x ½ inch
1 ounce fresh basil, julienned
1 teaspoon salt

1 teaspoon black pepper
2 teaspoons lemon juice
6 ounces Chablis wine
4 tablespoons scampi butter, softened
16 ounces capellini pasta, cooked al dente and kept warm
½ cup Parmesan cheese

Heat oil in a skillet over high heat until very hot but not smoking.

Dredge shrimp in flour, shake off excess and add to skillet. Sauté until opaque but not brown. Add tomato, basil, salt and pepper. Sauté 1 minute. Add lemon juice and toss to mix. Deglaze pan with wine and toss to mix and create a sauce. Add scampi butter and stir. Cook until sauce thickens and is creamy. Remove from heat.

Place drained, hot pasta in a serving bowl. Pour shrimp mixture over top. Sprinkle with cheese.

Scampi Butter: Combine 1 stick softened butter with 2 cloves minced garlic and 1 small minced shallot.

Yield: 2 to 3 servings

**The Prawnbroker Grill
3754 S.E. Ocean Blvd.
Stuart, Florida**

Shrimp and Lobster Linguine

½ cup butter
1 tablespoon olive oil
2 medium onions, chopped
2½ teaspoons minced fresh
garlic
5 tablespoons flour
2½ cups evaporated skim milk
or half-and-half
1 teaspoon dried basil
1 teaspoon dried thyme
½ cup snipped fresh parsley
½ cup cooking sherry
1½ teaspoons salt
½ teaspoon white pepper
½ teaspoon MSG (optional)
⅓ cup shredded mozzarella
cheese
⅓ cup shredded provolone
cheese
⅓ cup Asiago cheese
1 pound fresh shrimp
1 pound fresh lobster meat,
cut into chunks
1 pound dry linguine, cooked
al dente
Parmesan cheese

Heat butter and oil in a large skillet. Add onions and garlic and sauté 3 to 5 minutes. Stir in flour. Slowly whisk in milk. Cook and stir until thickened. Add basil, thyme, parsley, sherry, salt, pepper, MSG, mozzarella cheese, provolone cheese, Asiago cheese, shrimp and lobster. Sauté until shrimp are pink, lobster is white and cheeses are melted. Serve seafood mixture over drained, hot linguine. Serve Parmesan cheese on the side.

Italian Scallops

1 cup sliced fresh mushrooms
1 clove garlic, minced
½ cup diced onion
3 slices prosciutto, diced
1 tablespoon butter
1 pound large scallops, halved
1 tablespoon butter
½ cup half-and-half
1 tablespoon fresh dill
Salt and pepper to taste

Sauté mushrooms, garlic, onion and prosciutto in 1 tablespoon butter for 3 minutes. Set aside. In a separate pan, sauté scallops in 1 tablespoon butter until done. Set aside.

Add half-and-half to mushroom mixture and simmer until sauce is slightly reduced. Add dill, salt and pepper. Stir in scallops.

Mom's Shrimp Casserole Au Gratin

2 tablespoons butter	2 pounds cooked shrimp, cleaned and deveined
2 tablespoons flour	1¼ cups cooked rice
1⅔ cups tomato puree or juice	1 cup soft bread crumbs
½ teaspoon salt	2 tablespoons butter, melted
Dash of cayenne pepper	
1 packed cup shredded American cheese (no substitutions)	

Preheat oven to 375 degrees. Heat 2 tablespoons butter in a skillet. Blend in flour, then add tomato puree. Cook, stirring constantly, until thickened. Add salt, cayenne pepper and cheese. Stir until cheese melts. Mix in shrimp and rice.

Place shrimp mixture in a casserole dish. Mix together bread crumbs and 2 tablespoons melted butter and sprinkle over casserole. Bake until crumbs are browned.

Yield: 6 to 8 servings

Dolphin Bar and Shrimp House
Jensen Beach, Florida

Frogmore Stew

Serve Frogmore Stew the authentic way: cover the table with newspaper, place pot of stew in the center of table and go at it!

6	quarts water	2	pounds smoked sausage,
¼	cup seafood boil		cut into 2 inch pieces
1	teaspoon Tabasco sauce	12	ears corn, shucked and
3	tablespoons salt		broken into 3 to 4 inch
6	cloves garlic, peeled		pieces
4	extra large onions, halved	4	pounds large shrimp,
8-10	medium-size red potatoes, unpeeled		unpeeled

Combine 6 quarts water, seafood boil, Tabasco sauce, salt and garlic in a large stockpot. Bring to a boil. Add onions and potatoes and cook 15 minutes. Add sausage and cook 5 minutes. Add corn and cook 5 minutes. Stir in shrimp and cook about 3 minutes or until shrimp are pink. Drain immediately and serve.

Yield: 8 servings

Shrimp Victoria

Versatile Florida shrimp becomes gourmet fare in minutes – cooked in mushrooms, butter, sour cream and seasonings.

1	pound shrimp, peeled and deveined	1	tablespoon flour
½	cup finely chopped onion	¼	teaspoon salt
4	tablespoons margarine or butter		Dash of cayenne pepper
1	(6 ounce) can sliced mushrooms, or 1 cup sliced fresh	1	cup sour cream or plain yogurt
		1½	cups hot cooked rice

Sauté shrimp and onion in margarine for 5 minutes or until shrimp are tender. Add mushrooms and sauté 2 to 3 minutes longer. Sprinkle flour, salt and cayenne pepper over shrimp. Stir in sour cream and cook gently for 10 minutes, being careful not to boil. Serve over rice.

Yield: 4 to 6 servings

Pan Seared Jumbo
BBQ Shrimp, Country Style Grits
and Pineapple Salsa

Salsa
2 cups diced golden pineapple
1 red bell pepper, diced
1 yellow bell pepper, diced
1 jalapeño pepper, finely
   diced
¼ red onion, diced

1 bunch cilantro, stemmed
   and chopped
½ cup peach nectar
   Juice of 1 lime
   Salt and pepper to taste

Grits
1 cup chicken broth
2 cups instant grits

4 tablespoons unsalted butter
   Salt and pepper to taste

Shrimp
48 (16/20 count) shrimp
   Flour
   Salt

   Cayenne pepper
   Olive oil
1 cup your favorite BBQ sauce

Combine all salsa ingredients in a mixing bowl. Marinate in refrigerator 8 hours.

Bring chicken broth to a boil in a medium saucepan. Stir in grits and cook until thickened. Add butter, salt and pepper. Keep warm on the stove.

Lightly dust shrimp in a seasoned flour mixture of flour, salt and cayenne pepper. Heat olive oil in a large skillet until smoking hot. Add shrimp and sear very quickly on both sides until light golden brown. Pour BBQ sauce into pan and continue cooking 1 to 2 minutes or until shrimp are done.

To serve, ladle grits into small pasta bowls. Divide shrimp among bowls. Add ¼ cup salsa to each serving.

Yield: 8 servings

Tangos Restaurant
925 Bougainvillea Lane
Vero Beach, Florida

Minced Lobster

2	pounds lobster	¼	cup peeled, seeded and chopped tomato
¼	cup oil	½	teaspoon dried thyme
4	slices bacon, diced	½	teaspoon black pepper
1	large stalk celery, chopped		Salt to taste
1	medium onion, chopped	1	small jalapeño pepper, diced
1	medium green or red bell pepper, chopped		
¼	cup tomato paste	2	tablespoons water

Cook lobster in boiling water for about 15 minutes. Cool, shell and shred meat. Heat oil in a skillet. Add bacon and cook until it starts to brown. Add celery, onion, bell pepper and tomato paste. Cook 4 to 5 minutes over medium heat. Add tomato and lobster and cook 4 to 5 minutes. Stir in thyme, pepper, salt, jalapeño pepper and water. Simmer about 3 minutes to reduce liquid. Serve over rice.

Angel Hair Commotion

2½	tablespoons chopped garlic	¼	cup chopped roasted red bell pepper
2½	tablespoons olive oil	1	teaspoon chopped fresh basil
½	teaspoon truffle oil		
¼	cup white Zinfandel wine	1	pound dry angel hair pasta, cooked al dente
¼	cup chicken broth		
½	cup diced beefsteak tomato	1	pound Maryland jumbo lump crabmeat
½	cup sliced asparagus, blanched		
¼	cup chopped roasted yellow bell pepper		Salt and pepper to taste
		2	teaspoons pine nuts, toasted

Sauté garlic in olive and truffle oils in a skillet. Deglaze skillet with wine and broth. Add tomato, asparagus, bell peppers and basil. Toss. Cook mixture over medium heat until sauce is reduced. Add drained pasta. Fold in crabmeat and season with salt and pepper. Sprinkle with pine nuts.

Ballantrae River Room
3325 SE Ballantrae Blvd.
Port St. Lucie, Florida

Florida Lobster Pot Pie

1	(9 inch) round puff pastry	1	pound Florida lobster meat, shelled
1	egg, beaten	¼	cup flour
1	tablespoon olive oil	½	cup Chardonnay or Fumé Blanc
½	cup finely diced potato		
¼	cup chopped carrots, blanched	½	cup heavy cream
¼	cup finely diced celery	1	tablespoon butter
½	cup finely diced onion	¼	teaspoon sea or kosher salt
1	cup peas	½	teaspoon black pepper
¼	teaspoon sea or kosher salt		Fresh rosemary sprigs for garnish

Preheat oven to 375 degrees. Place pastry round on a baking sheet lined with parchment paper. Using a fork, prick holes evenly throughout pastry. Brush pastry with egg using a pastry brush. Place pastry over a round baking dish. Bake 10 to 15 minutes or until golden. Remove from oven and set aside.

Place a 1 quart saucepan over medium high heat. Add olive oil and heat for 1 minute. Add potato, carrot, celery, onion, peas and ¼ teaspoon salt. Bring to a boil. Reduce heat and simmer until potatoes are tender. Add lobster, cover and cook until lobster is tender.

Mix flour and wine in a small bowl until smooth. Blend into lobster mixture. Add cream, butter, ¼ teaspoon salt and pepper. Bring to a boil. Reduce heat and simmer until creamy. Pour mixture into a serving bowl. Place baked pastry on top and garnish with rosemary.

Jake's Blackened Lobster Tails with Spinach Fettuccine with Tomato-Basil Cream Sauce

Lobster

1 cup Paul Prudhomme's Seafood or Redfish Magic seasoning
Clarified butter

1-2 (4 to 6 ounce) lobster tails per serving, thawed and shelled

Fettuccine

1 tablespoon olive oil
1 tablespoon chopped fresh garlic
1 teaspoon chopped fresh basil

1 (14½ ounce) can Italian plum tomatoes, drained and chopped
¼ cup heavy cream
1 pound spinach fettuccine, cooked al dente

Combine seasoning and enough clarified butter to make a thin paste. Lightly coat lobster tails with seasoning paste. Place tails in a white-hot cast iron skillet until blackened on one side. Turn and blacken the other side. Cut meat into slices.

To make fettuccine, heat oil in a skillet. Add garlic and basil. Stir in tomatoes and cook until thick. When ready to serve, add cream and heat without boiling. Pour sauce over drained fettuccine; pasta should be just lightly sauced. Add lobster and toss to coat.

Baked Squid with Garlic Anchovy Pasta

1¼	pounds small squid, cleaned	1	large clove garlic, minced
1	cup plain dry bread crumbs	1	teaspoon anchovy paste
1	teaspoon oregano, crumbled	¼	cup olive oil
1	teaspoon freshly ground	8	ounces dry capellini pasta
	black pepper	1	tablespoon unsalted butter
1	teaspoon salt		Lemon wedges
6	tablespoons olive oil		

Preheat oven to 450 degrees. Slice bodies of squid into ¼ inch rings. Cut tentacles in half if large. In a large bowl, combine squid, bread crumbs, oregano, black pepper and salt. Toss. Spread in a single layer in a large baking dish. Sprinkle with any leftover crumbs. Drizzle 6 tablespoons oil on top. Bake 10 minutes or until squid is golden brown and crunchy.

Meanwhile, in a small saucepan, whisk together garlic, anchovy paste and ¼ cup oil. Bring to a simmer over low heat. Cook, whisking, 3 minutes or until fragrant but not browned.

Cook pasta in a large saucepan of boiling salted water for 3 minutes or until al dente. Drain and return pasta to saucepan. Add anchovy sauce and butter and toss to coat. Make a bed of pasta on a serving platter or on individual serving plates. Mound baked squid in center of pasta. Serve with lemon wedges.

Yield: 4 servings

Twisted Crab Cakes

¼ large onion, finely diced
½ cup butter
Dash dry English mustard
Pinch fresh basil
Pinch fresh parsley

1 egg
1 tablespoon lemon juice
1 pound jumbo lump crabmeat
½ cup bread crumbs

Sauté onion in butter until transparent. Cool. Combine mustard, basil, parsley, egg and lemon juice in a mixing bowl. Stir in crabmeat and cooled onion. Mix in bread crumbs. Shape mixture into crab cakes and sauté until brown.

Yield: 4 servings

The Twisted Grille
2111 E. Ocean Blvd.
Stuart, Florida

Maryland Jumbo Lump Crab Cakes

1 pound Maryland jumbo lump crabmeat
1 egg
5 ounces crushed saltines
2 ounces mayonnaise
Juice of 1 large lemon

1 teaspoon stone ground mustard
1 teaspoon Worcestershire sauce
Salt and pepper to taste

Combine all ingredients. Shape mixture into crab cakes and sauté until brown.

David's in the Courtyard
23 Osceola
Stuart, Florida

Poultry, Meat and Meatless

JEAN SANDERS
Living Room
Watercolor, 1999

Poultry, Meat and Meatless

Meatless

Kelly's Veggie
   Enchilada Casserole 111
Cheesy Broccoli-Corn Strudel 112
Lentil-Rice Burgers 113
Angel Hair Pasta
   with Lemon and Pine Nuts 113
Pizza Bianco 114
Angel Hair with Puttanesca Sauce 115
Rigatoni with Lemon Cream Sauce 115
Rigatoni con Zucchini 116
Rigatoni à la Vodka 117
Fresh Tomato Sauce for Pasta 117
Penne with Sun-Dried
   Tomato Sauce 118
Fusilli with Broccoli, Sicilian Style 119

Chicken and Turkey

Perfect Roast Chicken 120
Curry Cajun Chicken 120
Chicken Cacciatore 121
Southern Pecan Encrusted Chicken
   with a Warm Berry Sauce 121
Chicken French Country Style 122
Garlicky Chicken 122
Spinach Stuffed Chicken Breasts 123
Feta Stuffed Herbed
   Chicken Breasts 124
Opulent Chicken 125
Chicken Paprikash 125
North African Roast Chicken
   Thighs with Raisins, Almonds
   and Apricots 126
Nantucket Cassoulet 127
Quick Cassoulet 128
Moroccan Chicken 129
Texas Stir-Fry 130
Artichoke and Mushroom Chicken 130
Chicken Stir-Fry 131
Swiss Chicken Bake 131
Chicken Louisa 132
Apple Stuffed Chicken Breast 132
Mike Szary's Black Beans and Rice 133
Grilled Chicken Breast
   with Pineapple Salsa 134
Chicken and Rice Bake 134
Chicken Mushroom
   in Puff Pastry Shells 135
Chicken with Fig and Port Sauce 135
Chicken Dijon Parmesan 136
Chicken and Dumplings 136
Chicken Breast
   with Creamy Mustard Sauce 137
Lemon Chicken with Cashews 137
Chicken and Linguine 138
Turkey Casserole 138
Chicken Linguine with
   Sun-Dried Tomatoes and Olives 139

Turkey Meatloaf 139
Chicken Livers Fabuloso 140
Grilled Raspberry Game Hens 141

Beef

Savory Roast Fillet of Beef 142
Grilled Fillet of Beef 142
Beef Tenderloin 143
Tournedos of
   Beef Tenderloin Roquefort 143
Beef Wellington 144
Sabana (Beef Tenderloin Mexicana) 145
Prime Rib with Roasted
   Garlic and Horseradish Crust 146
Steak Diane 147
Top Round Steak
   with Jalapeño Marinade 147
Steak Fajitas 148
Beef Bourguignonne 149
Burgundy Stew 150
Mexican Lasagna 150
Stuffed Cabbage 151
The Best Chicken Fried Steak 152
Horseradish Meatloaf 152
Beef Bar-B-Que 153
Picadillo 153
Fred's Meatloaf 154

Veal

Capellini with Veal and Tomatoes 155
Dijon Veal 156
Veal Escalopes with Spinach 156
Veal Escalopes
   with Tomato Basil Sauce 157
Veal Piccata 157
Braised Veal Shanks (Osso Buco)
   with White Wine, Butter
   and Lemon Sauce 158
Veal Chop Sicilian 159
Veal Stew 159

Pork

Feta-Pesto Stuffed Pork Chops 160
Pork Chop Potato Bake 161
Angry Pork Tenderloin 161
Pork St. Hubert 162
Jambalaya 162
Herbed Pork Roast 163
Fresh Tomato Pizza with Sausage 163
Spaghetti Carbonara 164
Sausage-Spinach Soufflé 165
Straw and Hay Pasta 166

Lamb

Leg of Lamb 166
Perfect Roast Leg of Lamb 167
Lamb Chops with Caper Sauce 167
Curried Lamb with Cashews 168

Treasures of the Tropics

Kelly's Veggie
Enchilada Casserole

1	small white onion, finely chopped	3	cloves garlic, finely chopped, or to taste
1	small red onion, finely chopped	1	(16 ounce) can corn, drained
1	green bell pepper, finely chopped	1½-2	(10 ounce) cans enchilada sauce
1	jalapeño pepper, seeded and finely chopped	15	corn tortillas, torn in half or thirds
½	bunch cilantro, finely chopped, or to taste	1	(12 ounce) package shredded cheddar or Mexican cheese

Preheat oven to 350 degrees. Combine onions, peppers, cilantro, garlic and corn in a bowl.

Spread a thin layer of enchilada sauce in a large baking pan to prevent sticking. Layer in order tortillas, sauce, vegetable mixture and cheese, forming 3 to 4 layers and finishing with tortillas and cheese. Bake 15 to 20 minutes or until heated through.

For variety, beans, meat, olives or any other veggies can be used.

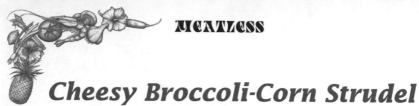

Cheesy Broccoli-Corn Strudel

1 cup part-skim ricotta cheese	¼ cup sliced green onions
1 (3 ounce) package Neufchâtel cheese, softened	1 (2 ounce) jar diced pimento, drained
1 (10 ounce) package frozen chopped broccoli, thawed and drained	½ teaspoon dried basil
	¼ teaspoon black pepper
1 cup whole kernel corn	12 sheets frozen phyllo pastry, thawed
½ cup shredded fontina cheese	¼ cup toasted wheat germ
½ cup egg substitute, thawed	1 teaspoon reduced-calorie margarine, melted

Preheat oven to 375 degrees. Combine ricotta and Neufchâtel cheeses and mix well. Add broccoli, corn, fontina cheese, egg substitute, green onions, pimento, basil and pepper. Mix well.

Place 4 sheets of phyllo pastry on wax paper, keeping remaining pastry covered. Coat with butter-flavored cooking spray. Sprinkle with 2 tablespoons wheat germ. Top with 4 more pastry sheets. Coat with cooking spray and sprinkle with remaining 2 tablespoons wheat germ. Place remaining 4 pastry sheets on top and coat with cooking spray.

Spoon cheese mixture lengthwise down half of phyllo stack, leaving a 1 inch margin on the long sides and a 1½ inch margin on the short sides. Roll stack jelly-roll fashion, starting with longest side. Tuck ends under and place diagonally, seam-side down, on a greased 15x10 inch jelly-roll pan. Brush with margarine. Use a sharp knife to cut diagonal slits, about ¼ inch deep, 2 inches apart across the top. Bake 30 minutes. Let stand 10 minutes before serving.

Yield: 7 servings

Lentil-Rice Burgers

¾ cup dry lentils	¼ cup chopped fresh parsley
¼ cup dry rice	Chopped green bell pepper
2½ cups water	Chopped carrot
1 egg, lightly beaten	½ teaspoon salt
½ cup shredded cheese	½ teaspoon black pepper
¼ cup chopped onion	½ teaspoon lemon pepper
¼ cup dry fine bread crumbs	Flour

Soak lentils and rice in water in a saucepan for 20 minutes. Bring to a boil. Reduce heat and simmer about 35 minutes or until soft. Drain, mash and cool slightly. Add egg, cheese, onion, bread crumbs and parsley to lentil mixture. Mix. Add bell pepper and carrot for color. Season mixture with salt, black pepper and lemon pepper.

Shape mixture into patties. Dust lightly with flour. Season with extra lemon pepper or seasoning of choice. Fry patties in a skillet or bake at 425 degrees for about 10 minutes.

Yield: 4 large patties

Angel Hair Pasta with Lemon and Pine Nuts

¾ teaspoon minced garlic	1½ teaspoons lemon zest
2 tablespoons olive oil	¼ cup minced flat-leaf parsley
2 tablespoons pine nuts, toasted golden and slightly crushed	Salt and pepper to taste
2 tablespoons fresh lemon juice	4 ounces dry angel hair or capellini pasta

Sauté garlic in oil in a small saucepan over medium-low heat until softened. Transfer to a large bowl. Add pine nuts, lemon juice, zest and parsley. Season with salt and pepper.

Cook pasta in a large saucepan of boiling salted water until al dente. Drain well, reserving 2 tablespoons of cooking water. Add pasta and reserved cooking water to lemon mixture and toss until mixture is well absorbed. Serve warm or at room temperature.

Pizza Bianco

Cheese Filling
½ cup ricotta cheese
¼ cup Parmesan cheese
¼ cup shredded mozzarella
    cheese
¼ cup shredded fontina cheese

1 tablespoon minced yellow
    onion
1½ tablespoons milk
¼ teaspoon salt

Crust
2 (6 inch diameter) ready-to-
    serve thick pizza crusts

Toppings
¼ cup sliced green onions
⅓ cup diced black olives
⅓ cup seeded and chopped
    tomato

½ cup shredded mozzarella
    cheese
1 tablespoon Parmesan cheese
    Sprinkle of dried oregano
    Sprinkle of dried basil

Preheat oven to 375 degrees. Combine all filling ingredients and mix thoroughly. Spread filling over crusts.

Sprinkle onions, olives and tomato over filling. Top with cheeses. Sprinkle with oregano and basil. Bake 8 to 10 minutes or until filling is hot and cheese is melted. Cut each pizza into 6 wedges.

Yield: 6 appetizer servings

The Olive Garden

Angel Hair
with Puttanesca Sauce

1	clove garlic, chopped	½	cup capers
2	tablespoons olive oil	4	anchovy fillets, mashed
1	(28 ounce) can pear tomatoes	2	pinches salt
1	teaspoon dried oregano	2	pinches black pepper
10	basil leaves, chopped	1	pound dry angel hair pasta, cooked al dente
¼	cup kalamata olives		

Sauté garlic in oil in a saucepan until lightly browned. Coarsely chop tomatoes in a blender and add to saucepan. Add oregano, basil, olives, capers, anchovy fillets, salt and pepper. Bring to a boil. Reduce heat and simmer over medium heat for 10 minutes. Serve sauce over hot pasta.

Yield: 4 servings

Mario's
1924 SE Federal Hwy.
Stuart, Florida

Rigatoni with
Lemon Cream Sauce

1	cup heavy cream	14	ounces dry pasta, such as rigatoni, cooked al dente
½	cup half-and-half	⅓	cup Parmesan cheese
¼	teaspoon dried hot pepper flakes or to taste		Salt and pepper to taste
2	tablespoons lemon zest	¼	cup chopped fresh parsley

Combine cream, half-and-half, pepper flakes and zest over medium-low heat for 20 minutes or until mixture is reduced to about 1 cup. Toss cream sauce with hot pasta and cheese. Season with salt and pepper. Sprinkle parsley on top.

Yield: 4 servings

Rigatoni con Zucchini

Rigatoni

⅓ cup olive oil
1 cup chopped onion
8 ounces mushrooms, minced
1½ teaspoons finely minced garlic
8 ounces mushrooms, quartered
3 cups crushed tomatoes
1 (16 ounce) can tomatoes, drained and diced
1½ cups tomato puree
1 cup sliced black olives

2 teaspoons capers, drained
½ teaspoon dried oregano
½ teaspoon dried basil
¼ teaspoon black pepper
¼ teaspoon dried red pepper flakes
½ teaspoon fennel seeds
½ teaspoon salt
1 (1 pound) package dry rigatoni pasta
Parmesan cheese

Zucchini

4 large zucchini
Dried basil
Dried oregano

Salt and pepper to taste
2 tablespoons olive oil

Heat ⅓ cup olive oil in a heavy Dutch oven over medium heat. Add onion and minced mushrooms and sauté 10 minutes or until onion is very soft. Add garlic and mushroom quarters and sauté 5 minutes. Stir in all tomatoes, puree, olives, capers, oregano, basil, black pepper, pepper flakes, fennel and salt. Cook rigatoni in a large pot of boiling water according to package directions.

Meanwhile, prepare zucchini. Cut ends off and slice zucchini lengthwise into ¼ inch thick rectangles. Sprinkle slices with basil, oregano, salt and pepper. Heat 1 tablespoon olive oil in a large skillet over medium heat. Place zucchini slices in pan and sauté 3 minutes on each side or until tender. Keep slices warm on a heated serving platter while sautéing remaining zucchini. Use remaining 1 tablespoon oil as needed.

To serve, drain rigatoni and transfer to a serving platter. Ladle mushroom sauce over pasta. Top with zucchini slices. Pass extra sauce and Parmesan cheese on the side.

Yield: 4 to 6 servings

The Olive Garden

Rigatoni à la Vodka

4 strips prosciutto or
   pancetta, shredded
Oil
3 cloves garlic, halved
1 small onion, diced
½ red bell pepper, diced
1 (14½ ounce) can diced
   tomatoes
1 (8 ounce) can tomato sauce
¼ cup vodka
Dried oregano to taste

Dried basil to taste
Fennel to taste
Dried hot pepper flakes to
   taste
Salt and cracked black
   pepper to taste
3 tablespoons heavy cream
3 tablespoons ricotta cheese
Rigatoni or penne pasta,
   cooked
Parmesan cheese

Sauté prosciutto in oil until brown. Add garlic, onion and bell pepper and sauté until onion is opaque. Stir in tomatoes and sauce. Simmer, uncovered, for 30 minutes. Add vodka, oregano, basil, fennel, pepper flakes, salt and black pepper. Cook 3 minutes. Stir in cream and ricotta cheese. Serve over hot pasta. Sprinkle Parmesan cheese on top before serving.

Fresh Tomato Sauce for Pasta

6 tomatoes
½ sweet onion, such as
   Florida, Vidalia or Texas,
   minced
Chopped fresh basil to taste
3 tablespoons olive oil

Salt and freshly ground
   black pepper to taste
Pasta, cooked al dente and
   drained
Olive oil for pasta
¼ cup freshly grated Parmesan
   or Romano cheese

Dip tomatoes in boiling water for 10 seconds. Remove skin and core; seed and dice. Combine diced tomato, onion, basil, 3 tablespoons oil, salt and pepper. Let stand at room temperature for 1 hour.

To serve, toss pasta with olive oil and ¼ cup Parmesan cheese. Pass sauce and extra cheese with the pasta.

Yield: 4 servings

A great accompaniment to veal piccata or grilled chicken breasts, or serve as a main dish.

Penne with Sun-Dried Tomato Sauce

1 tablespoon olive oil	½ cup pitted kalamata olives, chopped
1 tablespoon minced garlic	
1 (3 ounce) package sun-dried tomatoes, rehydrated and chopped	1 cup chopped fresh basil
	1 cup crumbled feta cheese
	¾ cup Parmesan cheese
1 (28 ounce) can diced tomatoes, undrained	1 pound dry penne pasta, cooked al dente
	Salt and pepper to taste

Heat oil in a heavy saucepan over medium heat. Add garlic and quickly sauté. Add sun-dried and canned tomatoes and olives. Bring to a boil. Reduce heat and simmer 4 to 5 minutes or until sauce is slightly thickened. Mix in basil and cheeses. Stir until cheese melts. Add cooked pasta to saucepan and toss. Season with salt and pepper. Transfer to a serving bowl.

Yield: 4 servings

An alternate method is to add only the feta cheese to the sauce and sprinkle Parmesan cheese on top as a garnish.

Fusilli with
Broccoli, Sicilian Style

1	large bunch broccoli, cut into florets and 1 inch stem pieces	8	sun-dried tomatoes, packed in oil, drained and minced
¼	cup extra virgin olive oil	½	cup golden raisins
3-4	leeks, white and tender green parts, trimmed and minced	⅓	cup pine nuts
		12	ounces dry fusilli, cooked al dente
4	cloves garlic, minced	¼	cup extra virgin olive oil
1	heaping tablespoon anchovy paste	4	ounces Romano pecorino cheese, freshly grated
	Pinch of saffron threads		Salt and freshly ground black pepper to taste

Blanch, steam or microwave broccoli until just slightly undercooked. Drain and set aside. Heat ¼ cup olive oil in a large skillet over medium-high heat. Add leeks and sauté 10 minutes or until very soft. Add garlic and sauté 1 minute longer. Stir in anchovy paste, saffron, tomatoes, raisins and pine nuts. Cook over low heat for 5 to 6 minutes to blend flavors. Stir in reserved broccoli.

Toss hot pasta with leek sauce, ¼ cup olive oil and Romano cheese. Season with salt and pepper. Serve immediately.

Yield: 4 servings

Perfect Roast Chicken

1	(3 to 4 pound) chicken Salt and freshly ground pepper	2	small, thin skinned lemons, washed and dried

Preheat oven to 350 degrees. Thoroughly wash chicken inside and out in cold water. Remove any loose fat. Let stand slightly tilted on a plate for 10 minutes to drain. Pat dry. Season chicken generously inside and out with salt and pepper. Rub in seasonings. Roll lemons on counter back and forth, pressing in with palm of hand. Puncture each lemon with a fork in at least 20 places. Place lemons in chicken cavity. Seal opening with toothpicks, closing it well but not airtight to prevent bursting. Use kitchen string to tie legs together at the knuckle.

Place chicken, breast-side down, in a roasting pan. Place it in the upper third of the oven. Bake 30 minutes. Carefully turn chicken over and bake 30 to 35 minutes longer. Increase heat to 400 degrees and bake 20 minutes. Carve chicken at table, leaving lemons inside until carved. Spoon juices that run out over the chicken.

Yield: 4 servings

Curry Cajun Chicken

⅓	cup honey	2-3	teaspoons curry powder
3	tablespoons mustard	2	tablespoons butter, melted
2-3	teaspoons Cajun seasoning	3	tablespoons water
1	teaspoon lemon juice	6	chicken breasts
1	clove garlic, chopped		

Preheat oven to 350 degrees. Combine honey, mustard, Cajun seasoning, lemon juice, garlic, curry powder, butter and water in a bowl. Add chicken breasts and mix to coat chicken with marinade.

Arrange chicken in a single layer in a 3 quart rectangular baking dish. Pour marinade over the top. Bake, uncovered, for 30 to 40 minutes. Serve over rice.

Chicken Cacciatore

9   pieces chicken
2-3 tablespoons vegetable oil
1   onion, chopped
3   cloves garlic, minced
½   cup white wine

1   (28 ounce) can chopped
     tomatoes
1   teaspoon dried oregano
1   teaspoon dried basil
     Salt and pepper to taste

Brown chicken in oil on both sides in a large skillet. Add onion and garlic and sauté 2 minutes. Stir in wine, tomatoes, oregano, basil, salt and pepper. Cover and cook 45 minutes. Serve over linguine.

Southern Pecan Encrusted Chicken with a Warm Berry Sauce

Warm Berry Sauce
1   cup frozen berries

2   cups sugar

Pecan Encrusted Chicken
1   cup flour
½   cup pecan pieces

4   boneless, skinless chicken
     breast halves
     Butter

Combine sauce ingredients in a saucepan. Cook over medium heat until sauce thickens.

To prepare chicken, preheat oven to 350 degrees. Blend flour and pecans in a food processor. Coat chicken with flour mixture. Melt enough butter in a skillet to cover the bottom. Add chicken and brown. Transfer to oven and bake 20 minutes or until chicken is done.

To serve, spoon berry sauce onto a serving plate. Place chicken on top and drizzle with more sauce.

Seminole Inn
Indiantown, Florida

Chicken French Country Style

Easy "do ahead" dish.

8	pieces chicken	1	tablespoon butter
2	tablespoons vegetable oil	2	roasted red bell peppers,
	Salt and pepper to taste		cut into 1 inch pieces
1	pound sweet sausage	¼	cup chopped fresh parsley
4	ounces mushrooms, quartered		

Preheat oven to 400 degrees. Sauté chicken in oil until golden. Season with salt and pepper and place in a large baking dish. Pierce skin of sausage and cook in ¾ inch boiling water, turning occasionally. When all water has cooked away, brown sausage over medium heat. Cut into bite-size pieces and add to baking dish.

Sauté mushrooms in butter and add to baking dish along with bell peppers. Bake 10 minutes or until heated through. Sprinkle with parsley.

Yield: 6 to 8 servings

Garlicky Chicken

6	skinless chicken breast halves, bone-in	1	teaspoon black pepper
½	cup olive oil	4	tablespoons Parmesan cheese
4-6	large cloves garlic, chopped	1	cup white wine
1	tablespoon dried oregano	2	tablespoons Parmesan cheese
2	teaspoons salt		

Place chicken in a baking pan.

Combine oil, garlic, oregano, salt, black pepper and 4 tablespoons Parmesan cheese. Spoon over chicken and marinate at least 1 hour.

When ready to bake, preheat oven to 350 degrees. Add wine to pan and sprinkle with 2 tablespoons Parmesan cheese. Bake 1 hour. Serve with linguine. Spoon pan juices over chicken and linguine. Sprinkle with extra Parmesan cheese, if desired.

Yield: 4 to 6 servings

Spinach Stuffed Chicken Breasts

½ teaspoon olive oil
2 cups diced mushrooms
1 large clove garlic, minced
4 green onions, diced
1 teaspoon black pepper
½ (10 ounce) package fresh
   spinach

4 boneless, skinless chicken
   breast halves
4 slices Gouda cheese
½ teaspoon olive oil
1 (1 ounce) package
   peppercorn sauce mix
¼ cup water
1 cup milk

Heat ½ teaspoon olive oil in a skillet. Add mushrooms, garlic and onions and sauté 3 minutes. Add black pepper and spinach. Heat, stirring occasionally, until spinach is wilted.

Cut a horizontal slit in each chicken breast. Fill each pocket with 2 tablespoons spinach mixture and a slice of cheese. Heat ½ teaspoon oil over medium heat in a clean skillet. Add chicken and cook 6 minutes on each side.

Meanwhile, in a small saucepan, mix sauce mix, ¼ cup water and milk. Stir until blended. Cook until hot. Serve hot sauce over chicken breasts.

Yield: 4 servings

Feta Stuffed Herbed Chicken Breasts

Chicken

3	slices bread
2	tablespoons chopped fresh parsley
2	tablespoons chopped fresh basil
1	tablespoon chopped fresh rosemary

4	boneless, skinless chicken breast halves, butterflied
4	slice roasted red bell pepper
½-¾	cup feta cheese
	Egg wash
2	tablespoons butter
1	tablespoon vegetable oil

Red Wine Reduction

2	tablespoons butter
½	cup red wine

1	teaspoon flour

Combine bread, parsley, basil and rosemary in a food processor. Blend until fine and set aside. Unfold chicken breasts to lay flat. Place a slice of roasted pepper on each breast. Top each with 2 to 3 tablespoons of feta cheese. Fold up breasts and secure with toothpicks. Dip chicken in egg wash and roll in bread crumb mixture. Refrigerate 1 hour.

When ready to cook, heat butter and oil in a skillet. Add chicken and cook over medium high heat for 15 minutes or until done, turning to brown on all sides.

To make wine reduction, melt butter in a saucepan. Whisk in wine and flour. Cook and stir over medium heat for 4 minutes. Serve with chicken breasts.

Yield: 4 servings

Opulent Chicken

8	boneless, skinless chicken breast halves	3	tablespoons flour
¼	teaspoon black pepper	1	(14½ ounce) can chicken broth
1½	teaspoons seasoned salt	¼	cup sherry
1	teaspoon paprika	1	(14 ounce) can artichoke hearts, drained
4	tablespoons butter		
8	ounces mushrooms, sliced		

Preheat oven to 375 degrees. Sprinkle chicken with pepper, seasoned salt and paprika. Melt half the butter in a skillet. Add chicken and brown. Remove chicken and add remaining half of butter to skillet. Add mushrooms and sauté. Stir in flour to make a roux. Stir in broth and sherry.

Place chicken in a baking dish. Sprinkle with artichoke hearts. Pour mushroom gravy over the top. Bake 45 to 60 minutes.

Chicken Paprikash

1	medium onion, finely chopped	4	cups sour cream
3	tablespoons butter		Salt to taste
3	pounds chicken parts or boneless breasts		Cayenne pepper to taste
1	tablespoon paprika, preferably Hungarian		Parsley, orange slices and paprika for garnish

Sauté onion in butter in a large skillet until softened but not browned. Add chicken and sprinkle with paprika. Cover and simmer 45 minutes or until chicken is tender.

Gently fold in sour cream. Season with salt and cayenne pepper. Cook until heated thoroughly; do not boil. Serve over large, flat egg noodles. Garnish as desired.

Yield: 6 servings

North African Roast Chicken Thighs with Raisins, Almonds and Apricots

12	skinless chicken thighs, bone-in	1	tablespoon ground turmeric
	Salt and freshly cracked black pepper to taste	1	teaspoon paprika
		2	teaspoons salt
2	tablespoons virgin olive oil	4	cups chicken broth
1	yellow onion, thinly sliced	2	tablespoons lemon juice
1	tablespoon minced garlic	¼	cup raisins
2	small to medium sweet potatoes, peeled and cut into bite-size chunks	¼	cup dried apricots, chopped
		¼	cup blanched almonds, coarsely chopped
1	tablespoon minced ginger	1	tablespoon minced fresh red or green chile pepper or your choice
1	tablespoon ground cumin		
1	tablespoon cinnamon		

Preheat oven to 350 degrees. Sprinkle chicken with salt and pepper. Heat oil in a large skillet over medium heat until hot but not smoking. Add chicken and cook, moving around every few minutes, for 5 to 7 minutes or until lightly browned on all sides. Remove chicken from skillet and set aside.

Add onion to skillet and sauté over medium heat for 5 to 7 minutes or until onions begin to brown. Add garlic and sauté 1 minute. Add sweet potatoes, ginger, cumin, cinnamon, turmeric, paprika and salt. Cook and stir 1 minute. Add broth, lemon juice, raisins, apricots, almonds, chile pepper and reserved chicken. Bring to a boil. Cover and transfer to oven. Bake 20 to 25 minutes or until chicken is tender and cooked through. Season with salt and pepper.

Nantucket Cassoulet

4	sweet Italian sausages	3-4	cloves garlic, chopped
4	hot Italian sausages	2	bay leaves
12	skinless chicken thighs, bone-in	3	sprigs fresh thyme, or 1 teaspoon dried
2	medium onions, sliced		Salt and pepper to taste
4	(16 ounce) cans white navy beans, drained and rinsed	¾	cup white wine
1	(28 ounce) can plum tomatoes, halved, juice reserved		Chopped fresh parsley

Preheat oven to 325 degrees. Cook sweet and hot sausages in a large skillet over medium heat until they render some fat. Add chicken and cook until sausages and chicken are browned, adding some olive oil if needed. Transfer meat to a bowl, reserving fat in skillet. Slice sausages into 1 inch pieces. Add onions to skillet and sauté over low heat for 10 to 15 minutes.

In a large casserole dish, make 2 layers in the following order: meat, beans, tomatoes, sautéed onions and garlic. Add bay leaves, thyme, salt and pepper. Pour wine and reserved tomato juice over top. Cover and bake 1 hour. Serve immediately garnished with parsley, or for best flavor, bake a day ahead and refrigerate. When ready to serve, bring to room temperature and reheat at 325 degrees for 30 minutes.

Yield: 6 servings

Quick Cassoulet

2	pounds kielbasa or other smoked sausage, sliced ½ inch thick
2	large onions, chopped (about 2 cups)
2	cups dry vermouth
2	cups chopped cooked chicken, turkey or beef
1	(16 ounce) can white beans, drained

1	(16 ounce) can kidney beans, drained
1	(16 ounce) can stewed tomatoes, undrained
1	tablespoon sugar
5	cloves garlic, finely minced
6	bay leaves
1	bunch parsley, chopped
1	tablespoon dried thyme
1	teaspoon allspice
6	slices bacon

Preheat oven to 350 degrees. Sauté sausage without extra oil over medium heat in a large skillet for 10 minutes or until meat has browned and edges have blistered slightly. Add onions and vermouth and simmer 1 hour or until liquid has almost completely evaporated, turning sausage occasionally. Transfer mixture to a 2 quart casserole dish.

Add chopped chicken, beans, tomatoes, sugar, garlic, bay leaves, parsley, thyme and allspice. Lay bacon slices over top. Cover and bake 45 minutes or until bacon is browned and juices are bubbling.

Yield: 8 servings

Moroccan Chicken

Has a nice, not too spicy, Mid-East flavor.

Chicken

6	boneless, skinless chicken thighs	½	cup orange juice
⅓-½	cup chopped onion	¼	teaspoon salt
1	large clove garlic, chopped	¼	teaspoon cinnamon
1	tablespoon margarine	⅛	teaspoon allspice
2	teaspoons orange zest	2	tablespoons honey

Couscous

2	cups water	1⅓	cups dry couscous
2	tablespoons lemon juice	½	cup currants
1	tablespoon olive oil	½	cup chopped green onions
½	teaspoon salt, or to taste		Orange wedges and fresh
⅛	teaspoon turmeric powder		mint for garnish

Sauté chicken, onion and garlic in margarine until brown. Add orange zest, orange juice and salt. Bring to a boil. Reduce heat and simmer 5 minutes. Sprinkle chicken with cinnamon and allspice. Drizzle with honey. Cover and simmer 5 to 10 minutes or until done.

Meanwhile, prepare couscous. Bring 2 cups water, lemon juice, oil, salt and turmeric to a boil in a saucepan. Stir in couscous and currants. Remove from heat and cover. Let stand 5 minutes or until water is absorbed. Fluff with a fork and stir in green onions. Serve chicken with couscous and garnish with orange wedges and mint.

Texas Stir-Fry

2 tablespoons vegetable oil
1 pound chicken fillets or pork tenderloin, cut into ½ inch strips
1-2 tablespoons chili powder
1 bunch green onions, cut into 1 inch pieces
2 cloves garlic, minced
1 red bell pepper, chopped
1 jalapeño pepper, seeded and chopped

1 (16 ounce) can black beans, drained and rinsed
1 bunch cilantro, chopped
3-4 plum tomatoes, seeded and chopped
1 cup frozen corn, thawed and drained
1 teaspoon cumin
1 teaspoon coriander
1 teaspoon salt
1-2 tablespoons lime juice

Heat oil in a skillet. Add chicken and chili powder and stir-fry until lightly browned. Remove chicken with a slotted spoon.

Add onions, garlic and peppers to skillet. Stir-fry 1 minute. Add beans, cilantro, tomatoes, corn, cumin, coriander, salt and lime juice. Stir-fry 2 to 3 minutes. Stir in chicken and cook until heated through. Serve over rice.

Artichoke and Mushroom Chicken

2 boneless, skinless chicken breasts, sliced
3 tablespoons flour
3 tablespoons olive oil
4 tablespoons butter
1 clove garlic, minced

1 (14 ounce) can artichoke hearts, quartered
10 medium mushrooms, sliced, or one (3½ ounce) can
½ cup dry white wine
1 teaspoon dried parsley
Salt and pepper to taste

Coat chicken in flour. Heat oil in a skillet over medium heat. Add chicken and sauté until golden brown. Transfer chicken to a serving platter and keep warm in a 200 degree oven.

Add butter, garlic, artichokes and mushrooms to skillet. Sauté 5 minutes. Mix in wine and parsley. Season with salt and pepper. Simmer 5 minutes. Spoon mushroom sauce over chicken and serve immediately.

Yield: 2 servings

Chicken Stir-Fry

1 (14½ ounce) can chicken broth
2 tablespoons cornstarch
2 tablespoons soy sauce
½ teaspoon garlic powder
½ teaspoon ginger
½ teaspoon black pepper
2 tablespoons sesame oil
1 pound boneless, skinless chicken breast, cut into strips
1 head broccoli, stem removed, florets chopped
1 (8 ounce) can sliced water chestnuts
2 carrots, julienned
½ cup frozen peas
¼ cup peanuts
3-4 cups cooked rice

Combine chicken broth, cornstarch, soy sauce, garlic powder, ginger and black pepper in a cup. Set aside.

Heat sesame oil in a wok over high heat. When oil begins to smoke, stir in chicken. Move chicken up the sides of wok as it gets done. Add broccoli, water chestnuts, carrots, peas and peanuts to center of wok and stir-fry. Push vegetables up the side of wok as they get almost but not completely cooked. Stir chicken broth mixture and add to wok. Continue to cook and stir until broth begins to thicken. Remove from heat. Serve over rice.

Swiss Chicken Bake

6 boneless, skinless chicken breast halves
6 slices Swiss cheese
1 (10¾ ounce) cream of chicken or mushroom soup
½ cup milk
2 cups Stove Top stuffing
2-4 tablespoons butter, melted

Preheat oven to 350 degrees. Pound chicken until even and fairly thin. Place in a casserole dish. Top each breast with a slice of cheese.

Combine soup and milk and pour over chicken and cheese. Sprinkle stuffing on top. Drizzle with butter. Bake 50 minutes.

Chicken Louisa

4	(⅓ inch thick) chicken cutlets	4-5	plum tomatoes, chopped
	Salt and pepper to taste	2	tablespoons chopped fresh
1	tablespoon olive oil		tarragon
1	tablespoon butter	½-1	chicken bouillon cube,
1	medium shallot, chopped		crumbled
½	cup dry white wine		Fresh chives for garnish
¾	cup heavy cream		

Pat chicken dry with paper towels. Season with salt and pepper. Heat oil and butter in a heavy skillet. Cook chicken, in 2 batches, for 3 minutes to brown on both sides. Transfer to a plate and cover to keep warm.

Add shallot to skillet and sauté 1 minute. Add wine and deglaze skillet by boiling over high heat, scraping up brown bits, until reduced by half. Stir in cream, tomatoes, tarragon and bouillon. Simmer and stir 3 to 4 minutes or until tomatoes are softened and sauce begins to thicken. Season with salt and pepper.

Return chicken, along with an accumulated juices on plate, to skillet. Simmer 4 to 5 minutes or until cooked through. Garnish with chives and serve immediately.

Apple Stuffed Chicken Breast

A fancy entrée without the fuss.

¼	cup slivered almonds	8	boneless chicken breast
½	apple, peeled and diced		halves
1	egg, lightly beaten		Cooking spray
1¾	cups dry plain bread crumbs		Salt and pepper to taste
1½	tablespoons brown sugar		Paprika to taste
¼	cup currants (optional)		

Preheat oven to 350 degrees. Place almonds in a skillet and toast over medium heat for about 5 minutes. Combine almonds, apple, egg, bread crumbs, sugar and currants in a large bowl. Mix well.

Rinse chicken and pat dry. Cut a pocket into each breast. Stuff bread crumb mixture into each pocket. Place stuffed chicken on a jelly-roll pan. Spray breasts with cooking spray. Season with salt, pepper and paprika. Bake 30 minutes.

Mike Szary's
Black Beans and Rice

1 pound dried black beans	3 cups chicken broth
1½ pounds boneless, skinless chicken breasts	Juice of 2 lemons
¼ cup extra virgin olive oil	1 tablespoon plus 1 teaspoon sugar
2 tablespoons minced garlic	2 teaspoons chili paste with garlic
1 large red bell pepper, diced	Salt to taste
1 large green bell pepper, diced	3-4 tablespoons cornstarch
1 large yellow bell pepper, diced	Steamed jasmine rice
1 large yellow onion, diced	6 green onions, chopped

Boil beans in salted water until soft. Drain, cool and set aside. Grill or broil chicken. Cool, dice and set aside.

Heat oil a 2 quart saucepan. Add garlic and sauté until opaque. Add peppers and onion and sauté briefly. Stir in cooked chicken, drained beans and chicken broth. Bring to a boil. Add lemon juice, sugar, chili paste and salt. Bring to a boil. Cook until vegetables are crisp-tender.

Mix cornstarch with enough water to make a paste. Stir into saucepan and cook until thickened. Serve with rice and garnished with green onions.

Yield: 8 servings

This recipe is very flexible. Substitute any meat, seafood or poultry for the chicken, or serve as a vegetarian dish. Adjust the richness (olive oil), sweetness (sugar), sourness (lemon juice) and seasoning (chili paste) to suite your taste.

Sailfish Point Country Club
Stuart, Florida

Grilled Chicken Breast with Pineapple Salsa

Pineapple Salsa

1	small pineapple, finely diced		1½	teaspoons ground cumin
1	red bell pepper, finely diced		1½	teaspoons black pepper
1	green bell pepper, finely diced		½	cup pineapple juice
1	small onion, finely diced		1	teaspoon lime zest
1	tablespoon finely chopped fresh jalapeño pepper		1	tablespoon finely chopped cilantro
2	teaspoons finely chopped garlic		¼	cup rice wine vinegar

Chicken

4   boneless, skinless chicken breast halves

Combine all salsa ingredients in a large bowl. Mix and refrigerate 20 minutes.

Grill chicken until done. Serve salsa over chicken.

Orchid Bay Golf and Beach Club
One Beachside Drive
Vero Beach, Florida

Chicken and Rice Bake

1¼	cups dry long grain rice		1	cup sliced mushrooms
1	(10¾ ounce) can condensed cream of chicken soup		1	chicken, cut into pieces
1¾	cups water		½	teaspoon salt
½	cup diced celery		¼	teaspoon paprika
			¼	teaspoon poultry seasoning

Preheat oven to 350 degrees. Mix rice, soup, 1¾ cup water, celery and mushrooms in a baking dish.

Season chicken with salt, paprika and poultry seasoning. Lay chicken over rice. Bake 45 to 60 minutes.

Chicken Mushroom in Puff Pastry Shells

"An elegant entrée that is simple to prepare."

6	puff pastry shells	1	tablespoon cornstarch
3	tablespoons butter	2	tablespoons water
3	shallots, chopped	½	cup heavy cream
3	cups thinly sliced mushrooms		Dash of poultry seasoning
1	cup chicken broth		Dash of nutmeg
2	boneless, skinless chicken breasts, cooked and chopped		Slivered almonds

Prepare pastry shells as directed on package. Melt butter in a skillet. Add onion and mushrooms and sauté until tender. Add broth and chopped chicken. Cook 10 minutes.

Dissolve cornstarch in 2 tablespoons water and add to skillet along with cream, poultry seasoning and nutmeg. Cook until sauce thickens. To serve, spoon chicken mixture into pastry shells. Sprinkle slivered almonds on top.

Chicken with Fig and Port Sauce

2	chicken breast halves, cut into bite size pieces	¼	cup water
	Seasoned flour	1	chicken bouillon cube, crumbled
	Butter for sautéing	2	tablespoons cream
5	dried figs, sliced		Mashed potatoes
1	tablespoon port wine		Paprika
¼	cup white wine		

Toss chicken in seasoned flour. Sauté in butter in a skillet until done. Transfer chicken to a plate. Add figs, wines, ¼ cup water and bouillon to skillet. Bring to a boil. Reduce heat and simmer until slightly reduced. Add chicken to skillet and heat thoroughly. Stir in cream.

Spoon mashed potatoes onto individual serving plates. Make a well in center of potatoes and sprinkle with paprika. Fill well with chicken mixture. Serve immediately or keep warm in oven until ready to serve.

Chicken Dijon Parmesan

1 cup butter, melted	3 cups freshly grated Parmesan cheese
1 tablespoon Dijon mustard	3 cups fresh bread crumbs
1 tablespoon Worcestershire sauce	12 sprigs parsley, chopped
1 clove garlic, crushed	8 boneless, skinless chicken breast halves

Preheat oven to 350 degrees. Combine butter, mustard, Worcestershire sauce and garlic in a shallow dish. In a separate shallow dish, mix cheese, bread crumbs and parsley. Dip chicken in butter mixture, then coat with breading mixture. Roll each breast and dust with breading.

Place on a baking sheet. Bake about 30 minutes or until done. Remove from baking sheet and let stand 5 minutes before serving.

Yield: 8 servings

Chicken and Dumplings

"My family's favorite - great for using after Thanksgiving turkey"

1 turkey carcass with some meat on	Chicken base or bouillon cubes to taste
1 whole chicken, or chicken pieces of your choice	1 (16 ounce) package frozen mixed vegetables
1 onion, quartered	2 cups baking mix
2 stalks celery, cut into 3 inch chunks	1 cup milk

Place turkey carcass and chicken in a large stew pot. Add onion, celery, chicken base and enough water to cover. Cook until meat is tender and falling off the bone. Strain broth through a colander and return broth to pot. Cool chicken, cut into bite-size pieces and add to broth. Add mixed vegetables and simmer 10 minutes.

To make dumplings, combine baking mix and milk. Mix. Drop by teaspoonfuls into simmering stew. Cover and cook 10 minutes. Remove cover and cook 10 minutes longer. If stew is too thin, cook longer. If stew is too thick, add water until desired consistency is reached.

Chicken Breast
with Creamy Mustard Sauce

1	teaspoon butter	½	cup plain yogurt
1	teaspoon vegetable oil	2	tablespoons Dijon mustard
8	boneless, skinless chicken breast halves		

Heat butter and oil in a large skillet over medium heat. Add chicken and brown until no longer pink. Transfer chicken to a plate and keep warm.

Add yogurt to drippings in skillet. Add mustard and stir 30 to 40 seconds. Add chicken and cook until heated.

Lemon Chicken with Cashews

Stir-Fry

1	tablespoon vegetable oil	2	bell peppers, sliced
2½	teaspoons Asian sesame oil	1	(7 ounce) package frozen snow peas, halved on the diagonal
½	teaspoon chili oil		
1	pound boneless, skinless chicken breasts, cut into strips	2	cups shredded lettuce
		½	cup cashews or to taste

Sauce

1	teaspoon minced fresh ginger	3	tablespoons lemon juice
1	clove garlic, minced	1	teaspoon lemon zest
2	tablespoons soy sauce	⅛	teaspoon cayenne pepper
2	tablespoons dry sherry	1½	teaspoons cornstarch dissolved in 2 tablespoons cold water
2	tablespoons chicken broth		
1½	teaspoons sugar		

Heat oils in a skillet. Add chicken, bell peppers, snow peas and lettuce and stir-fry until chicken is done and vegetables are crisp tender.

Combine all sauce ingredients and pour over stir-fry mixture. Cook until sauce thickens. Serve with rice and garnish with cashews.

Chicken and Linguine

8   ounces dry linguine pasta, cooked and drained
½   teaspoon garlic powder
2   tablespoons butter, melted
1   teaspoon salt
2   tablespoons Parmesan cheese
4   cups cooked and chopped chicken

2-3 (4 ounce) cans sliced mushrooms, drained, juice reserved
1   (10¾ ounce) can cream of mushroom soup
1   (10¾ ounce) can cream of chicken soup
2   tablespoons pimento
¼   cup white wine or sherry
½   cup Parmesan cheese

Preheat oven to 350 degrees. Combine pasta, garlic powder, butter, salt and 2 tablespoons Parmesan cheese. Spread mixture in a greased shallow baking dish. Arrange chicken on pasta mixture. Sprinkle mushrooms over the top.

Mix soups, pimento, wine and reserved mushroom liquid in a bowl. Spread evenly over casserole. Top with ½ cup Parmesan cheese. Bake 30 minutes.

Dish can be prepared a day ahead. Bake when ready to serve, adjusting baking time as needed.

Turkey Casserole

4   cups cooked and chopped turkey
1   cup mayonnaise
3   cups herb seasoned stuffing
1   (10¾ ounce) can cream of mushroom soup

1   (10¾ ounce) can cream of chicken soup
1   (8 ounce) can sliced water chestnuts, drained
2   (8 ounce) cans sliced mushrooms, drained

Preheat oven to 350 degrees. Combine all ingredients and put in a 9x13 inch casserole dish. Bake 40 minutes. Cut into squares and serve.

Chicken Linguine with Sun-Dried Tomatoes and Olives

2 tablespoons virgin olive oil
2 boneless, skinless chicken breasts, cut into strips
1 ounce garlic, chopped
1 ounce sun-dried tomatoes, rehydrated and cut into thin strips
½ ounce pine nuts, toasted
½ cup crumbled feta cheese
½ cup crumbled goat cheese
2 teaspoons chopped fresh basil
1 ounce pitted kalamata olives
6 ounces dry linguine, cooked al dente
2 tablespoons virgin olive oil
2 teaspoons Parmesan cheese

Heat 2 tablespoons olive oil in a skillet until hot. Add chicken, garlic, tomatoes and pine nuts and sauté for 1 minute. Add feta and goat cheeses and basil. Stir in olives, drained linguine and 2 tablespoons olive oil and toss. Transfer to a serving bowl. Top with Parmesan cheese.

Yield: 2 servings

Disney's Vero Beach Resort
9250 Island Grove Terrace
Vero Beach Florida

Turkey Meatloaf

3 pounds ground turkey
1 cup dry bread crumbs
1½ teaspoons seasoned salt
1 tablespoon dried oregano
1 tablespoon dried parsley
1 teaspoon dried basil
1 teaspoon dried rosemary
1 teaspoon dried thyme
1 teaspoon onion powder
1 teaspoon garlic powder
½ teaspoon black pepper
2 eggs, beaten
1 cup shredded cheese

Preheat oven to 350 degrees. Combine all ingredients in a large bowl. Form into a loaf and place in a lightly greased shallow roasting pan. Bake 1½ hours.

Chicken Livers Fabuloso

1 pound bacon	1 (8 ounce) can whole water chestnuts, halved
2-3 medium onions, sliced	Worcestershire sauce to taste
1 red bell pepper, cut into strips	Sherry to taste
1 green bell pepper, cut into strips	Teriyaki or tamari sauce to taste
1 pound mushrooms, halved or quartered if large	Salt to taste
1½ pounds chicken livers, halved if large	Cayenne pepper to taste
	Parsley for garnish (optional)

Cook bacon in a large skillet or microwave oven until done. Drain off grease, reserving 2 tablespoons. Cut bacon into 2 to 3 inch pieces and place in a casserole dish.

Wipe out skillet with paper towels and add reserved bacon grease to skillet. Add onions, bell peppers, mushrooms and livers and sauté. Stir in water chestnuts and cook until heated. Season with Worcestershire sauce, sherry, teriyaki sauce, salt and cayenne pepper. Add mixture to casserole dish. Garnish with parsley. Serve with white rice.

Grilled Raspberry Game Hens

Marinade

¾ cup pureed fresh or frozen unsweetened raspberries

1 cup raspberry vinegar
Zest of 1 lemon

1 tablespoon minced garlic or shallot

2 tablespoons chopped fresh mint

⅓ cup olive oil

Game Hens

4 (1 pound) game hens
Salt and pepper to taste

Fresh raspberry and mint sprigs for garnish

Glaze

⅓ cup seedless raspberry preserves or jam

1 teaspoon orange zest

¼ cup Grand Marnier

Combine all marinade ingredients with a whisk or food processor. Split game hens in half and rinse well. Pat dry with paper towels and season with salt and pepper. Place in a glass or plastic container. Pour marinade over hens to coat well. Refrigerate overnight, turning hens occasionally.

When ready to serve, heat grill. Remove hens from marinade, reserving marinade for basting. Grill hens, skin-side down, for 10 minutes. Turn and baste. Discard marinade.

Meanwhile, combine all glaze ingredients in a small saucepan. Heat and stir until preserves melt. Remove from heat.

When hens have cooked for about 25 minutes total, begin brushing on the glaze, watching carefully to prevent burning. Cook for a total of 35 to 40 minutes or until juices run clear when pierced with a fork. Serve immediately or refrigerate and serve at room temperature as a luncheon entrée. Garnish with raspberries and mint.

Yield: 6 to 8 servings

Savory Roast Fillet of Beef

1	(8 pound) beef tenderloin		Juice of 2 lemons
1	tablespoon salt	⅔	cup steak sauce
1	tablespoon black pepper	¼	cup Worcestershire sauce
2	teaspoons celery salt	2	ounces paprika
2	teaspoons onion salt		

Wash beef and pat dry. Rub salt, pepper, celery salt and onion salt into meat. Rub well to get into all crevices. In a small bowl, combine lemon juice, steak sauce and Worcestershire sauce. Rub sauce mixture into meat, setting extra sauce aside.

Place beef in a shallow roasting pan. Coat with paprika. Marinate in refrigerator for 8 to 10 hours, turning 2 to 3 times. Bring to room temperature before roasting. To cook, preheat oven to 550 degrees. Pour leftover sauce and any accumulated meat juices over beef, draining any excess liquid from pan. Roast, uncovered, for 10 minutes. Reduce heat to 450 degrees and roast 8 to 10 minutes per pound.

Yield: 8 to 10 servings

Grilled Fillet of Beef

1	(6 to 8 pound) beef tenderloin, trimmed	2	medium-size yellow onions, thinly sliced
2	bay leaves	10-12	black peppercorns
1	(750 ml) bottle red wine	⅓	cup olive oil
10-12	sprigs parsley		Salt and pepper to taste

Fold under and tie thin end of tenderloin. Place beef in a large zip-top bag. Combine bay leaves, wine, parsley, onions, peppercorns, oil, salt and pepper in a large bowl. Pour mixture over meat and seal bag. Marinate in refrigerator overnight.

To cook, heat grill. Remove beef from bag, discarding marinade. Cook beef 25 to 30 minutes, depending on desired degree of doneness. Remove string and beef stand for 5 minutes before slicing. Serve with Marchant de Vin or peppercorn sauce.

Beef Tenderloin

1 whole beef tenderloin, trimmed	Coarse grain mustard Crushed peppercorns

Preheat oven to 500 degrees. Cover tenderloin with mustard and peppercorns. Bake 20 minutes. Remove from oven and cover with foil. Let stand 20 minutes. Slice thin and serve warm or at room temperature.

Tournedos of Beef Tenderloin Roquefort

1 cup crumbled Roquefort cheese	Black pepper to taste
½ cup coarsely chopped walnuts	4 (4 ounce, 1 inch thick) beef tournedos steaks
2 tablespoons butter, softened	Salt to taste Chopped parsley for garnish

Preheat broiler. Combine cheese, walnuts, butter and pepper in a small bowl. Season steaks on both sides with salt and pepper. Broil, 3 to 4 inches from the heat source, for 3 to 4 minutes on each side for rare, 4 to 5 minutes for medium or 7 to 8 minutes for well-done.

Two minutes before steaks are done cooking, sprinkle with cheese mixture and return to broiler until cheese melts. Serve hot, garnished with parsley.

Yield: 4 servings

Yacht and Country Club
3883 SE Fairway East
Stuart, Florida

Beef Wellington

Beef

2	teaspoons olive oil
2	pounds beef fillet
12	ounces veal
8	ounces ham
4	ounces pork
1	onion, chopped
½	cup butter
¼	cup sherry
½	cup beef broth

½	(10 ounce) bag spinach leaves, chopped
2	bay leaves
	Salt and pepper to taste
2	egg yolks
½	cup Parmesan cheese
1	(15 ounce) package refrigerated pie crusts (2 crusts), room temperature

Périgourdine Sauce

1½	tablespoons butter
1½	tablespoons flour
1	(10½ ounce) can beef broth
1	tablespoon butter
1	small onion, chopped
1	shallot, minced

1	(4 ounce) can mushrooms, drained
½	cup Madeira wine
	Dash of salt
⅛	teaspoon cayenne pepper

Heat oil in a large skillet. Sear beef in oil on all sides. Remove and cool.

To make a filling, put veal, ham and pork through a grinder or food processor. Sauté onion in butter for 3 minutes. Add ground meat and sauté 3 minutes. Stir in sherry, broth, spinach, bay leaves, salt and pepper. Cook about 7 minutes. Remove from heat and discard bay leaves. Stir in egg yolks and Parmesan cheese. Cool.

Preheat oven to 450 degrees. Connect sides of pie crusts, forming one long crust. Spread filling over crust, leaving a 1 inch border on all sides. Lay fillet on top of filling. Wrap crust around fillet, turning ends under and sealing all edges. Place seam-side down on a baking sheet. Bake for 10 minutes. Reduce heat to 425 degrees and bake 20 minutes for medium rare. Test with meat thermometer for desired doneness. Remove from oven and let stand 10 minutes. Slice in 1½ to 2 inch slices.

To make sauce, melt 1½ tablespoons butter in a saucepan. Blend in flour and cook over low heat until brown. Combine broth with enough water to equal 2 cups and add to saucepan. Bring to a boil. Reduce heat and simmer 30 minutes, stirring occasionally. In a separate saucepan, melt 1 tablespoon butter. Add onion and shallot and sauté 3 minutes. Add brown sauce, mushrooms, wine, salt and cayenne pepper. Heat through. Serve with sliced fillet.

Sabana
(Beef Tenderloin Mexicana)

*In this traditional Mexican dish, tenderloins of beef
are pounded thin, like a sheet, or sabana. They are then briefly
seared and laid across a layer of black beans, topped with
onions and peppers. The meat is so tender you could eat it with
a spoon. Great for an elegant meal or a small dinner party.*

⅓ cup dried black beans,
    washed and picked over
2 cups water
3 slices bacon, cut into ½ inch
    pieces
½ onion, diced
½ teaspoon salt
½ teaspoon black pepper
2 (8 ounce) beef tenderloin
    fillets

Salt and pepper to taste
2 teaspoons vegetable oil
1 tablespoon unsalted butter
1 bunch green onions, white
    and light green parts,
    thinly sliced on the diagonal
3 red or green hot chiles,
    stemmed, seeded and
    julienned
Juice of 1 lime

Place beans and 2 cups water in a saucepan. Bring to a boil. Reduce
heat and simmer, uncovered, for 1 hour, 15 minutes or until soft.
Remove from heat. Cook bacon until golden. Spoon off extra fat. Add
onion and sauté until golden. Add beans with their liquid, ½ teaspoon
salt and ½ teaspoon pepper and cook 2 minutes longer. Keep warm.

Flatten fillets or have butcher do this when buying them. Season fillets
to taste with salt and pepper. Heat oil in a very large nonstick skillet.
Add fillets one at a time and sear 30 to 40 seconds on each side.

Spread bean mixture over 2 large serving plates. Top each with a hot
steak. For a garnish, melt butter in a small skillet over medium-high
heat. Add green onions, chiles and lime juice. Season to taste with
salt and pepper. Sauté for 1 minute. Sprinkle over steaks and serve
immediately.

Yield: 2 servings

Prime Rib with Roasted Garlic and Horseradish Crust

30 large cloves garlic, unpeeled	½ teaspoon coarse salt
¼ cup olive oil	1 (6 pound) boneless beef rib
⅓ cup prepared white cream- style horseradish	roast, well trimmed Salt and pepper to taste

Preheat oven to 350 degrees. Toss garlic cloves and oil in a small baking dish. Cover and bake 35 minutes or until garlic begins to brown. Drain oil into a food processor and cool 15 minutes. Peel garlic and place in processor. Add horseradish and coarse salt and puree until almost smooth.

Place a wire rack on a large rimmed baking sheet. Sprinkle beef with salt and pepper. Spread a thin layer of garlic mixture on underside of beef. Place beef, garlic mixture-side down, onto wire rack. Spread beef with remaining garlic mixture. Cover and refrigerate at least 3 hours or up to 1 day.

When ready to serve, preheat oven to 350 degrees. Position rack in bottom third of oven. Roast beef, uncovered, for 1 hour, 45 minutes or until a meat thermometer inserted into top registers 150 degrees for medium-rare. Transfer beef to a platter and let stand 30 minutes. Pour pan juices into a small saucepan. To serve, slice beef crosswise. Rewarm pan juices and drizzle over beef.

Yield: 8 servings

Steak Diane

2	(6 ounce) beef filet mignon	1	tablespoon lemon juice
⅛	teaspoon salt	1½	teaspoons Worcestershire
⅛	teaspoon freshly ground		sauce
	black pepper	1	tablespoon minced fresh
2	tablespoons butter		chives
1	teaspoon Dijon mustard	1	tablespoon brandy
2	tablespoons minced shallots	1	tablespoon minced fresh
1	tablespoon butter		parsley

Season steaks with salt and pepper. Melt 2 tablespoons butter in a heavy skillet. Add mustard and shallots and sauté over medium heat for 1 minute. Add steaks and cook about 3 minutes on each side for medium-rare. Remove steaks and keep warm.

Add 1 tablespoon butter, lemon juice, Worcestershire sauce and chives to pan drippings in skillet. Cook 2 minutes. Stir in brandy and pour over steaks. Sprinkle with parsley.

Yield: 2 servings

Top Round Steak
with Jalapeño Marinade

3	fresh jalapeño peppers,		Fresh parsley
	seeded	1	teaspoon salt
⅔	cup dry red wine	½	teaspoon black pepper
⅓	cup olive oil	1	(2½ pound) beef top round
2	cloves garlic		steak

Combine jalapeño, wine, oil, garlic, parsley, salt and pepper in a food processor and blend. Transfer to a plastic zip-top bag. Score beef and add to marinade in bag. Marinate at least 6 hours.

When ready to serve, preheat grill. Grill steak, turning and brushing with marinade, for 14 to 16 minutes for rare or 18 to 20 minutes for medium. Carve thin slices diagonally across the grain and serve.

Steak Fajitas

1	(2 pound) beef skirt steak	1	green bell pepper, cut into ½ inch rings
⅓	cup tequila	1	red onion, cut crosswise into ½ inch slices
¼	cup fresh lime juice		
2	tablespoons vegetable oil	1	yellow onion, cut crosswise into ½ inch slices
2	cloves garlic, minced		
½	teaspoon salt		Olive oil
½	teaspoon dried red pepper flakes	12	flour tortillas
2	red bell peppers, cut into ½ inch rings		Guacamole, salsa, sour cream and shredded cheese for toppings

Place steak in a flat pan or a plastic zip-top bag. Whisk together tequila, lime juice, vegetable oil, garlic, salt and pepper flakes in a bowl. Pour over steak and marinate in refrigerator for at least 3 hours, turning several times.

When ready to cook, preheat grill. Remove meat from marinade and pat dry, reserving marinade. Arrange pepper rings and onion slices on grill and brush with olive oil. Grill 3 minutes, turn and brush again with oil. Grill 3 minutes longer. Transfer to a platter and cover to keep warm.

Grill steak to desired degree of doneness, turning and brushing with marinade every 2 minutes. Cook about 8 minutes for rare or 10 minutes for medium. To serve, cut steak in thin slices diagonally across the grain. Mound steak on onions and peppers on platter. Serve with warm tortillas and guacamole, salsa, sour cream and cheese for toppings.

Beef Bourguignonne

1	cup dry red wine	6	small white onions, peeled
2	tablespoons olive oil	8	large mushrooms, quartered
1	large onion, sliced	2	tablespoons flour
½	teaspoon dried thyme	½	cup brandy
1	tablespoon dried parsley flakes	2	green onions, cut into 1 inch pieces
1	teaspoon crumbled bay leaves	1	teaspoon salt or to taste
		1	teaspoon dried orange peel
¼	teaspoon black pepper	¾	cup water
2	pounds beef stew meat	1	bouillon cube
2	thick slices bacon, diced	4	medium potatoes, peeled and quartered
1	tablespoon olive oil		

Combine wine, 2 tablespoons olive oil, sliced onion, thyme, parsley, bay leaves and black pepper in a plastic zip-top bag. Add stew meat and marinate at least 3 hours or up to 8 hours. In a heavy saucepan, brown bacon in 1 tablespoon olive oil. Remove bacon to paper towels, reserving drippings in pan. Add small onions to pan and sauté 5 to 10 minutes. Remove and set aside. Add mushrooms to pan and sauté. Remove from pan and set aside.

Drain meat and pat dry, reserving marinade. Add to pan drippings in saucepan, a few pieces at a time, and cook until browned. When all meat is browned, return meat to saucepan and sprinkle with flour. Stir until flour is absorbed.

Pour brandy into saucepan. Scrape sides and simmer until brandy is almost evaporated. Strain marinade, if desired, and add to meat mixture. Stir in green onions, salt, orange peel, ¾ cup water and bouillon. Bring to a boil. Reduce heat, cover and simmer 2 hours. Add bacon, sautéed onions, mushrooms and potatoes. Cover and simmer 40 minutes. Add more water and wine as needed. Add another bouillon cube if necessary.

For variety, omit the potatoes and serve with rice or noodles.

Burgundy Stew

2 pounds boneless beef chuck, cut into bite-size pieces
2 cups sliced carrots
1 cup sliced celery
2 medium onions, sliced
3 tablespoons flour
1 tablespoon sugar
1 tablespoon salt
1 teaspoon dried basil or marjoram
1 (16 ounce) can tomatoes
1 cup Burgundy wine
1 (8 ounce) can mushrooms, drained
1 (8 ounce) can sliced water chestnuts

Preheat oven to 300 degrees. Combine beef, carrots, celery and onions in a casserole dish. Mix together flour, sugar, salt, basil, tomatoes and wine. Pour over beef mixture. Cover tightly. Bake 3 to 3½ hours. Stir in mushrooms and water chestnuts and cook 10 minutes longer.

Mexican Lasagna

1½ pounds ground beef
1 onion, diced
1 (10 ounce) can enchilada sauce
1 (10 ounce) can Rotel tomatoes and green chiles
1 (16 ounce) can creamed corn
Dash of ground cumin
Dash of dried oregano
Dash of garlic powder
1 jalapeño pepper, seeded and chopped (optional)
10-12 ounces soft corn tortillas
1 (8 ounce) package shredded cheddar cheese
1 (8 ounce) package Monterey Jack cheese, shredded

Preheat oven to 350 degrees. Brown ground beef and onion. Add enchilada sauce, tomatoes and chiles, corn, cumin, oregano, garlic powder and jalapeño. Simmer 10 minutes.

In a baking dish, layer tortillas, ⅓ of beef mixture and cheddar cheese. Repeat layers twice. Top with Monterey Jack cheese. Bake 30 minutes.

Stuffed Cabbage

2	large heads cabbage	4	teaspoons salt
2	cups chopped onions	¼	teaspoon black pepper
¾	cup raisins	3	pounds ground beef
2	(15 ounce) cans tomato sauce	1½	cups dry long grain rice
½	cup dark brown sugar	4	eggs
¼	cup lemon juice	1	tablespoon onion salt

Discard dark outer leaves of cabbages and core. Fill a 12 quart saucepan three-fourths full with water. Bring to a boil. Place one head of cabbage at a time in water, core-side up. Separate leaves as they soften, removing 16 large leaves from each head. Drain in a colander, discarding all but 2 cups of cooking liquid. Coarsely chop remaining cabbage and return to saucepan. Add onions and raisins to pan. Set aside.

In a medium bowl, combine tomato sauce, brown sugar, lemon juice, salt and ¼ teaspoon pepper. In a large bowl, mix ground beef, rice, eggs, onion salt and black pepper to taste.

To make rolls, place 2 tablespoons of meat mixture in the center of each cabbage roll and shape mixture into a 3 inch cylinder. Fold 2 sides of leaf toward the center, then roll up jelly-roll fashion starting at a short end. Place half the rolls, seam-side down, on cabbage mixture in saucepan. Top with half of tomato sauce mixture. Add remaining rolls and spoon remaining tomato sauce on top. Pour in reserved 2 cups of cooking liquid and add enough water to just cover cabbage. Bring to a boil. Reduce heat to low and cover. Simmer 2½ hours. Uncover and cook 15 minutes longer.

Yield: 16 servings

If desired, after cooking, half of the rolls can be frozen in a 9x13 inch baking dish for a later use.

The Best Chicken Fried Steak

¼	cup all-purpose flour		Vegetable oil
½	teaspoon salt	3	tablespoons all-purpose
½	teaspoon black pepper		flour
	Lemon pepper to taste	1¼	cups chicken broth
1	pound cubed beef steaks	½	cup milk
1	egg, lightly beaten		Dash of Worcestershire
2	tablespoons milk		sauce
1	cup crushed saltine crackers		Dash of hot pepper sauce

Combine ¼ cup flour, salt, black pepper and lemon pepper. Sprinkle mixture over both sides of steaks. Combine egg and milk in a shallow dish. Dip steaks in egg mixture, then dredge in cracker crumbs.

Pour oil to a depth of ½ inch in a large skillet. Heat oil until hot. Add steaks and fry over medium heat, turning once, until browned. Reduce heat and cover. Simmer, turning occasionally, for 15 minutes or until tender. Remove steaks, drain on paper towels and keep warm. Drain all but 3 tablespoons drippings from skillet.

Add 3 tablespoons flour to skillet and stir until smooth. Cook and stir 1 minute. Gradually add broth and milk. Cook over medium heat, stirring constantly, until gravy is thickened and bubbly. Stir in Worcestershire sauce and pepper sauce. Serve gravy with steaks and rice or mashed potatoes.

Yield: 4 servings

Horseradish Meatloaf

2	pounds ground beef chuck, or 1½ pounds chuck and ½ pound veal or pork	¼	cup ketchup
		2	cups bread crumbs
		¼	cup prepared horseradish
2	eggs	2	teaspoons salt
2	green onions, minced	1	teaspoon dry mustard
1	medium onion, minced	½	cup ketchup
¼	cup milk		

Preheat oven to 400 degrees. Combine meat, eggs, onions, milk, ¼ cup ketchup, crumbs, horseradish, salt and mustard. Mix well and shape firmly into a 5x10 inch loaf in a 9x13 inch baking pan. Spread ½ cup ketchup over top of loaf. Bake 1 hour.

Yield: 8 servings

Beef Bar-B-Que

A good way to use up leftover beef or pork.

1 cup chopped onion	2 teaspoons Worcestershire sauce
1 cup chopped celery	
Vegetable oil or shortening	1 (12 ounce) bottle chili sauce
1½ pounds ground beef, or leftover beef or pork	Salt and pepper to taste
	3 dashes Tabasco sauce
1 cup ketchup	2 tablespoons brown sugar
2 tablespoons mustard	

Sauté onion and celery in vegetable oil until translucent. Add beef and cook until browned. Stir in ketchup, mustard, Worcestershire sauce, chili sauce, salt, pepper, Tabasco sauce and brown sugar. Simmer 30 minutes. Serve on toasted buns.

Picadillo

Ernest Hemingway used to serve guests this exotic concoction at his home, Finca Vigia, in Cuba. He had a talent for budget, as well as taste — the main ingredient is ground beef. The dish is even better the next day.

2 cups raisins	2 cloves garlic, minced
½ cup hot beef broth	½ teaspoon dried oregano
2 tablespoons vegetable oil	¼ teaspoon ground cloves
2 pounds lean ground beef	¼ teaspoon black pepper
2 cups red wine	2 green bell peppers, chopped
¾ cup finely chopped green onions with tops	¾ cup slivered almonds
	Snipped fresh watercress for garnish (optional)
2 teaspoons salt	

Soak raisins in broth for 10 minutes or until plump; drain.

Heat oil in a large skillet. Add beef and quickly brown. Stir in wine, onions, salt, garlic, oregano, cloves and black pepper. Simmer 15 minutes. Stir in bell pepper and cook 5 minutes longer. Add almonds and raisins. Serve over rice garnished with watercress.

Yield: 8 servings

Conchy Joe's Seafood
3945 N.E. Indian River Drive
Jensen Beach, Florida

Fred's Meatloaf

A recipe that evolved over the last half of the
20th century, created by Fred Ayres, Dolphin Bar owner.

1	very large red onion, chopped	1	green bell pepper, sliced large julienne
1	medium white onion, chopped	3	jalapeño peppers, very thinly sliced
2	pounds meat loaf mix (pork, beef and veal)	4	teaspoons Dijon mustard
2	pounds ground beef	4	teaspoons distilled vinegar
3	pounds ground lamb	4	teaspoons Worcestershire sauce
1	(10 ounce) can mushroom pieces	1	tablespoon salt
1	(1 ounce) package onion soup mix	1	teaspoon garlic powder
2	red bell peppers, sliced large julienne	1	teaspoon black pepper
		3	eggs
		3½	cups Special K cereal

Preheat oven to 400 degrees. Combine all ingredients in a large bowl and mix well. Spread in two 9x13 inch pans. Cover with a decorative ketchup grid or with canned green chiles.

Bake 20 minutes to sear meat. Reduce heat to 325 degrees and bake 1½ to 2 hours.

Dolphin Bar and Shrimp House
1405 NE Indian River Drive
Jensen Beach, Florida

Capellini with Veal and Tomatoes

1 (16 ounce) package capellini pasta
2 slices bacon, cut into 1 inch pieces
1 large onion, thinly sliced
8 ounces veal cutlets, cut into 1 inch strips
2 tablespoons instant-blending flour
½ cup Chablis or other dry white wine
2 cloves garlic, minced

2 tablespoons extra virgin olive oil
½ teaspoon salt
½ teaspoon dried oregano
½ teaspoon dried thyme
5 medium tomatoes, cut into wedges
10 pitted black olives, halved
2 ounces prosciutto, cut into 1 inch strips
2 tablespoons chopped fresh parsley

Cook pasta according to package directions. Drain and set aside, keep warm. Cook bacon in a large skillet over medium heat until transparent. Add onion and sauté until bacon is crisp and onion is tender.

Sprinkle veal with flour. Add veal to skillet and cook, stirring constantly, until veal is lightly browned. Stir in wine, garlic, oil, salt, oregano and thyme. Bring to a boil. Reduce heat and cover. Simmer 8 to 10 minutes or until veal is almost tender. Add tomato wedges and olives. Cover and simmer 5 to 7 minutes or until thoroughly heated. Stir in prosciutto, cover and let stand 2 minutes. Serve over pasta and garnish with parsley.

Yield: 6 servings

Dijon Veal

1	(8 ounce) jar Dijon mustard	1	(10½ ounce) can beef broth
½	cup butter, melted	¼	cup sherry
1	small leg of veal, boned and rolled	1	tablespoon chopped fresh parsley

Preheat oven to 300 degrees. Blend mustard and butter and pour over veal in a shallow pan. Bake 4 hours. During the last hour, baste every 20 minutes with a mixture of broth and sherry. Use pan dripping to make a gravy. Garnish with parsley.

Veal Escalopes with Spinach

¼	cup flour	½	cup sliced sun-dried tomatoes, drain oil
½	teaspoon salt		
½	teaspoon black pepper	1	(10 ounce) package fresh spinach, washed and stemmed
1	teaspoon garlic powder		
6	veal escalopes, pounded thin		
		6	thin slices prosciutto (optional)
1	tablespoon olive oil		
1	tablespoon butter	6	slices mozzarella cheese
1	onion, chopped	1	(10½ ounce) can beef broth
8	ounces mushrooms, sliced	2	tablespoons Marsala wine
		2	tablespoons flour

Preheat oven to 350 degrees. Combine ¼ cup flour, salt, pepper and garlic powder. Dredge veal in flour mixture. Heat oil and butter in a skillet. Add veal and sauté on both sides until brown. Remove from skillet. Add onion, mushrooms and tomatoes to skillet and sauté.

Spread spinach in a large baking dish. Place veal over spinach and lay prosciutto over veal. Top with sautéed vegetables. Place mozzarella slices over vegetables. Combine broth and wine. Blend in 2 tablespoons flour. Pour mixture over veal. Bake until heated through.

Veal Escalopes
with Tomato Basil Sauce

3	tablespoons butter	¾	cup chicken broth
1	tablespoon vegetable oil	¾	cup half-and-half
12	(⅛ inch thick) veal escalopes	2	tomatoes, peeled, seeded and finely chopped
2	tablespoons chopped shallots	½	cup chopped fresh basil
¾	cup dry white wine		Salt and pepper to taste

Heat butter and oil in a large skillet over medium-high heat. Quickly sauté veal in batches until both sides are lightly browned. Remove from skillet and keep warm.

Remove all but 2 tablespoons of pan drippings from skillet. Add shallots and sauté 1 minute. Add wine and broth and bring to a boil. Reduce liquid to ½ cup. Add half-and-half and cook until slightly thickened. Stir in tomatoes and basil. Season with salt and pepper. Return veal to skillet and heat gently until just warm.

Veal Piccata

8	thin slices veal	⅓	cup chicken broth
	Salt and pepper to taste	¼	teaspoon dried oregano
	Flour	8	thin lemon slices
⅓	cup olive oil	2	teaspoons chopped fresh parsley
4	tablespoons butter		
¼	cup lemon juice		

Season veal with salt and pepper. Dust lightly with flour. Sauté quickly in oil in a skillet. Discard pan drippings and cook veal briefly in skillet, turning once. Squeeze a few drops of lemon juice over veal. Remove veal from pan.

Add butter, lemon juice, broth and oregano to skillet and scrape brown bits off bottom of pan. Add veal, simmer a few minutes and turn. Twist lemon slices and place a slice on each piece of veal. Simmer a few minutes longer. Transfer veal to a warm serving plate. Spoon some of sauce over veal. Garnish with parsley.

Yield: 4 servings

Braised Veal Shanks (Osso Buco) with White Wine, Butter and Lemon Sauce

I invented this for my husband who doesn't like garlic or tomatoes.

4   veal shanks
½   teaspoon Season All
     seasoned salt
½   teaspoon black pepper
     Flour
4   tablespoons butter
2-4 tablespoons olive oil
2   cups water

1½ tablespoons chicken base or
     bouillon
1   cup dry white wine
     Juice of 1 lemon
½   teaspoon dried thyme
½   teaspoon dried rosemary
½   cup dry white wine

Rub veal shanks with Season All and black pepper and dredge in flour. Heat butter and oil in a deep skillet. Brown veal in skillet. Add 2 cups water, chicken base, 1 cup wine, lemon juice, thyme and rosemary. Cover and bake at 350 degrees or simmer on stovetop for 1½ hours or until meat falls off the bone.

Stir in ½ cup wine. Adjust seasonings as needed. Serve with rice or noodles to which butter and poppy seeds have been added.

For variety, add chopped celery and carrots to the skillet after browning the veal. Add extra flavor with 2 cloves minced garlic and 1 (15 ounce) can chopped tomatoes.

Veal Chop Sicilian

1	bell pepper, cut into 1 inch strips
¼	cup olive oil
2-4	rib or loin veal chops
¼	cup chicken broth
¼	cup white wine

Salt and pepper to taste
Rosemary to taste
Thyme to taste
Oregano to taste
Basil to taste

Sauté bell pepper in oil. Add veal and cook over medium heat for 10 minutes or until brown on both sides. Remove from heat and deglaze pan with broth and wine.

Season with salt, pepper, rosemary, thyme, oregano and basil. Excellent served with risotto.

Veal Stew

3	pounds veal stew meat
2	tablespoons butter
2	tablespoons vegetable oil
2	large onions, chopped
¼	cup flour
½	cup dry white wine
3	cups chicken broth

¼	teaspoon dried thyme
1	bay leaf
	Salt and pepper to taste
8	ounces mushrooms, sliced or quartered
1	tablespoon butter
	Chopped fresh parsley

Dry veal well with paper towels. Heat 2 tablespoons butter and oil in a saucepan. Add veal and brown. Remove meat. Add onions to skillet and sauté 5 minutes. Stir in flour and cook 2 to 3 minutes. Deglaze skillet with wine and broth. Return veal to pot. Add thyme, bay leaf, salt and pepper. Simmer slowly for about 1½ hours or until tender.

About 15 minutes before stew is ready, sauté mushrooms in 1 tablespoon butter for 3 to 4 minutes. Add mushrooms to stew. Adjust seasonings as needed. Garnish with parsley. Serve with rice or orzo pasta.

Yield: 6 to 8 servings

Feta-Pesto Stuffed
Pork Chops

Pork Chops

3   tablespoons crumbled feta cheese
2   tablespoons purchased pesto
1   tablespoon pine nuts, toasted

4   (1¼ inch thick) pork chops
1   tablespoon balsamic vinegar
2-3 tablespoons purchased pesto
2   tablespoons jalapeño jelly

Rub

1   teaspoon minced garlic
1   teaspoon black pepper
½   teaspoon crushed fennel seeds

¼   teaspoon ground cumin
½   teaspoon cayenne pepper
½   teaspoon celery seed
¼   teaspoon dried thyme

Preheat grill. Make a stuffing by combining feta, 2 tablespoons pesto and pine nuts in a small bowl. Trim fat from pork chops. Cut a horizontal slit in each chop, starting at the edge and going to the bone. Spoon stuffing into pockets and secure each with a toothpick, if necessary. Combine vinegar, 2-3 tablespoons pesto and jelly in a small saucepan. Heat over low heat until jelly melts.

Mix all rub ingredients. Rub seasoning mix over both sides of chops. Grill chops over medium heat for 35 to 40 minutes or until juices run clear. Brush with jalapeño glaze during the last 10 minutes, turning once during that time to glaze the other side.

Yield: 4 servings

Pork Chop Potato Bake

6	(¾ to 1 inch thick) boneless pork loin chops	1	(32 ounce) package frozen loose-pack hash browns, thawed
2	tablespoons vegetable oil		
2	(10¾ ounce) cans cream of mushroom soup	1	(8 ounce) package shredded cheddar cheese
1	(8 ounce) container sour cream	1	(2.8 ounce) can French fried onion rings
½	cup milk		

Preheat oven to 350 degrees. Brown chops in hot oil in a large skillet over medium-high heat for 1 to 2 minutes on each side. Set aside.

Combine soup, sour cream and milk. Stir in hash browns and half the cheese. Spread mixture in a greased 3 quart rectangular baking dish. Arrange chops on top. Cover and bake 1¼ to 1½ hours or until potatoes in the center of dish are tender. Sprinkle remaining cheese and onion rings on top. Bake, uncovered, for 5 minutes.

Yield: 6 servings

Angry Pork Tenderloin

This is served as one of the main dishes at "La Fiesta Mexicana" — auctioned at the Hibiscus Children's Center's Fall Benefit.

1	(8 ounce) can chipotle chiles, drained	¼	cup fresh lime juice
12	cloves garlic	¼	cup brown sugar
3	shallots, peeled	1	teaspoon freshly ground black pepper
1	jalapeño pepper, seeded and chopped	½	cup orange juice
½	cup malt vinegar	¼	cup olive oil
		4	(1 pound) pork tenderloins, trimmed of fat and skin

Combine chiles, garlic, shallots, jalapeño, vinegar, lime juice, brown sugar, black pepper and orange juice in a blender. Puree. With motor running, drizzle in oil. Marinate pork in pureed mixture for at least 1 hour in a zip-top bag.

Preheat grill. Grill pork over medium-high heat until cooked to desired degree of doneness. Cut into ½ inch slices. Serve with Pam's Black Bean Mango Salsa.

Pork St. Hubert

2	(1 pound) pork tenderloins	4	tablespoons butter
	Salt and pepper to taste	1	cup chicken broth
¼	cup vegetable oil	⅓	cup currant jelly
¼	cup Dijon mustard	1	tablespoon honey
¼	cup red wine vinegar	1	tablespoon cornstarch
4	shallots, chopped	¼	cup Madeira wine

Cut tenderloins into ½ inch thick slices. Season with salt and pepper. Combine oil, mustard and vinegar and pour over pork in a zip-top bag. Refrigerate 2 hours or overnight.

In a large skillet, sauté shallots in butter until tender. Drain mustard marinade from meat and reserve. Add meat to skillet and cook 3 to 4 minutes or until brown on all sides. Transfer meat to a serving plate and keep warm.

Add broth, jelly, honey and reserved marinade to skillet. Cook until reduced by a third. Dissolve cornstarch in wine and add to skillet. Bring to a boil, stirring constantly. Cook 5 minutes or until sauce is clear. Spoon some of sauce over meat and serve immediately.

Yield: 6 servings

Jambalaya

2	pounds hot Italian sausage, casing removed	2	(14½ ounce) cans diced tomatoes
1	large onion, chopped	¼	teaspoon dried thyme
⅓	cup chopped fresh parsley		Salt and pepper to taste
1	clove garlic, chopped	2	cups dry rice
2½	cups water	1	pound peeled shrimp or chopped cooked chicken

Cook sausage in a heavy skillet. Add onion, parsley and garlic and sauté. Stir in 2½ cups water, tomatoes, thyme, salt and pepper. Bring to a boil. Stir in rice and shrimp. Cover and cook over low heat for 30 minutes, stirring as little as possible while cooking.

Herbed Pork Roast

3	tablespoons vegetable oil	1	clove garlic, crushed
1	teaspoon dry mustard	1	(4 to 5 pound) rolled
1	teaspoon dried thyme		boneless pork loin roast
1	teaspoon dried marjoram	1	banana leaf, washed
½	teaspoon salt		(optional)
½	teaspoon black pepper	¾	cup dry white wine

Preheat oven to 325 degrees. Combine oil, mustard, thyme, marjoram, salt, pepper and garlic. Score roast and rub with seasoning mixture. Wrap roast in aluminum foil and refrigerate 8 hours.

Remove roast from foil. If using, wrap roast in banana leaf. Place roast, fat-side up, on a rack in a shallow roasting pan. Insert a meat thermometer, making sure it is not inserted into fat. Bake, uncovered, for 2 to 2½ hours or until thermometer registers 160 degrees (30 to 35 minutes per pound). Baste frequently with wine while baking. Remove from oven and let stand 10 to 15 minutes before slicing.

Yield: 12 servings

Fresh Tomato Pizza with Sausage

1	cup pizza sauce	2	tablespoons Parmesan
1	(16 ounce) Boboli pizza		cheese
	crust	1	cup shredded mozzarella
1	large yellow onion, sliced		cheese
1	clove garlic, chopped	2	fresh tomatoes, sliced
1	pound ground sausage	2	tablespoons diced red onion
	Black pepper to taste		Olive oil
	Italian seasoning to taste		

Preheat oven to 450 degrees. Spread sauce over crust. Sauté yellow onion and garlic until caramelized and spread over sauce. Sauté sausage, drain and spread over onion. Season with pepper and Italian seasoning. Sprinkle with cheeses. Arrange tomato slices over cheese in a single layer. Season with Italian seasoning. Top with red onion and drizzle with olive oil.

Bake 10 minutes or until heated in the center. Top with extra Parmesan cheese, if desired. Slice and serve.

Spaghetti Carbonara

Spaghetti Carbonara

24	extra thick slices bacon	3	cups Béchamel Sauce (recipe below)
1	pound dry spaghetti		Freshly ground black pepper
¼	cup virgin olive oil	2	teaspoons minced fresh parsley
8	ounces fresh mushrooms, sliced ¼ inch thick		Salt to taste
6	tablespoons finely minced shallots	¼	cup freshly grated Parmesan cheese

Béchamel Sauce

6	tablespoons butter or margarine	6	tablespoons all-purpose flour
		3	cups whole milk

Cook bacon until fully cooked but not crisp. Drain on paper towels, reserving ¼ cup bacon drippings. Cut cooked bacon into ½ inch strips. Set aside. Cook spaghetti according to package directions. Drain and toss with olive oil to prevent sticking. Keep warm.

Add reserved bacon drippings, or substitute olive oil, to a large, heavy skillet. Heat over medium heat until fragrant. Add mushrooms and shallots and sauté until golden but not brown. Add bacon strips, stir well and remove from heat. Add warm spaghetti and mix thoroughly. Stir in béchamel sauce, pepper, parsley and salt and blend thoroughly. Place on a heated serving dish or individual serving plates. Sprinkle generously with Parmesan cheese and serve immediately.

To make béchamel sauce, melt butter in a heavy non-aluminum saucepan. Blend in flour and cook over medium heat for 2 minutes, stirring constantly with a wire whisk. Do not allow roux to darken more than a blond color. Whisk in milk and heat to just below boiling point. Remove from heat and keep warm.

Yield: 6 to 8 servings

The Olive Garden

Sausage-Spinach Soufflé

White Sauce

4	tablespoons butter	5	teaspoons cornstarch
1	teaspoon salt	2	cups milk
¼	teaspoon black pepper	2	eggs, separated

Soufflé

1	medium onion, minced	2	(10 ounce) boxes frozen
1	cup minced celery		chopped spinach, thawed
2	tablespoons vegetable oil		and squeezed dry
1	pound lean ground sausage	2	cups White Sauce

Preheat oven to 325 degrees. To make sauce, melt butter in a saucepan. Add salt, pepper and cornstarch and blend to make a roux. Gradually stir in milk and bring to a boil. Cook 2 minutes. Slightly beat egg yolks and add to sauce. Beat egg whites until stiff and fold into sauce.

For soufflé preparation, sauté onion and celery in oil. Set aside. Brown sausage and mix into sautéed vegetables. Drain well. Mix in spinach. Fold mixture into white sauce. Transfer to a soufflé pan. Bake 45 minutes.

Chopped broccoli can be substituted for the spinach.

Straw and Hay Pasta

2	tablespoons butter	¼	cup brandy
½	onion, chopped	1	cup half-and-half
2	tablespoons chopped fresh parsley	¼	teaspoon salt
		¼	teaspoon black pepper
1½	cups sliced fresh mushrooms	4	quarts water
		6	ounces egg fettuccine
4	ounces smoked ham, cut into strips	6	ounces spinach fettuccine
		1	cup Parmesan cheese

Heat butter in a skillet over medium-high heat. Add onion and parsley and sauté. Stir in mushrooms and ham. Cook about 5 minutes, stirring until mushrooms are tender. Stir in brandy and cook until liquid evaporates. Stir in half-and-half, salt and pepper. Bring to a boil. Reduce heat and simmer, uncovered, for 15 minutes or until thickened.

Meanwhile, bring 4 quarts water to a boil. Add pasta and cook 3 to 4 minutes or until al dente. Drain; do not rinse. Mix pasta with cream sauce. Top with cheese.

Leg of Lamb

½	cup Dijon mustard	1	tablespoon olive oil
¼	cup white wine	2	cloves garlic, minced
½	teaspoon dried rosemary	½	teaspoon dried basil
¼	teaspoon dried oregano	¼	teaspoon dried thyme
¼	teaspoon black pepper	1	boneless leg of lamb

Combine all ingredients except lamb to make a marinade. Butterfly leg of lamb and lay flat on a pan. Brush marinade over lamb. Marinate 1 hour.

When ready to cook, preheat grill. Grill lamb over low heat for 45 to 60 minutes, basting frequently with marinade.

Perfect Roast Leg of Lamb

Lamb

1 (6 pound) leg of lamb,
   trimmed of fat
2 cloves garlic, minced
1 tablespoon paprika

1 tablespoon chopped fresh
   rosemary, or 1½ teaspoon
   dried
2 teaspoons salt
½ teaspoon freshly ground
   black pepper

Orange Basting Sauce

4 tablespoons butter
1 (6 ounce) can frozen orange
   juice concentrate

¼ cup dry red wine

Preheat oven to 350 degrees. Cut 12 slits into lamb. Combine garlic, paprika, rosemary, salt and pepper. Press some of seasoning mixture into each slit. Insert a meat thermometer into the thickest part of the meat. Roast 12 to 15 minutes per pound for rare, 20 minutes per pound for medium and 30 to 35 minutes per pound for well done or 160 degrees on the thermometer.

Meanwhile, prepare basting sauce. Combine sauce ingredients in a saucepan. Simmer, uncovered, for 15 minutes. After lamb has cooked for 1 hour, baste with sauce frequently until lamb is done. Let stand 15 minutes before slicing.

Lamb Chops with Caper Sauce

4 lamb chops
2 tablespoons butter
2 tablespoons quick-
   dissolving flour
½ cup chicken broth

3 tablespoons sherry
4 teaspoons capers
1 teaspoon brown sugar
   Salt and pepper to taste

Brown lamb in butter for about 3 minutes in a skillet. Remove lamb. Add flour, broth, sherry, capers, sugar, salt and pepper to skillet. Bring to a simmer. Add lamb back to skillet. Simmer 15 minutes.

Curried Lamb with Cashews

Marinated Lamb

½ cup plain yogurt
¼ teaspoon minced fresh ginger
    Salt and pepper to taste

1½ pounds lamb loin or shoulder, cut into 1½ inch cubes

Curry Paste

¼ cup raw cashews
3 red chiles, seeded
1 (1 inch) piece fresh ginger
1 cup water
1 cinnamon stick, crushed

¼ teaspoon cardamom seeds
3 cloves garlic
2 tablespoons poppy seeds
1 teaspoon cumin seeds

Assembly

¼ cup boiling water
½ teaspoon saffron threads
6 tablespoons clarified butter
1 cup chopped onion
1 teaspoon salt
    Curry Paste
    Marinated Lamb

¼ teaspoon turmeric
¼ teaspoon ground coriander
    Dash of cinnamon
1 tablespoon curry powder
2 tablespoons chopped fresh cilantro
1 tablespoon fresh lemon juice

Combine yogurt, ginger, salt, pepper and lamb. Marinate at room temperature for 30 minutes.

To make curry paste, combine cashews, chiles, ginger and water in a food processor. Blend until smooth. Add cinnamon, cardamom, garlic, poppy seeds and cumin seeds. Blend again and set aside.

To assemble dish, pour boiling water over saffron. Soak 10 minutes. Heat butter in a skillet. Add onion and sauté 7 to 8 minutes. Stir in salt and curry paste. Add marinated lamb. Cook and stir 5 minutes. Add turmeric, coriander, cinnamon and curry powder. Mash saffron against side of bowl and add with liquid to skillet. Reduce heat, cover and cook 20 minutes. Sprinkle with cilantro and cook 10 minutes longer. Serve on rice and sprinkle with lemon juice.

Yield: 4 servings

Side Dishes

Succulent

ROBIN LEE MAKOWSKI
Succulent!
Watercolor, 2000

Side Dishes

Vegetables

Broccoli with
Deviled Cream Sauce 169
Sweet-and-Sour Broccoli 169
Broccoli Soufflé with Almonds 170
Broccoli and Rice Casserole 170
Baked Lima Beans 171
Spinach Soufflé 171
Green Beans with Pecans 172
Zucchini Stuffed
with Corn and Cheese 172
Zucchini with Bacon 173
Spaghetti Squash Florentine 173
Lucy's Marinated Carrots 174
Swiss Vegetable Medley 174
Cheesy Summer Squash 175
Squash Pie 175
Posh Squash 176
Vegetable Casserole 176
Eggplant with Kalamata Olives 177
Onion Rings 177
Whole Baked Eggplant 178
Mom's Onion Shortcake 179
Sauerkraut and Apples 179
Southern Corn Pudding 180
Corn and Cheese Pie with Chiles 180
Chiles Rellenos Casserole 181

North Carolina Tomato Pie 181
Roasted Tomatoes 182
Gratin of Cherry Tomatoes 182
Grilled Portobello Mushrooms 183
Don's Slow Cooked Baked Beans..... 183
Savory Cream Peas 184
Roquefort Potato Gratin 184
Cottage Potatoes 185
Southwest Potato Casserole............ 185
Broque Potatoes 186
Holiday Sweet Potatoes 186
Virginia's Holiday
Mashed Potatoes 187

Rice and Pasta

Baked Orzo 187
Bahamian Pigeon Peas and Rice 188
Classic Creamy Risotto 188
Oriental Rice 189
Basmati Rice
with Dried Fruits and Nuts 189
Coconut Rice 190
Spiced Rice 190
Rice and Onion Casserole 191
Quick and Easy
Macaroni and Cheese 191
Cheesey Rigatoni 192
Noodles and Sauerkraut 192

Broccoli with
Deviled Cream Sauce

3	(10 ounce) packages frozen broccoli spears, or 3 pounds fresh	1	teaspoon brown sugar
2	tablespoons butter	½	teaspoon Worcestershire sauce
2	tablespoons flour	¼	teaspoon salt
1½	teaspoons dry mustard	1	cup milk
		½	cup sour cream

Cook broccoli until tender; drain. Arrange broccoli in a shallow baking dish.

To make a cream sauce, melt butter in a saucepan. Blend in flour, mustard, sugar, Worcestershire sauce and salt. Add milk all at once. Cook and stir until smooth and bubbly. Stir a small amount of hot mixture into sour cream, then stir sour cream mixture into hot mixture. Heat but do not bring to a boil. Pour sauce over broccoli.

Yield: 10 servings

Sweet-and-Sour Broccoli

3	cups broccoli florets	1	tablespoon balsamic vinegar
1	tablespoon olive oil		Salt and pepper to taste
1	large shallot, minced	2	tablespoons chopped walnuts
½	teaspoon sugar		

Steam broccoli for 5 minutes or until tender.

Heat oil in a skillet. Add shallot and sauté 3 minutes or until tender. Stir in sugar and vinegar. Add broccoli and cook until heated through, stirring frequently. Season with salt and pepper. Stir in walnuts. Serve warm or at room temperature.

Broccoli Soufflé with Almonds

2	(10 ounce) packages frozen chopped broccoli	¾	cup grated Swiss cheese
3	tablespoons butter	½	cup slivered almonds
3	tablespoons flour	1	teaspoon salt
¼	cup chicken broth	½	teaspoon black pepper
1	cup sour cream	½	teaspoon nutmeg
⅓	cup minced green onion	½	pound mushrooms, thinly sliced
3	eggs, lightly beaten	1	tablespoon butter

Preheat oven to 350 degrees. Cook broccoli until tender; drain. Pulse in a food processor to coarsely chop.

Melt butter in a saucepan. Blend in flour. Mix in broth. Gradually stir in sour cream and onion. Cook and stir until thick and blended. Stir eggs into sour cream mixture. Cook, stirring constantly, for 1 minute. Blend in cheese until melted. Add broccoli, almonds, salt, pepper and nutmeg. Spoon into a greased 1 quart ring mold. Bake in a hot water bath for 50 minutes. Unmold soufflé and top with mushrooms sautéed in butter.

Double recipe if using a Bundt pan.

Broccoli and Rice Casserole

1	(10 ounce) package frozen chopped broccoli	1	(8 ounce) jar Cheez Whiz
4	cups cooked rice	1	(10¾ ounce) can condensed cream of mushroom soup
1	(8 ounce) can sliced water chestnuts	1	cup flavored bread crumbs, buttered

Preheat oven to 350 degrees. Blanch broccoli and drain. Combine broccoli, rice, water chestnuts, Cheez Whiz and soup. Place in a baking dish. Top with bread crumbs. Bake 35 minutes.

Baked Lima Beans

3	(10 ounce) packages frozen large lima beans	½	cup butter
1	cup sour cream	2	tablespoons molasses
¾	cup light brown sugar	1	teaspoon salt

Preheat oven to 350 degrees. Cook lima beans as directed on package, drain. While hot, add sour cream, sugar, butter, molasses and salt to beans. Place in a baking dish. Bake, covered, about 1 hour.

Spinach Soufflé

½	cup butter	1	(8 ounce) can sliced water chestnuts, drained
1½	(8 ounce) packages cream cheese	1	(14 ounce) can artichoke hearts, chopped and drained
4	(10 ounce) packages frozen chopped spinach		

Preheat oven to 350 degrees. Melt butter and cream cheese together. Blend until smooth.

In a greased baking dish, make two layers of ingredients in the following order: spinach, cream cheese mixture, water chestnuts and artichokes. Bake 45 minutes.

Yield: 6 servings

Green Beans with Pecans

2	pounds green beans, trimmed	4	teaspoons minced lemon zest
5	tablespoons butter	⅓	cup chopped fresh Italian
¾	cup quartered pecans		parsley

Steam green beans about 5 minutes. Drain, rinse in cold water and drain again. Refrigerate.

Melt butter over medium heat in a large, heavy skillet. Add pecans and sauté 3 minutes or until nuts are crisp and butter is brown, about 3 minutes. Add beans to skillet and cook and toss about 5 minutes or until heated through. Mix in zest and cook 1 minute. Add parsley and serve.

Zucchini Stuffed with Corn and Cheese

2	(6 to 7 inch) narrow zucchini or yellow squash	1-2	tablespoons snipped fresh chives
1	cup corn kernels		Salt and pepper to taste
½-⅔	cup ricotta cheese	¾	cup shredded cheddar cheese

Preheat oven to 350 degrees. Cook whole squash in boiling salted water for 5 minutes. Rinse under cold water and drain. Halve squash lengthwise and scoop out seeds to form cavities.

Coarsely puree corn and ricotta cheese in a food processor. Add chives and season with salt and pepper. Fill squash halves with mixture, mounding slightly. Sprinkle with cheddar cheese. Place in a greased casserole dish. Bake, covered, for 15 minutes. Uncover and bake 20 to 25 minutes longer or until squash is tender and topping is browned.

Zucchini with Bacon

4	strips bacon, diced	⅓	cup freshly shredded
1	onion, chopped		Parmesan cheese
2	zucchini, sliced		

Cook bacon in a skillet. Remove bacon, leaving some of drippings in the skillet. Add onion to skillet and sauté 2 minutes. Add zucchini and bacon to skillet. Top with cheese. Cook, covered, over medium-low heat for about 20 minutes or until tender.

Spaghetti Squash Florentine

1	spaghetti squash	½	cup shredded Gruyère cheese
¼	cup flour		
⅛	teaspoon cayenne pepper	1	(10 ounce) package frozen chopped spinach, squeezed dry
2	cups milk		
½	cup chopped onion		
3	cloves garlic, chopped	⅔	cup chopped prosciutto

Cut squash in half lengthwise. Remove and discard seeds with a spoon. Place squash in a shallow pan. Add water to pan to ½ inch in depth. Cover and microwave 15 minutes or until fork tender. Cool. Scrape squash with a fork onto a plate, breaking up strands.

Preheat oven to 375 degrees. Place flour and cayenne pepper in a bowl. Gradually add milk, blending with a whisk until smooth. Coat a skillet with cooking spray. Add onion and garlic and sauté over medium-high heat for 1 minute. Add milk mixture and cook, stirring constantly, 6 minutes or until thickened. Add cheese and spinach to skillet, stirring well. Remove from heat and stir in 5 cups of squash and prosciutto. Pour into a 9x13 inch casserole dish sprayed with cooking spray. Bake 25 minutes.

Yield: 10 servings

Lucy's Marinated Carrots

1	pound carrots, cut into sticks	½	teaspoon red pepper flakes
1	tablespoon salt	1	large clove garlic
½	medium onion, chopped	½	cup sugar
1	teaspoon dill seed	½	cup vinegar

Combine carrot sticks, salt, onion, dill, pepper flakes and garlic in a glass jar. Bring sugar and vinegar to a boil and cook until sugar dissolves. Pour over carrot mixture. Cool. Cover jar with a lid and refrigerate 5 days.

Swiss Vegetable Medley

1	(16 ounce) package frozen broccoli, carrots and cauliflower mix, thawed and drained	¼	teaspoon black pepper
		1	(4 ounce) jar chopped pimento, drained (optional)
1	(10¾ ounce) can condensed cream of mushroom soup	1	(2.8 ounce) can French fried onions
½	cup shredded Swiss cheese	½	cup shredded Swiss cheese
⅓	cup sour cream		

Preheat oven to 350 degrees. Combine vegetable mix, soup, ½ cup cheese, sour cream, pepper, pimento and half the onions. Pour into a 1 quart casserole dish.

Bake, covered, for 30 minutes. Top with ½ cup cheese and remaining onions. Bake, uncovered, 5 minutes longer.

Yield: 6 servings

To prepare in microwave, prepare as above. Cook, covered, on high for 8 minutes, turning halfway through. Top with cheese and remaining onions and cook, uncovered, on high for 1 minute or until cheese melts.

Cheesy Summer Squash

1	pound yellow squash, sliced	1	egg, beaten
1	onion, minced	¼	teaspoon nutmeg
1	cup shredded cheddar cheese		Salt and pepper to taste
½	cup half-and-half	½	cup Ritz cracker crumbs
		2	tablespoons butter, melted

Preheat oven to 350 degrees. Steam squash and onion about 4 minutes. Combine squash, onion, cheese, half-and-half, egg and nutmeg. Season with salt and pepper. Place mixture in a greased casserole dish.

Combine cracker crumbs and butter and sprinkle over casserole. Bake 25 to 30 minutes or until lightly browned on top.

Squash Pie

4½	cups sliced yellow squash	2	tablespoons minced onion
1½	teaspoons salt	½	cup shredded carrot
1	cup sour cream	1	(16 ounce) package Pepperidge Farm cornbread stuffing mix
1	(10¾ ounce) can condensed cream of chicken soup		

Preheat oven to 350 degrees. Cook squash with salt in boiling water until tender. Drain well. Add sour cream, soup, onion and carrot. Mix well.

Sprinkle half of stuffing mix into a greased casserole dish. Pour squash mixture over stuffing. Top with remaining stuffing mix. Bake 30 to 45 minutes.

Posh Squash

3	yellow squash, sliced	1	small onion, chopped
1	egg, beaten	½-¾	cup shredded cheddar cheese
1	cup mayonnaise		Dash of paprika

Cook squash in a small amount of water in microwave for 15 minutes or until tender. Drain. Combine squash, egg, mayonnaise and onion and place in a greased casserole dish. Top with cheese and sprinkle with paprika. Microwave 12 minutes.

Vegetable Casserole

1	(16 ounce) can French-style green beans, drained	1	(4 ounce) can mushrooms, drained
1	(16 ounce) can shoe peg corn, drained	1	(10¾ ounce) can condensed cream of celery soup
½	cup chopped celery	1	(8 ounce) container sour cream
½	cup chopped green bell pepper	¾	sleeve Ritz cracker, crushed
½	cup chopped onion	½	teaspoon paprika
		½	cup margarine

Preheat oven to 350 degrees. Combine green beans, corn, celery, bell pepper, onion, mushrooms, soup and sour cream. Place in a greased 11x8½ inch casserole dish.

Sprinkle with cracker crumbs and paprika. Dot with margarine. Bake 45 minutes.

Eggplant
with Kalamata Olives

2	small eggplants	1	teaspoon marjoram
2	tablespoons olive oil	½	cup chopped Kalamata
1	small onion		olives
3	cloves garlic, chopped	½	cup bread crumbs
2	medium tomatoes, diced	⅓	cup Parmesan cheese
	and drained		Salt and pepper to taste

Preheat oven to 350 degrees. Cut eggplants in half lengthwise and drizzle with oil. Bake 30 minutes. Cool. Scoop out pulp and chop, leaving skin intact to form a shell. Set aside.

Sauté onion and garlic 2 minutes. Add tomatoes and marjoram and cook 2 minutes longer. Cool. When cool, add olives, bread crumbs and cheese to onion mixture. Mix well. Add eggplant pulp. Season with salt and pepper. Stuff mixture into eggplant shells. Bake 15 minutes or until golden brown.

Onion Rings

2	large onions, cut into	2	cups buttermilk
	½ inch slices		Vegetable oil for frying
1½	cups flour		Salt to taste
½	cup cornmeal		Cayenne pepper to taste

Separate onion slices into rings. Combine flour and cornmeal in a dish. Pour buttermilk into a separate dish. Dip onion rings in buttermilk, then dredge in flour mixture. Repeat buttermilk and flour mixture steps.

Fry rings in hot oil for about 3 minutes. Drain on paper towels. Season with salt and cayenne pepper.

Whole Baked Eggplant

2	large tomatoes, or 4 plum tomatoes		Salt and pepper to taste
3	tablespoons virgin olive oil	2	cloves garlic, thinly sliced
1	pound yellow onions, quartered	2	small bay leaves
¼	teaspoon fennel seeds, crushed	6-8	sprigs thyme
		12	(3 to 4 inch) eggplants
½	teaspoon Herbes de Provence	1	tablespoon virgin olive oil
		12-18	niçoise olives
		⅓	cup wine or water
		1-2	tablespoons virgin olive oil

Preheat oven to 400 degrees. Cut tomatoes in half, then into slices ½ inch thick. Heat 3 tablespoons oil in a skillet. Add onions, fennel seeds and Herbes de Provence. Cook over low heat for 3 minutes or until softened. Season with salt and pepper. Lay most of onions along with tomatoes, garlic, bay leaves and 3 to 4 thyme sprigs in the bottom of a gratin dish.

In a separate dish, toss eggplants with 1 tablespoon oil and season with salt. Nestle eggplants among the onions. Tuck olives between eggplants and scatter remaining onions and thyme on top. Add wine and drizzle with 1 to 2 tablespoons oil. Cover dish with foil. Bake 35 to 45 minutes or until eggplants are very soft. Serve warm or at room temperature. Allowing eggplants to sit after baking helps the flavors to develop and strengthen.

Mom's Onion Shortcake

1	pound Bermuda onions, sliced	½	cup shredded cheddar cheese	
4	tablespoons butter or margarine	1	(16 ounce) can creamed corn	
1	cup sour cream	1	egg, beaten	
¼	teaspoon salt	⅓	cup milk	
1	teaspoon dill	1½	cups corn muffin mix	
		2	drops Tabasco sauce	
		½	cup shredded cheddar cheese	

Preheat oven to 425 degrees. Sauté onion in butter. Add sour cream, salt, dill and ½ cup cheese.

In a bowl, mix corn, egg, milk, muffin mix and Tabasco sauce. Pour mixture into an 8x8 inch pan. Pour onion mixture over corn mixture. Sprinkle with ½ cup cheese. Bake 30 to 40 minutes.

Yield: 8 servings

Sauerkraut and Apples

1	(2 pound) package sauerkraut, rinsed and drained	½	cup light brown sugar, or to taste
3	tart apples, peeled and cut into thick pieces	1	teaspoon prepared mustard
1	medium onion, diced	1	teaspoon caraway seeds
		½	cup dry white wine or vermouth

Preheat oven to 325 degrees. Spread sauerkraut in the bottom of a roasting pan. Combine apples, onion, sugar, mustard and caraway seeds in a bowl. Scatter mixture over sauerkraut. Drizzle with wine and cover pan. Bake 1½ hours. Serve with pork roast or kielbasa.

Southern Corn Pudding

2	(16 ounce) cans creamed corn	4	tablespoons butter, melted
2	tablespoons flour	½	cup sugar
6	eggs, beaten		Salt and pepper to taste

Preheat oven to 325 degrees. Mix together all ingredients in order listed. Pour into a greased casserole dish. Bake 1 hour or until a knife inserted near the center comes out clean.

Yield: 8 servings

Corn and Cheese Pie with Chiles

1	(8 ounce) can creamed corn	1	(4 ounce) can chopped green chiles
1	(10½ ounce) can niblets corn		
½	cup butter, melted	4	ounces Monterey Jack cheese, diced
2	eggs, beaten		
½	cup yellow cornmeal	4	ounces diced sharp cheddar cheese, diced
1	cup sour cream		
½	teaspoon salt		

Preheat oven to 350 degrees. Combine all ingredients and blend well. Pour into a greased 9 or 10 inch pie plate or square glass dish. Bake 1 hour. Serve warm.

If making ahead, cool dish, then refrigerate for up to 3 days, or freeze. Thaw, if necessary, and reheat at 350 degrees for about 20 minutes or until hot.

Yield: 8 servings

Chiles Rellenos Casserole

4	ounces Monterey Jack cheese, cut into strips	½	cup milk
1	(8 ounce) can whole green chiles	½	cup flour
4	eggs	½	teaspoon baking powder
		1	cup shredded cheddar cheese

Preheat oven to 375 degrees. Place a strip of Monterey Jack cheese in each chile. Lay chiles in a shallow baking dish. Mix eggs, milk, flour and baking powder and pour over chiles. Sprinkle cheddar cheese on top. Bake 30 minutes.

North Carolina Tomato Pie

1	frozen deep dish pie crust	¾	cup Hellmann's mayonnaise
3-4	tomatoes, sliced	1	cup shredded sharp cheddar cheese
2-3	green onions, chopped		
5-6	slices bacon, cooked and crumbled		

Partially bake pie crust according to package instructions, baking for about three-fourths of time indicated.

Preheat oven to 350 degrees. Arrange a layer of tomato slices in crust. Sprinkle onions and bacon over tomatoes. Repeat tomato, onion and bacon layers. Combine mayonnaise and cheese and spread over top of pie. Bake 30 minutes.

Yield: 6 servings

Roasted Tomatoes

4 Roma tomatoes, halved lengthwise, ends trimmed flat	Dried basil
	Dried oregano
Coarse salt	4 cloves garlic, minced
Freshly cracked black pepper	Balsamic vinegar
	Olive oil

Preheat oven to 350 degrees. Sprinkle each tomato half with salt, pepper, basil, oregano, garlic, vinegar and oil in order listed. Place in a shallow baking dish. Bake 45 minutes.

Gratin of Cherry Tomatoes

1½ pints cherry tomatoes	2 slices homemade-style white bread
Salt and freshly ground black pepper to taste	½ cup coarsely chopped fresh parsley
2 teaspoons Herbes de Provence	½ cup freshly grated Parmesan cheese
2 large cloves garlic, peeled	⅓ cup extra virgin olive oil

Preheat oven to 400 degrees. Arrange tomatoes in an ovenproof gratin dish just large enough for them to fit compactly in a single layer. Season with salt, pepper and Herbes de Provence.

Combine garlic, bread, parsley and cheese in a food processor. Process until finely minced. With motor running, add olive oil and process until well blended. Sprinkle bread mixture evenly over tomatoes. Bake 40 to 45 minutes or until crumbs are crusty brown and the juices from the tomatoes are bubbling. Allow to cool a few minutes. Serve hot, warm or at room temperature.

Yield: 6 servings

Grilled Portobello Mushrooms

1 (4 inch) portobello mushroom cap per serving	Italian seasoning to taste
Olive oil	Crumbled blue, Gorgonzola
Salt and pepper to taste	or feta cheese

Preheat grill. Wash mushroom caps. Drizzle with oil and season with salt, pepper and Italian seasoning. Grill mushroom caps on a covered grill over medium-high heat, underside down, for about 8 minutes. Turn and cook 8 minutes longer. Sprinkle with cheese and serve.

Don's Slow Cooked Baked Beans

1 pound ground beef, cooked and drained	1 (16 ounce) can black-eyed peas
¾ pound bacon, diced and cooked	1 cup ketchup
1 cup diced onion	1 tablespoon liquid smoke
3 tablespoons vinegar	1 cup brown sugar
3 (16 ounce) cans pork and beans	Salt and pepper to taste

Combine all ingredients in a crockpot the morning of serving. Cook all day on the low setting.

Savory Cream Peas

4	slices bacon, chopped	⅛	teaspoon black pepper
1	tablespoon chopped onion	1	cup milk
¼	teaspoon flour	1	(16 ounce) can Le Sueur
¼	teaspoon salt		peas, drained

Cook bacon and remove from pan to drain; reserve 1 tablespoon bacon drippings in pan. Add onion and sauté. Stir in flour, salt and pepper. Add milk and whisk until smooth. Stir in peas and cook until heated.

Roquefort Potato Gratin

2½	pounds russet potatoes	1⅓	cups canned low-salt chicken broth
8	ounces Roquefort cheese or other blue cheese, crumbled	2	tablespoons butter, cut into small pieces
	Salt and pepper to taste		

Preheat oven to 350 degrees. Arrange one-third of potato slices in the bottom of a greased 9x13 inch glass baking dish, overlapping slightly. Sprinkle half the cheese over the potatoes and season with salt and pepper. Repeat layers, using half of remaining potatoes and all of remaining cheese. Arrange remaining potato slices on top in a decorative fashion.

Pour broth over potatoes and dot with butter pieces. Bake 1 hour, 40 minutes or until top is golden brown, potatoes are tender and liquid thickens. Tilt pan occasionally while baking to baste top layer of potatoes with broth mixture. Cool on a wire rack 5 minutes. Serve hot.

Yield: 6 servings

Cottage Potatoes

6	large potatoes	8	ounces Velveeta, diced
1	large red bell pepper, diced		Salt and pepper to taste
1	large onion, diced	½	cup butter, melted
2	slices white bread, cubed		Milk

Preheat oven to 350 degrees. Cook potatoes in skin until tender; peel and dice. In a large bowl, mix diced potatoes, bell pepper, onion, bread, Velveeta, salt and pepper. Pour into a 9x13 inch glass baking dish. Drizzle butter over potato mixture. Add enough milk to go halfway up side of dish. Bake 1 hour.

Southwest Potato Casserole

½	cup chopped onion	1	(16 ounce) can corn, drained
½	cup chopped red bell pepper	1	(4 ounce) can chopped green chiles
3	cloves garlic, chopped		
1	jalapeño pepper, seeded and chopped	1	(10 ounce) can enchilada sauce
1	tablespoon oil or as needed	1	cup shredded cheddar cheese
1	(20 ounce) package Simply Potatoes Southwest-Style hash browns		

Preheat oven to 350 degrees. Sauté onion, bell pepper, garlic and jalapeño in oil until crisp-tender. Add hash browns and cook until brown and tender, turning occasionally with a spatula and adding more oil if needed. Add corn, chiles and enchilada sauce to hash brown mixture. Pour into a greased 9x13 inch baking dish. Top with cheese. Bake about 30 minutes or until hot and bubbly.

Broque Potatoes

6	tablespoons unsalted butter, melted	1½	teaspoons dried rosemary
3	tablespoons olive oil	1½	teaspoons paprika
2	tablespoons lemon juice		Dash of cayenne pepper
3	large cloves garlic, crushed	½	teaspoon salt
½	cup chopped fresh parsley	3	pounds small new potatoes
½	teaspoon dried thyme		Salt and pepper to taste

Preheat oven to 375 degrees. Combine butter, oil, lemon juice, garlic, parsley, thyme, rosemary, paprika, cayenne pepper and salt. Roll potatoes in seasoning mixture and place in a baking dish. Bake about 40 minutes. Season with salt and pepper.

Yield: 8 to 10 servings

Holiday Sweet Potatoes

Potatoes

1	(40 ounce) can sweet potatoes, drained	½	cup brown sugar
		½	cup orange juice
6	tablespoons butter, melted		Dash of salt
1	teaspoon vanilla		

Pecan Topping

2	tablespoons butter, cold	½	teaspoon cinnamon
½	cup brown sugar	⅓	cup chopped pecans
2	tablespoons flour		

Preheat oven to 350 degrees. Mash sweet potatoes. Stir in butter, vanilla, sugar, orange juice and salt. Spoon mixture into a shallow baking dish.

To make topping, cut butter into sugar, flour and cinnamon until crumb-like. Stir in pecans and sprinkle evenly over potatoes. Bake 30 minutes or until brown.

Virginia's
Holiday Mashed Potatoes

4	pounds potatoes	½	cup sour cream
1	(8 ounce) package cream cheese, softened and cubed	½	cup milk
		2	eggs, lightly beaten
		¼	cup minced onion or chives
5	tablespoons butter, cut into pieces	1	teaspoon salt
		1	teaspoon black pepper

Preheat oven to 350 degrees. Cook potatoes. Peel potatoes while still hot and mash until smooth in a large bowl. Add cream cheese and butter. Beat until cheese and butter are melted and completely mixed in. Stir in sour cream.

Combine milk, eggs and onion. Add to potato mixture along with salt and pepper. Beat well until fluffy and light. Place in a greased 9 inch round casserole dish. Refrigerate if not serving right away. Bake 45 minutes or until lightly browned.

Yield: 8 to 12 servings

Baked Orzo

1	pound dry orzo pasta	¼	cup cream
2	(14 ounce) cans chicken broth	¼	cup olive oil
			Salt and pepper to taste
1	cup water		Freshly grated Parmesan cheese
3	tablespoons dried dill		
8	ounces feta cheese		

Preheat oven to 350 degrees. Boil pasta in broth and 1 cup water until tender. Drain and rinse in cold water. Combine cooked orzo with dill, feta cheese, cream and oil. Season with salt and pepper and place in a baking dish. Bake, covered, for 25 minutes. Uncover and sprinkle with Parmesan cheese. Bake 10 minutes longer.

Bahamian Pigeon Peas and Rice

Serve with Marinated Mahi Mahi, Conch Fritters and Key Lime Pie.

2 thick strips bacon, diced	1 cup chicken broth or water
1 tablespoon butter	½ teaspoon dried thyme or more to taste
¼ cup diced onion	2 bay leaves
1 stalk celery, diced	1 (16 ounce) can pigeon peas
1 tablespoon tomato paste	Salt and pepper to taste
1 cup dry long grain rice	

Sauté bacon in butter 2 to 3 minutes. Add onion and celery and sauté 3 to 5 minutes. Add tomato paste and cook 1 minute. Stir in rice and sauté 1 minute. Add broth, thyme, bay leaves and peas. Bring to a boil. Reduce heat and simmer, covered, for about 25 minutes or until rice is tender. Season with salt and pepper.

Classic Creamy Risotto

2 cups chicken broth	¼ cup olive oil
2 cups water	1 cup pine nuts, toasted
2 cups heavy cream	1 cup julienned roasted red bell pepper
2 cups dry Arborio rice	½ teaspoon white pepper
1 cup Parmesan cheese, shredded	¼ teaspoon salt

Bring broth, 2 cups water and cream to a boil in a large pot. Add rice and reduce heat to medium. Cook, stirring constantly to prevent sticking, for about 15 minutes or until liquid is absorbed and risotto is thickened. Add cheese, oil, pine nuts, bell pepper, white pepper and salt. Stir until well blended.

Oriental Rice

1 (6 ounce) package Uncle Ben's wild rice mix	1 tablespoon soy sauce
1 cup chopped onion	1 (3 ounce) can mushrooms, drained
1 cup chopped celery	1 (5 ounce) can water chestnuts, drained
⅓ cup slivered almonds	
3 tablespoons butter	

Prepare rice as directed on package. Preheat oven to 350 degrees. Sauté onion, celery and almonds in butter. Combine cooked rice, sautéed mixture, soy sauce, mushrooms and water chestnuts. Place in a 1½ quart casserole dish. Bake 20 minutes.

Yield: 6 to 8 servings

Basmati Rice
with Dried Fruits and Nuts

4 tablespoons unsalted butter	¼ teaspoon allspice
1 small yellow onion, minced	¼ cup raisins
1½ cups dry basmati rice	¼ cup dried cherries or cranberries
3¼ cups water	½ cup dried apricot halves, quartered
¾ teaspoon salt	½ cup pecans, toasted and coarsely chopped
Freshly ground black pepper to taste	
¼ teaspoon cinnamon	

Melt butter in a saucepan over medium heat. Add onion and sauté about 10 minutes or until softened.

Meanwhile, rinse rice well and drain. Add rice, 3¼ cups water, salt, pepper, cinnamon, allspice, raisins, cherries and apricots to sautéed onion. Bring to a boil. Reduce heat to low and cover. Cook, without stirring or removing cover, for 20 minutes. Uncover to check if rice is tender and liquid is absorbed. If not, re-cover and cook a few minutes longer until done. Add pecans and toss to combine. Transfer to a warmed serving dish and serve immediately.

Yield: 6 servings

Coconut Rice

1½ cups dry rice	2 tablespoons butter or margarine
1 onion, chopped	2½ cups chicken broth
½ cup shredded coconut	⅓ cup cream of coconut
1 tablespoon curry powder	½ teaspoon salt

Sauté rice, onion, coconut and curry in butter until coconut is lightly toasted. Add broth, cream of coconut and salt. Simmer until rice is tender.

Yield: 6 servings

Cream of coconut, such as Coco Lopez brand, can be found with the drink mixes in the grocery store.

Spiced Rice

4 tablespoons butter	¼ teaspoon cinnamon
1 medium onion, minced	¼ teaspoon allspice
¼ cup coarsely chopped fresh parsley	3 tablespoons currants
	Salt and pepper to taste
2½ cups chicken broth	1 cup dry rice

Heat butter in a heavy saucepan. Add onions and sauté until tender. Add parsley, broth, cinnamon, allspice, currants, salt and pepper. Stir well and bring to a boil.

Stir in rice and cover. Reduce heat and simmer 20 to 25 minutes. Remove from heat and let stand 5 minutes before serving. Serve with chicken or pork.

Rice and Onion Casserole

4	tablespoons butter	1	cup shredded Jarlsberg or
8	onions, cut into chunks		Swiss cheese
½	cup dry rice	⅔	cup half-and-half
5	cups boiling salted water		

Preheat oven to 325 degrees. Melt butter in a skillet. Add onions and sauté. Cook rice in 5 cups boiling salted water for 5 minutes. Drain well. Mix rice into onions. Add cheese and half-and-half. Place in a shallow baking dish. Bake 1 hour.

Yield: 8 servings

Quick and Easy Macaroni and Cheese

1	(8 ounce) package large elbow macaroni, cooked and drained	1	(10¾ ounce) can condensed cream of mushroom soup
1	(8 ounce) package shredded sharp cheddar cheese	½	cup mayonnaise
		½	cup milk

Preheat oven to 375 degrees. Combine all ingredients in a lightly greased 2½ quart baking dish. Bake 25 minutes.

Low fat cheese, soup, mayonnaise and milk can be substituted, if desired.

Cheesey Rigatoni

1   (1 pound) package rigatoni, cooked and drained
2   (8 ounce) packages extra sharp white cheddar cheese, sliced

1   (16 ounce) ball mozzarella cheese, sliced
¼   cup Parmesan cheese
    Black pepper to taste
    Milk

Preheat oven to 350 degrees. Layer rigatoni, cheddar cheese and mozzarella cheese in a baking dish. Repeat layers three times, sprinkling between layers with Parmesan cheese and pepper. Add milk to about 1 to 2 inches in depth. Bake 45 minutes.

Noodles and Sauerkraut

1   large onion, sliced
2   cups sliced fresh mushrooms
2   cups butter

2   (14½ ounce) cans or 1 (2 pound) bag sauerkraut, drained
1   pound dry spiral pasta, cooked and drained

Sauté onion and mushrooms in butter. Add sauerkraut and cook until heated through. Add pasta and toss until mixed.

Desserts

NORMA DESANTIS
Summer Table
Watercolor, 2000

Desserts

Cakes

Aspirin Cake 193
Red Velvet Cake 193
Sinful Chocolate Cake 194
Death By Chocolate 194
Winner's Chocolate Cake 195
Macadamia Fudge Torte 196
Chocolate, Chocolate Chip
    Cake with Powdered Sugar 197
Low-Fat Chocolate Torte 197
Fresh Fruit Cake 198
Out Of This World Fruitcake 199
Banana Split Cake 199
Mandarin Orange Cake 200
Three-Ginger Gingerbread 200
Lite Angel Food Torte 201
Apple Pound Cake 201
The Best Carrot Cake 202
Granny Shear's
    1-2-3-4 Pound Cake 203
Popcorn Cake 203
Classic Tiramisu 204
Miracle Cake................................. 204
Apple or Pear Cake 205
Old Fashion Prune Cake................. 205
Almond Cake with Plum Compote .. 206
Frosting Cake 206

Cheesecakes and Custards

White Chocolate Cheesecake 207
Cheesecake 208
Warm Chocolate Gâteau 208
Turtle Pecan Cheesecake 209
Chocolate Pudding or Pie Filling 210
Chocolate Fondue.......................... 210
Chocolate Mousse 211
Mexican Flan 211
Frozen Chocolate Crêpes
    with Vanilla Custard Sauce 212
Bread Pudding 213
Bread and Butter Pudding 214
Australia's Finest
    Sticky Toffee Pudding 215
Pumpkin Delight............................ 216

Pies and Pastry

Caramel-Coconut Pie 216
Summer Fruit "Tart" 217
Fabulous Pecan Pie 217
Pumpkin Ice Cream Pie 218
Chocolate Pecan Pie 218
Chocolate Peanut Butter Pie 219
Key Lime Mousse Tart 220
Frozen Key Lime Pie 220
Apple Ding-A-Lings 221
Sasha's Key Lime Pie 221
Robin's Blue Ribbon Apple Pie 222
Pat's Florida Key Lime Pie 222
Crustless Pear Tart 223
Calamondin Pie 224
Strawberry Pie 224
Kentucky Pecan Pie 225
Chocolate Silk Pie 225
Hershey Pie 226
Apple Strudel 226
Fruit Cobbler 227
Cherry Cobbler.............................. 227

Cookies, Candy and Ice Cream

Neiman Marcus' $250
    Chocolate Chip Cookies 228
Everyday Cookies 228
Special Chocolate Chip Cookies 229
Potato Chip Cookies 229
Peanut Butter Cookies 230
Coconut-Almond Macaroons 230
Butter Snowballs 231
Coconut Macaroons Claudet 231
Bumblebee Cookies 232
Sue's Hermit Cookies 232
Holiday Fruit Drops 233
Overnight Meringues 233
Cherries and Cream
    Sweetheart Scones 234
Chocolate Raspberry Bars 235
Macadamia Nut Bars 236
Magnificent Brownies 236
Lemon Bars Deluxe........................ 237
Julie's Killer Brownies 237
Caroline's Brownies 238
Peanut Butter Bars 238
Texas Sheet Cake 239
Pecan Dainties 239
Peanut Butter Fudge 240
Butter Crunch Candy 240
Brandy Alexander Ice Cream 241
Speedy Peach Ice Cream 241
The World's Best
    By Far Lime Ice Cream 241

Dessert Sauces

Piña Colada Fruit Dip 242
Grand Marnier Sauce 242
Raspberry Chocolate Sauce............. 243
Black Cherry Sauce 243

Treasures of the Tropics

Aspirin Cake

Preheat oven to 375 degrees. Turn down TV. Remove toys from countertop. Measure 2 cups of flour. Get baking powder. Remove Benjamin's hand from flour. Put flour, baking powder and salt into sifter. Vacuum mixture off kitchen floor. (Benjamin spilled it.) Get an egg. Answer phone. Separate egg and warm baby Adam's bottle. Help Mary figure out a new math problem the old way. Grease pan. Salesman at door. Take ¼ inch of salt from greased pan and look for Benjamin. Put mess in wastebasket and dishes in dishwasher. Call the bakery and take two aspirins.

Red Velvet Cake

A popular Southern treat.

Cake

2½	cups self-rising flour	1½	cups sugar
1	cup buttermilk	1	teaspoon vinegar
1½	cups vegetable oil	2	eggs
1	teaspoon vanilla	1	teaspoon baking soda
¼	cup red food coloring	3	tablespoons cocoa

Frosting

⅔	cup butter, softened	1½	cups chopped pecans
1¼	(8 ounce) packages cream cheese, softened	½	cup chopped pecans for garnish
1	(1 pound) package powdered sugar		

Preheat oven to 350 degrees. Combine all cake ingredients with an electric mixer. Divide cake batter among 3 greased cake pans. Bake 20 minutes or until a toothpick inserted near the center comes out clean. Cool briefly before removing from pans to cool completely.

To make frosting, cream butter and cream cheese. Add powdered sugar and 1½ cups pecans. Frost cooled cake. Use ½ cup pecans to garnish top of cake.

Sinful Chocolate Cake

1 (5 ounce) package cook and serve chocolate pudding	5 tablespoons chocolate chips
2 cups milk	5 rounded tablespoons whipped topping
1 (18 ounce) package chocolate cake mix	1 (1 pound) container dark chocolate frosting

Preheat oven to 350 degrees. Prepare pudding as directed on package, using 2 cups milk. After pudding has boiled 1 minute, remove from heat and stir in cake mix. Pour batter into a greased and floured 8 inch springform pan. Sprinkle chocolate chips over batter. Bake 35 minutes.

Transfer hot cake to freezer for 5 minutes. Remove from freezer and spoon topping on cake. Return to freezer for 10 minutes. Remove from freezer and ice with frosting.

Death By Chocolate

1 (18 ounce) package chocolate cake mix	6 Heath English toffee candy bars, crumbled
3 (3.9 ounce) boxes instant chocolate pudding mix	1 (12 ounce) container frozen whipped topping
4 cups milk	

Prepare cake according to package directions; cool. Crumble cake when cooled. Mix pudding and milk; chill.

In a 4 quart serving bowl, layer crumbled cake, pudding, candy and whipped topping in order listed, using half of each ingredient. Repeat layers with remaining ingredients. Cover and chill before serving.

Winner's Chocolate Cake

This dense, flourless fudge-like cake should be served in small wedges.

Cake

8	ounces bittersweet or semisweet chocolate, chopped
2	ounces unsweetened chocolate, chopped

½	cup plus 6 tablespoons unsalted butter
1	cup sugar
5	eggs, separated
3	tablespoons ground almonds

Glaze

½	cup heavy cream
3	tablespoons unsalted butter
4	ounces bittersweet or semisweet chocolate, chopped

4	ounces milk chocolate, chopped
	Fresh raspberries (optional)
	Fresh mint leaves (optional)

Preheat oven to 350 degrees. To make cake, melt chocolates and butter in a heavy medium saucepan over medium-low heat, stirring constantly until smooth. Pour mixture into a large bowl and cool slightly. Add sugar, egg yolks and almonds to bowl and whisk until smooth.

Use an electric mixer to beat egg whites in a large bowl until stiff, but not dry. Fold whites into batter in two additions. Pour batter into a greased and floured 9 inch springform pan. Bake about 40 minutes or until top is dry and begins to crack and a toothpick inserted in the center comes out with moist crumbs attached. Cool in pan on a wire rack for 15 minutes. Press down gently on top of cake to even edges. Cool completely.

For glaze, bring cream and butter to a simmer in a heavy medium saucepan. Reduce heat and add chocolates. Stir until smooth. Let stand about 1 hour or until cool but still able to pour.

Invert cake onto an 8 inch round tart pan bottom or cardboard round. Place cake on a rack set over a baking sheet. Pour glaze over cake, spreading with a spatula to coat top and sides. Refrigerate 1 hour or until glaze sets. Transfer cake to a serving platter. Garnish with raspberries and mint.

Yield: 10 servings

Cake can be prepared one day ahead and kept refrigerated. Let cake stand at room temperature for 2 hours before serving.

CAKES

Macadamia Fudge Torte
Winner of a Pillsbury Bakeoff

Filling

⅓ cup low-fat condensed milk

½ cup semisweet chocolate chips

Cake

1 (15 ounce) can sliced pears in light syrup, drained

1 (18 ounce) package Pillsbury Moist Supreme Devil's Food cake mix

1½ teaspoons cinnamon

⅓ cup oil

2 eggs

⅓ cup chopped macadamia nuts

2 teaspoons water

Sauce

⅓ cup milk

1 (17 ounce) jar Mrs. Richardson's butterscotch caramel topping, or ½ jar butterscotch and ½ jar caramel topping

Preheat oven to 350 degrees. Combine filling ingredients in a small saucepan. Cook over low heat, stirring constantly, until melted. Set aside.

To make cake, puree pears in a blender. In a large bowl, combine cake mix, cinnamon and oil. Blend with an electric mixer on low speed for 20 to 30 seconds. In a separate bowl, combine 2½ cups of cake mixture, pureed pears and eggs. Beat on low speed until mixed. Increase speed to medium and beat 2 minutes.

Spread batter in a greased 10 inch springform pan. Drop filling by spoonfuls over batter.

Stir nuts and 2 teaspoons water into remaining cake mixture. Sprinkle over filling. Bake 45 to 60 minutes or until top springs back when touched. Cool 10 minutes. Remove from pan and cool 1½ hours.

When ready to serve, combine milk and topping in a saucepan. Cook over low heat for 3 to 4 minutes. Spoon 2 tablespoons warm sauce onto each individual serving plate. Top with a wedge of torte.

Yield: 10 to 12 servings

Chocolate, Chocolate Chip Cake with Powdered Sugar

1 (18 ounce) package
chocolate cake mix
1 (3 ounce) package instant
chocolate pudding mix
1½ cups chocolate chips

½ cup vegetable oil
3 eggs
1 cup water
Powdered sugar

Preheat oven to 350 degrees. Combine all ingredients except powdered sugar. Pour batter into a greased Bundt pan. Bake 1 hour. Remove from pan and sprinkle with powdered sugar while still warm.

Low-Fat Chocolate Torte

Simple, yet looks elegant

1 (12 ounce) container frozen
whipped topping, thawed
2 (3½ ounce) containers
(individual serving size)
prepared fat-free vanilla
pudding

1 (16 ounce) package light
chocolate graham crackers

Mix half of whipped topping and pudding. Spread a one-eighth inch layer of pudding mixture over each cracker. Stack crackers on top of each other. Turn stack on its side and coat with remaining whipped topping. Refrigerate several hours.

To serve, slice diagonally. Serve with raspberries or strawberries.

Fresh Fruit Cake

*Mary, a home economist for the Virginia Egg Council,
made up this recipe. Not your typical fruitcake.*

3 cups all-purpose flour
1 tablespoon baking powder
1 teaspoon cinnamon
½ teaspoon baking soda
¼ cup brandy
1 medium unpeeled orange,
   sliced
2 slices unpeeled lemon

1 banana, sliced
1 cup cubed apple
½ cup whole fresh cranberries
1 cup butter, softened
1½ cups sugar
6 eggs
1½ cups raisins
½ cup chopped walnuts

Preheat oven to 350 degrees. In a medium bowl, stir together flour, baking powder, cinnamon and baking soda. Set aside.

Place brandy, orange, lemon and banana in a blender. Blend at medium speed until finely chopped. Add apple and cranberries. Blend at medium speed until finely chopped and evenly combined. Set aside.

Cream butter and sugar with an electric mixer at medium speed until light and fluffy. Beat in eggs until well blended. At low speed, gradually beat in dry ingredients alternately with fruit mixture until thoroughly blended. Blend in raisins and walnuts. Pour into a greased and floured 10 inch tube pan. Bake 60 to 70 minutes or until a toothpick inserted in the center comes out clean. Cool completely on a wire rack before removing from pan.

Yield: 12 to 16 servings

Out Of This World Fruitcake

1 cup margarine	2 cups chopped walnuts
2 cups granulated sugar	1 (7 ounce) can flaked coconut
4 eggs	3½ cups flour
1 teaspoon baking soda	2 cups powdered sugar
½ cup buttermilk	1 cup freshly squeezed
1 pound chopped dates	orange juice
1 pound chopped orange	
jellied candies	

Preheat oven to 250 degrees. Cream margarine and granulated sugar. Beat in eggs one at a time. Dissolve baking soda in buttermilk and add to creamed mixture.

Combine dates, orange candies, walnuts and coconut. Toss with flour and blend into creamed mixture. Pour batter into a greased and floured Bundt pan. Bake 2½ hours.

Combine powdered sugar and orange juice. Pour over hot cake and let stand overnight.

Banana Split Cake

½ cup butter, melted	3-4 bananas, sliced
2 cups graham cracker crumbs	1 (8 ounce) can crushed pineapple, drained
½ cup butter, softened	2 pints fresh strawberries, sliced
2 cups powdered sugar	Frozen whipped topping, thawed
1 (8 ounce) package cream cheese, softened	

Combine melted butter and cracker crumbs. Press mixture into the bottom of a 9x13 inch pan.

Cream softened butter, sugar and cream cheese together. Spread over cracker crust. Add layers of bananas, pineapple and strawberries. Top with whipped topping.

Mandarin Orange Cake

Cake

1 (18 ounce) package light yellow cake mix
3 eggs

½ cup oil
1 (11 ounce) can Mandarin oranges, undrained

Topping

1 (8 ounce) can crushed pineapple, undrained
1 (3 ounce) package instant vanilla pudding mix

1 (8 ounce) container frozen whipped topping, thawed

Preheat oven to 350 degrees. Combine cake mix, eggs and oil. Stir in oranges and pour into a greased 9x13 inch baking pan. Bake 20 to 25 minutes. Cool.

To make topping, mix pineapple and pudding mix. Fold in whipped topping. Spread over cooled cake.

Three-Ginger Gingerbread

3 cups all-purpose flour
1 tablespoon cinnamon
2 teaspoons baking soda
1½ teaspoons ground cloves
1 teaspoon ground ginger
¾ teaspoon salt
1½ cups sugar
1 cup vegetable oil

1 cup light molasses
½ cup water
2 eggs
1 tablespoon minced fresh ginger
½ cup chopped crystallized ginger

Preheat oven to 350 degrees. Sift flour, cinnamon, baking soda, cloves, ginger and salt into a medium bowl.

In a large bowl, combine sugar, oil, molasses, water, eggs and fresh ginger. Blend in dry ingredients. Stir in crystallized ginger. Pour batter into a greased and floured 10 inch springform pan. Bake 50 to 60 minutes. Cool 30 minutes before removing from pan. Bread may sink in the center and crack as it cools.

Yield: 10 servings

Lite Angel Food Torte

1 (18 ounce) package angel
food cake mix
1 (20 ounce) can crushed
pineapple, undrained
1 (3 ounce) package instant
vanilla pudding mix

1 (16 ounce) container light
frozen whipped topping,
thawed
1 (11 ounce) can Mandarin
oranges, drained

Prepare cake mix according to package directions. Cool. Slice cake into 3 layers horizontally.

Combine pineapple and pudding. Mix in whipped topping. Use mixture to ice between layers and on top and sides. Arrange oranges on top. Refrigerate.

Apple Pound Cake

4½ cups peeled and sliced apple
3 cups sugar
5 eggs
2¼ cups vegetable oil
½ tablespoon baking soda

2½ teaspoons vanilla
4½ cups flour
½ tablespoon salt
½ tablespoon cinnamon
1 teaspoon ground cloves

Preheat oven to 350 degrees. Spray the inside of 2 large loaf pans with cooking spray. Line inside bottom of pan with parchment paper and lightly spray paper with cooking spray. Place sliced apples in water until needed. Add a small amount of lemon juice to water to prevent apples from discoloring.

Combine sugar, eggs, oil, baking soda and vanilla in a mixing bowl. Mix with an electric mixer on low speed until well blended. Add flour, salt, cinnamon and cloves. Mix until blended.

Drain apples and pat dry with a clean towel. Using a rubber spatula, fold apples into batter until incorporated. Pour batter into prepared pans, filling about three-fourths full. Bake about 35 to 40 minutes.

Orchid Island Golf and Beach Club
One Beachside Drive
Vero Beach, Florida

The Best Carrot Cake

Cake

3 cups unbleached all-purpose flour
3 cups granulated sugar
1 teaspoon salt
1 tablespoon baking soda
1 tablespoon cinnamon
1½ cups corn oil

4 eggs, lightly beaten
1 tablespoon vanilla
1½ cups chopped walnuts
1½ cups shredded coconut
1½ cups pureed cooked carrot
¾ cup drained crushed pineapple

Cream Cheese Frosting

6 tablespoons unsalted butter, softened
1 (8 ounce) package cream cheese, softened

3 cups powdered sugar
1 teaspoon vanilla
Juice of ½ lemon

Preheat oven to 350 degrees. Combine flour, sugar, salt, baking soda and cinnamon in a bowl. Add oil, eggs and vanilla. Beat well. Fold in walnuts, coconut, carrot and pineapple. Pour batter into two greased 9 inch springform pans.

Bake in center of oven for 50 minutes or until edges pull away from the sides and a toothpick inserted in the center comes out clean. Cool on a rack 3 hours before removing from pans.

To make frosting, cream together butter and cream cheese. Add sugar and beat until smooth. Stir in vanilla and lemon juice. Spread frosting between cake layers and on outside of cake.

Granny Shear's 1-2-3-4 Pound Cake

Granny's recipe made in the 1920's and still yummy!

1	cup butter	1	tablespoon vanilla
2	cups sugar	2	teaspoons baking powder
3	cups flour	¼	teaspoon salt
4	eggs	1	cup milk

Preheat oven to 350 degrees. Cream butter and sugar. Add eggs one at a time, beating after each addition. Blend in vanilla.

Sift together flour, baking powder and salt in a medium bowl. Add dry ingredients alternately with milk to creamed mixture. Mix until smooth. Pour batter into a greased and floured tube pan. Bake 1 hour.

Popcorn Cake

This colorful treat is great for the holidays. Kids as well as adults love the taste.

12	cups popped popcorn, unpopped kernels discarded	1	(6½ ounce) can cocktail peanuts
1	(1 pound) package M&M's plain candies	1	(1 pound) package marshmallows
		½	cup margarine or butter

Combine popcorn, M&M's and peanuts in a bowl. Heat marshmallows and margarine until melted. Pour over popcorn mixture and stir until mixed well.

Press mixture into an angel food cake pan. When cool, invert onto a serving plate.

Classic Tiramisu

An Italian temptation

6 egg yolks
¾ cup sugar
10 ounces mascarpone cheese
6 ounces chocolate, melted and cooled (optional), or 6 ounces pureed fresh fruit such as raspberries, strawberries or mango (optional)

1 quart heavy cream
Sponge cake or 2 dozen lady fingers, halved
½ cup Kahlúa liqueur
2 cups espresso coffee
Semisweet ground cocoa powder

Beat egg yolks and sugar in a mixing bowl until almost white. Fold in cheese. Add chocolate or fruit, if using. Whip cream until stiff peaks form. Fold cream into egg mixture and beat again until stiff.

Cut sponge cake to form a ¼ inch layer over the bottom of a 12x18 inch baking pan or line pan with halved lady fingers. Combine Kahlúa and coffee and mix well. Cool and pour over cake. Spread cream mixture over cake and sprinkle with cocoa powder. Chill overnight. Cut into squares and serve.

Create great chocolate curls to garnish tiramisu. Wrap a piece of milk chocolate in plastic wrap and hold between hands up to 30 seconds until chocolate just begins to soften. Remove plastic to expose a portion of chocolate. Carefully make curls with a vegetable peeler, working over tiramisu so curls fall directly onto dessert.

Miracle Cake

Mayo makes it very moist.

2 cups flour
1 cup sugar
¼ cup cocoa powder
1½ teaspoons baking soda
¼ teaspoon salt

1 cup Miracle Whip salad dressing
1 cup cold water
1 tablespoon vanilla

Preheat oven to 325 degrees. Sift together flour, sugar, cocoa powder, baking soda and salt in a bowl. Stir in salad dressing, water and vanilla. Pour batter into a Bundt pan. Bake 1 hour or until a toothpick inserted in the center comes out clean.

Apple or Pear Cake

6 apples or pears, or combination, sliced
5 tablespoons sugar
5 teaspoons cinnamon
3 cups flour
1 tablespoon baking powder

1 teaspoon salt
2 cups sugar
¼ cup orange juice
1 cup vegetable oil
1 teaspoon vanilla
4 eggs

Preheat oven to 350 degrees. Combine fruit, 5 tablespoons sugar and cinnamon. Set aside. Mix flour, baking powder, salt, 2 cups sugar, orange juice, oil and vanilla in a bowl until well blended. Add eggs and blend.

Layer fruit and batter in a tube pan. Bake 1¼ hours.

Old Fashion Prune Cake

3 eggs
2 cups sugar
1 cup corn oil
2 cups self-rising flour

2 teaspoons allspice
2 teaspoons cinnamon
1 cup stewed prunes
1 cup chopped nuts

Preheat oven to 350 degrees. Beat eggs. Add sugar and beat well. Beat in oil. Combine flour, allspice and cinnamon. Blend dry ingredients into egg mixture. Stir in prunes and nuts. Pour batter into a tube pan.

Bake 1 hour or until a knife inserted in the center comes out clean.

Almond Cake
with Plum Compote

Cake

7½	ounces almond paste		Zest of 1½ oranges
1	cup sugar	1½	cups cake flour
¾	cup butter, softened	¾	teaspoon baking powder
5	eggs		Pinch of salt

Plum Compote

1	cup sugar	½	vanilla bean, scraped
1	cup water	½	lemon
1	cinnamon stick	1½	pounds plums, quartered

Preheat oven to 325 degrees. Grease a 9 inch cake pan and line with wax paper. Use an electric mixer to cream almond paste, sugar and butter until fluffy. Continue beating while gradually adding eggs and zest. Beat until mixture is smooth and fluffy.

Sift together flour, baking powder and salt. Fold dry ingredients into creamed mixture. Pour into prepared pan. Bake until a knife inserted in the center comes out clean.

To make compote, combine sugar, water, cinnamon stick and vanilla bean in a saucepan. Squeeze in juice from lemon into saucepan and then add lemon half to saucepan. Bring to a boil. Add plums and simmer 3 to 4 minutes or until softened. Remove lemon half. Serve compote with cake and whipped cream.

Frosting Cake

1	(18 ounce) package yellow cake mix	1	cup water
4	eggs	1	(1 pound) box coconut pecan frosting mix
1	cup oil	½	cup pecans

Preheat oven to 350 degrees. Combine cake mix, eggs, oil and 1 cup water. Mix well. Stir frosting into batter and mix well. Blend in pecans. Pour into a greased and floured Bundt pan. Bake on top rack of oven for 45 to 60 minutes. Remove from pan while hot.

White Chocolate Cheesecake

Crust

1   (9 ounce) package chocolate wafer cookies, broken into small pieces

½   cup unsalted butter, melted

Filling

1   pound good quality white chocolate, finely chopped

4   (8 ounce) packages cream cheese, softened

1   cup sugar

¼   teaspoon salt

4   eggs

1   cup sour cream

½   cup heavy cream

2   tablespoons vanilla

Garnish

1   good quality dark chocolate bar

1   good quality white chocolate bar

Preheat oven to 325 degrees. Grease a 10 inch springform pan and wrap outside with foil.

Grind cookies in a food processor. Add butter and blend until crumbs are moistened. Press into bottom and 2 inches up the sides of prepared pan. Bake in center of oven for 15 minutes. Cool crust on a wire rack.

To prepare filling, stir white chocolate in the top of a double boiler set over barely simmering water until melted and smooth. Cool to lukewarm, stirring occasionally. Meanwhile, beat cream cheese in a large bowl with an electric mixer for 3 minutes or until fluffy. Gradually blend in sugar and salt. Beat until smooth. Add eggs one at a time, beating well after each addition. Beat in sour cream, heavy cream and vanilla until blended. Gradually add melted white chocolate, beating until smooth. Pour into crust.

Bake at 325 degrees for 1 hour, 20 minutes or until top begins to brown but center still moves slightly when pan is gently shaken. Turn off heat and open oven door slightly. Leave cake in oven 30 minutes. Transfer to refrigerator and chill, covered, overnight or up to 2 days. When ready to serve, run a small knife between pan and cake. Release sides of pan. Use a vegetable peeler to shave chocolate bars over cake for garnish.

Cheesecake

1	pound ricotta cheese	3	large eggs
2	cups sour cream	3	tablespoons flour
2	(8 ounce) packages cream cheese, softened	3	tablespoons cornstarch
1½	cups sugar	5	teaspoons vanilla
½	cup butter, softened	5	teaspoons fresh lemon juice

Preheat oven to 350 degrees. Combine ricotta cheese and sour cream with an electric mixer in a bowl. Beating slowly, add cream cheese, sugar and butter. Increase to medium speed and add eggs, flour, cornstarch, vanilla and lemon juice. Increase to highest speed possible without spattering and beat 5 minutes. Pour into a 10 inch springform pan.

Bake 1 hour. Turn off heat and leave in oven with door closed for 1 hour longer. Cool on a wire rack.

Warm Chocolate Gâteau

4	ounces chocolate	½	cup sugar
7	tablespoons butter	½	cup sugar
4	eggs, separated		

Preheat oven to 375 degrees. Melt chocolate and butter together. Cool. Add egg yolks, beating in one at a time, to chocolate mixture when cool. Whisk in ½ cup sugar. Beat egg whites until soft peaks form. Gradually beat in ½ cup sugar. Fold whites into chocolate mixture.

Spoon mixture into greased molds or ramekins, filling each half full. Bake 15 minutes or until a toothpick comes out clean.

Yield: 8 servings

Turtle Pecan Cheesecake

Cheesecake

2	cups crushed chocolate cookies	¼	teaspoon salt
4	tablespoons butter, melted	1	teaspoon vanilla
2½	(8 ounce) packages cream cheese, softened	3	eggs
1	cup sugar	2	tablespoons heavy cream
1½	tablespoons flour	½	cup chocolate chips
			Pecans

Caramel Topping

½ (14 ounce) package caramels   ⅓ cup heavy cream

Chocolate Topping

1	(4 ounce) package German sweet chocolate	1	teaspoon butter
		2	tablespoons heavy cream

Preheat oven to 450 degrees. Combine crushed cookies and butter and press into the bottom of a 9 inch springform pan. Beat cream cheese in a large bowl until creamy. Mix in sugar, flour, salt and vanilla. Add eggs one at a time, beating well after each addition. Blend in cream. Pour batter over cookie crust. Sprinkle chocolate chips on top. Bake 10 minutes. Reduce oven temperature to 200 degrees and bake 35 to 40 minutes longer or until set. Cool. Remove sides of pan.

To make caramel topping, combine caramels and cream in a small saucepan. Stir over low heat until smooth.

For chocolate topping, heat and stir chocolate, butter and cream in a small saucepan over low heat until smooth. Drizzle toppings over cheesecake. Top with pecans. Refrigerate.

Chocolate Pudding
or Pie Filling

1½ cups sugar	1 tablespoon butter
¼ cup cornstarch	1½ teaspoons vanilla
½ teaspoon salt	3 (1 ounce) squares
3 cups whole milk	unsweetened chocolate,
3 egg yolks, beaten	melted

Mix sugar, cornstarch and salt in a saucepan. Gradually stir in milk. Cook over medium heat, stirring constantly, until mixture thickens and boils. Boil 1 minute and remove from heat.

Slowly stir half of milk mixture into egg yolks, then stir back into hot mixture in saucepan. Bring to a boil and boil 1 minute, stirring constantly. Remove from heat. Stir in butter, vanilla and chocolate.

Yield: Fills 1 (9 inch) pie crust

Chocolate Fondue

A fun dessert for kids and adults

Fondue

1 (12 ounce) package	2 tablespoons Cointreau,
semisweet chocolate chips	brandy or kirsch
¾ cup light cream	

Dippers

Fresh strawberries	Angel food cake
Sliced bananas	Apple wedges
Pineapple chunks	Maraschino cherries
Mandarin orange segments	

Heat chocolate and cream over low heat until melted. Remove from heat and stir in liqueur. Transfer mixture to a fondue pot and keep warm. Arrange dippers on a platter and let guests choose their favorites.

Chocolate Mousse

This one takes only 5 to 10 minutes to make and is really good.

1	pound semisweet chocolate chips	2	teaspoons 151 Proof rum or other liqueur or to taste (optional)
12	extra large or jumbo eggs, separated		Whipped cream

Melt chocolate in a large bowl by microwaving on high for about 2½ minutes. Stir.

Beat egg whites in a separate bowl until stiff. Add egg yolks to chocolate and stir to mix. Blend in rum. Mix a small amount of stiff egg whites into chocolate mixture. Fold in remaining whites.

Refrigerate for 8 hours or overnight. Serve with whipped cream.

Mexican Flan

Served as one of the desserts at "La Mexicana Fiesta" — auctioned at the Hibiscus Children's Center's Fall Benefit.

½	cup sugar	6	eggs
1	(14 ounce) can sweetened condensed milk	1	teaspoon vanilla
2	cups whole milk		Fresh strawberries or raspberries for garnish

Preheat oven to 350 degrees. Heat sugar in a heavy skillet, shaking and tilting constantly, until liquid and brown. Pour hot sugar into the bottom of individual baking dishes.

Blend milks, eggs and vanilla with an electric mixer. Pour gently into baking dishes. Bake in a water bath for 1 hour or until firm. To serve, run a knife around the edge of the baking dishes and invert onto serving plates. Garnish with berries.

Yield: 4 to 6 servings

Frozen Chocolate Crêpes with Vanilla Custard Sauce

This is served as one of the desserts at "La Mexicana Fiesta" — auctioned at the Hibiscus Children's Center's Fall Benefit.

Crêpes

2	eggs	1	cup milk
½	cup flour	1	tablespoon butter, melted
¼	cup sugar	1	teaspoon vanilla
2	tablespoons unsweetened cocoa powder		

Chocolate Mousse

2	cups semisweet chocolate chips		Pinch of salt
1½	teaspoons vanilla	1½	cups heavy cream
		6	egg yolks

Vanilla Custard Sauce

4	egg yolks	1½	cups half-and-half
½	cup sugar		Cinnamon
1	vanilla bean, split		

Combine all crêpe ingredients in a blender. Mix on low speed for 30 seconds or until just combined; do not over blend. Cover and allow to stand 1 hour. Heat a 7 inch nonstick crêpe or omelet pan. Add enough batter to cover bottom. Cook crêpe, turning once. Place cooked crêpes on wax paper to cool.

To make mousse, combine chocolate chips, vanilla and salt in a blender. Mix 30 seconds. Bring cream to a boil and add to blender. Mix 30 seconds or until the chocolate is completely melted. Add yolks and mix about 5 seconds. Transfer to a bowl to cool.

To assemble, spoon 1 heaping tablespoon of mousse onto each cooled crêpe and roll cigar-fashion. Place seam-side down on a baking sheet and freeze. When firm, wrap carefully and store in freezer until ready to serve.

When ready to serve, prepare custard. Combine egg yolks and sugar in a small bowl. Scrape soft inside of vanilla bean into yolk mixture with the point of a sharp knife; reserve pod. Beat mixture until light and fluffy. Place half-and-half and bean pod in a 2 quart saucepan. Bring to a boil over high heat, then remove pod. Beating constantly,

(Frozen Chocolate Crêpes continued)

very slowly pour boiling mixture into yolk mixture. Pour back into saucepan. Cook and stir constantly over low heat for about 20 minutes or until custard coats back of a metal spoon. Spoon warm custard over crêpes. Dust with cinnamon and serve.

Yield: 12 servings

Bread Pudding

Original recipe from Bonton's restaurant in New Orleans.

Pudding

1	loaf French bread, cut into cubes	2	cups sugar	
1	quart milk	2	tablespoons vanilla	
3	eggs	1	cup raisins	
		3	tablespoons butter, melted	

Whiskey Sauce

½	cup butter	1	egg, well beaten	
1	cup sugar		Whiskey to taste	

Preheat oven to 350 degrees. Soak bread in milk. Stir by hand until well mixed. Add eggs, sugar, vanilla and raisins; stir well. Pour butter into a baking pan. Add bread mixture. Bake until firm. Cool.

To make sauce, heat butter and sugar until very hot and dissolved. Add egg and whip quickly to prevent egg from curdling. Cool and add whiskey.

When ready to serve, cube cooled pudding and place into individual serving dishes. Pour sauce over pudding and heat under the broiler.

Bread and Butter Pudding

¾ cup butter, very softened
25 slices white bread, Pullman-style preferred
1 quart half-and-half
6 eggs
5 egg yolks

1 generous cup granulated sugar
1 teaspoon vanilla
¼ cup granulated sugar
2 teaspoons cinnamon
Powdered sugar
Caramel sauce

Preheat oven to 350 degrees. Butter one side of each slice of bread. Toast each bread slice under the broiler, buttered side up. Trim crusts away and divide each toast slice into two equal triangles. With the right angle of each piece of bread pointing up, spiral the bread slices into a greased 1x10 inch cake pan from the edge to the center, overlapping each slice.

Combine half-and-half, eggs, egg yolks, 1 cup sugar and vanilla. Beat until smooth. Pour custard mixture over bread in thirds, letting the pudding stand about 5 minutes between each addition.

Combine ¼ cup sugar and cinnamon and sprinkle over pudding. Bake in a water bath, with ½ inch of water in a pan, for about 45 minutes. To check for doneness, gently pull apart two slices of bread. If liquid is present, the pudding needs to bake longer. When done, cool briefly and serve warm. Dust with powdered sugar and serve with caramel sauce.

Yield: 10 servings

Do not allow water to boil in water bath while baking. This could cause pudding to fall when cooled.

Sailfish Point Country Club
Stuart, Florida

Australia's Finest
Sticky Toffee Pudding

Pudding

8	ounces pitted dates, chopped	2	eggs
1	teaspoon baking soda	1¼	cups flour
½	cup butter, cut into 8 pieces	½	teaspoon salt
5	tablespoons sugar	½	teaspoon vanilla
		1¾	tablespoons baking powder

Sauce

½	cup butter	½	teaspoon vanilla
¼	cup heavy cream	1	pint heavy cream, chilled and whipped
½	cup brown sugar		

Preheat oven to 350 degrees. To make pudding, place dates in a saucepan. Cover dates with water and bring to a boil. Reduce heat and simmer 3 minutes. Add baking soda; set aside. Cream butter and sugar in a bowl. Beat in eggs one at a time. Gently fold in flour, salt and vanilla. Slowly stir in baking powder and ¼ cup of cooking liquid from date mixture. Pudding mixture should resemble thick pancake batter. Stir in remaining date mixture. Pour into a greased 8 or 9 inch high-sided baking pan. Bake 30 to 40 minutes or until a toothpick inserted in the center comes out clean.

Meanwhile, prepare sauce by combining butter, ¼ cup cream, brown sugar and vanilla in a saucepan. Bring to a boil. Reduce heat and simmer 3 minutes.

To serve, drizzle sauce over warm pudding. Top with whipped cream and drizzle with more sauce. Serve extra sauce and whipped cream on the side.

Yield: 8 to 10 servings

Pumpkin Delight

1 (15 ounce) can pumpkin
4 eggs
1½ cups sugar
1 (12 ounce) can evaporated
   milk
3 tablespoons pumpkin pie
   spice

1 (18 ounce) package yellow
   cake mix
1 cup margarine, melted
¾ cup chopped nuts
   Whipped topping or ice
   cream

Preheat oven to 350 degrees. Beat pumpkin, eggs, sugar, milk and spice together and pour into a greased 9x13 inch baking dish.

Sprinkle cake mix over pumpkin layer. Drizzle margarine over cake mix and top with nuts. Bake 1 hour. Serve with whipped topping or ice cream.

Caramel-Coconut Pie

Makes 2 pies — one for now and one for later.

4 tablespoons butter or
   margarine
1 (7 ounce) package flaked
   coconut
½ cup chopped pecans
1 (8 ounce) package cream
   cheese, softened

1 (14 ounce) can sweetened
   condensed milk
1 (16 ounce) container frozen
   whipped topping, thawed
2 (9 inch) pie crusts, baked
1 (12 ounce) jar caramel ice
   cream topping
   Pecan halves for garnish

Melt butter in a large skillet. Add coconut and chopped pecans. Sauté until golden. Set aside to cool slightly. Combine cream cheese and milk. Beat with an electric mixer at medium speed until smooth. Fold in whipped topping.

Layer one-fourth of cream cheese mixture in each pie crust. Drizzle a fourth of caramel topping over each pie. Sprinkle each with one-fourth of coconut mixture. Repeat layers with remaining ingredients. Cover and freeze pies at least 8 hours.

To serve, let pies stand at room temperature for 5 minutes before slicing. Garnish with pecan halves.

Summer Fruit "Tart"

	Bread crumbs	½	cup butter, melted and
2	eggs		cooled
½	cup sugar	2	cups peaches, apricots or
1	cup all-purpose flour		cherries, peeled if
2	teaspoons baking powder		necessary and cut into
¼	teaspoon salt		1 inch pieces
½	teaspoon cinnamon	4	teaspoons sugar

Preheat oven to 350 degrees. Lightly grease a 10 inch springform pan and coat with bread crumbs. Whisk eggs and ½ cup sugar 8 minutes or until pale. Sift together flour, baking powder, salt and cinnamon. Fold dry ingredients into egg mixture. Mix a small amount of batter into butter, then fold back into remaining batter.

Pour into prepared pan and top with fruit. Sprinkle with 4 teaspoons sugar. Bake 35 to 40 minutes. Cut into eighths and serve with praline or toffee ice cream.

Yield: 8 servings

John's Island Country Club
Vero Beach, Florida

Fabulous Pecan Pie

3	eggs	1	teaspoon vanilla
1	cup dark corn syrup	⅛	teaspoon salt
1	cup sugar	1	cup pecans
2	tablespoons butter or	1	(9 inch) pie crust, unbaked
	margarine, melted		

Preheat oven to 400 degrees. Beat eggs lightly. Mix in corn syrup, sugar, butter, vanilla and salt. Stir in nuts. Pour into pie crust. Bake 15 minutes. Reduce oven temperature to 350 degrees and bake 30 to 35 minutes or until filling is just slightly less set in center than around edge.

Pumpkin Ice Cream Pie

Crust

¾ cup graham cracker crumbs   4 tablespoons margarine,
½ cup ginger snap crumbs   softened
                                    ¼ cup sugar

Filling

1 quart vanilla ice cream,   ½ teaspoon ground ginger
    softened   ½ teaspoon cinnamon
1 cup canned pumpkin   ½ teaspoon nutmeg
¾ cup sugar   1 (1.3 ounce) envelope Dream
½ teaspoon salt   Whip topping, whipped

Preheat oven to 350 degrees. Mix cracker and ginger snap crumbs. Stir in margarine and sugar. Press into a 9 inch pie plate. Bake 5 minutes. Chill. Spread ice cream over crust; freeze.

To make filling, mix pumpkin and sugar together. Add salt, ginger, cinnamon and nutmeg. Fold in whipped topping. Spread over ice cream; freeze.

Chocolate Pecan Pie

⅔ cup evaporated milk   2 tablespoons flour
2 tablespoons butter   ¼ teaspoon salt
1 (6 ounce) package chocolate   1 tablespoon vanilla
    chips   1 cup pecans
2 eggs, beaten   1 pie crust, unbaked
1 cup sugar

Preheat oven to 350 degrees. Combine milk, butter and chocolate in a double boiler. Cook until melted. Add eggs, sugar, flour, salt, vanilla and pecans. Pour into pie crust. Bake 30 to 40 minutes.

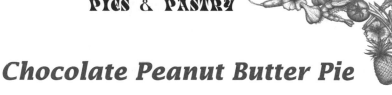

Chocolate Peanut Butter Pie

Graham Cracker Crust

¾ cup graham cracker crumbs	2 tablespoons brown sugar
¼ cup granulated sugar	4 tablespoons butter, melted

Filling

1½ cups heavy cream	¾ cup sugar
1 (8 ounce) package cream cheese, softened	1 cup peanut butter
	1 tablespoon vanilla

Chocolate Sauce

¾ cup heavy cream	8 ounces semisweet chocolate

Blend cracker crumbs and sugars in a food processor. With motor running, drizzle in butter and process until all ingredients are moist. Press into a 9 inch pie pan. Freeze 1 hour.

To make filling, whip cream until soft peaks form. Set aside. Beat cream cheese in a large mixing bowl until smooth. Add sugar and mix well. Add peanut butter and vanilla. Fold in whipped cream. Spoon filling into frozen crust. Freeze 1 hour.

For sauce, bring cream to a boil in a saucepan. Turn off heat, add chocolate and cover saucepan for 10 minutes. Stir chocolate until melted and smooth. Pour sauce over pie. Refrigerate until serving.

"11 Maple Street" Restaurant
3224 N.E. Maple Avenue
Jensen Beach, Florida

Key Lime Mousse Tart

Shortbread Crust
½   cup butter
1   teaspoon salt

¼   cup light brown sugar
1   cup all-purpose flour

Key Lime Filling
3   eggs
1   (14 ounce) can sweetened
     condensed milk

½   cup fresh key lime juice
     (about 6 key limes)
⅓   cup sugar

Preheat oven to 350 degrees. In a mixing bowl with a paddle attachment, whip butter until soft. Blend in salt and sugar. Mix in flour until incorporated. Knead quickly and lightly into an oblong ball. Press into a greased tart pan, forming a thin layer. Bake 12 to 15 minutes. Cool.

To make filling, separate eggs with yolks in one bowl, white in another. Whip yolks with an electric mixer until pale yellow and slightly fluffy. Add milk and lime juice and blend well. Set aside. Whip whites until white and foamy. Slowly mix in sugar. Whip until mixture is white and shiny. Lightly fold yolk mixture into whites with a rubber spatula until blended. Pour over crust in tart pan. Bake at 350 degrees for about 15 minutes. Serve topped with whipped cream.

Frozen Key Lime Pie

Make ahead and keep in the freezer for a great, quick dessert.

1   (14 ounce) can sweetened
     condensed milk
¾   cup lime juice, regular or
     Key lime or combination

2   teaspoons lime zest
1   (12 ounce) container frozen
     whipped topping, thawed
1   pie crust, baked

Mix milk, lime juice and zest. Fold in whipped topping. Pour into pie crust and freeze. To serve, remove from freezer 10 minutes before serving.

Apple Ding-A-Lings

**This is an original recipe devised
during a Maine Noreaster in the 1950's.**

Your favorite crust recipe
  for 2 crust pie
½ cup butter, melted

4-5 Granny Smith or Cortland
    apples
½ cup sugar
1-2 teaspoons cinnamon

Preheat oven to 350 degrees. Roll out pie crust on a floured cloth to
form a rectangle about ⅛ inch thick. Brush crust with melted butter.
Cut crust into 3 inch squares. Cut each apple into 8 wedges. Place
one apple wedge corner to corner on a pastry square. Pull opposite
edges of pastry over apple wedge and pinch together.

Combine sugar and cinnamon. Sprinkle mixture over each apple
pastry. Place pastries on an ungreased baking sheet. Drizzle
remaining butter over top. Bake 15 minutes or until lightly browned.

Sasha's Key Lime Pie

The lightest and most delicious Key lime pie I've ever tasted.

1 (8 ounce) package cream
    cheese
1 (14 ounce) can sweetened
    condensed milk
½ cup freshly squeezed Key
    lime juice
⅓ cup light rum

1 pie crust, baked
    Whipped cream or whipped
    topping
    Lime peel shavings or
    calamondin peel or
    sections for garnish

Beat cream cheese with an electric mixer until smooth. Add milk and
beat until blended. Add lime juice all at once. Mix in rum. Pour
mixture into pie crust.

Freeze pie for several hours or until somewhat firm. Spread whipped
cream on top and garnish.

Robin's Blue Ribbon Apple Pie

A county fair submission
that won my daughter a blue ribbon.

Crust

1½	heaping cups flour	1	tablespoon sugar
⅔	cup vegetable oil	1	tablespoon cinnamon
2	tablespoons whole milk		

Filling

3	pounds apples, peeled and sliced (about 5 cups)	2	tablespoons flour
		2	tablespoons cinnamon
3	tablespoons butter or margarine, cut into pieces	½	cup sugar
			Chopped nuts (optional)

Topping

4	tablespoons cold butter or margarine	⅔	cup flour
		⅔	cup brown sugar

Preheat oven to 400 degrees. Combine all crust ingredients in a 9 inch pie plate and pat into a mound. Press with knuckles into bottom of pan and up the sides, fluting the edges high.

Toss together all filling ingredients and put into crust.

Crumble together topping ingredients or cut together with 2 knives. Sprinkle over top of pie. Bake on a baking sheet for 50 to 60 minutes or until filling bubbles.

Pat's Florida Key Lime Pie

	Juice of 5-6 limes, Key limes preferred	1	(9 inch) pie crust, baked and cooled
1	(14 ounce) can sweetened condensed milk	1	cup heavy cream
		2	teaspoons powdered sugar
3	egg yolks, beaten		Shavings of lime peel for garnish

Preheat oven to 300 degrees. Combine lime juice, milk and egg yolks. Pour into pie crust. Bake 15 minutes. Refrigerate 6 hours or overnight. When ready to serve, whip cream with powdered sugar. Spread over pie. Garnish with lime peel.

Crustless Pear Tart

6 ounces whole, blanched almonds	4 tablespoons unsalted butter, melted
½ cup sugar	1 pound Bosc or Bartlett pears, peeled, halved and cored
⅓ cup flour	
⅛ teaspoon salt	1½ tablespoons sugar
2 eggs	1 tablespoon butter, cut into pieces
¼ cup milk	

Preheat oven to 350 degrees. Blend almonds with ½ cup sugar in a food processor until finely ground. Transfer mixture to a medium bowl. Stir in flour and salt. In a separate bowl, whisk eggs until frothy. Whisk in milk and melted butter. Add mixture to almond mixture and stir until well blended. Pour batter into a greased and floured 9½ inch ceramic dish or tart pan. Spread to form an even layer.

Cut each pear half crosswise into thin slices, keeping slices intact while cutting. Slide each pear half onto a palette knife and transfer to top of batter, slightly fanning slices. Press fanned slices into batter so only the surface of the slices show. Sprinkle tart with 1½ tablespoons sugar and dot with butter pieces.

Bake in upper third of oven for 45 minutes or until batter is puffed and golden. Cool on a rack. Serve directly from the baking dish with whipped cream or ice cream.

Yield: 8 servings

Calamondin Pie

1 cup calamondin puree	1 graham cracker crust, baked
3 eggs, separated	Sugar to taste
1 (14 ounce) can sweetened condensed milk	

Preheat oven to 250 degrees. To prepare calamondin puree, half calamondin and remove seeds. Place halves in blender and process briefly. Beat egg yolks until fluffy. Beat in milk. Stir in puree. Beat one egg white until stiff and fold into yolk mixture. Pour into pie crust.

Beat remaining 2 egg whites with sugar to taste until peaks form. Spread over pie. Bake 15 minutes. Chill before serving.

Strawberry Pie

Meringue Crust

4 egg whites	½ cup granulated sugar
Pinch of cream of tartar	

Filling

1 quart fresh strawberries, sliced	Dash of powdered sugar
	1 pint heavy cream, whipped

Preheat oven to 275 degrees. Beat egg whites and cream of tartar until stiff. Add granulated sugar and beat until smooth. Spoon into a pie pan and spread to form a crust.

Bake 2 hours. Turn off oven but leave crust in oven until cool. Combine strawberries and powdered sugar and place in cooled crust. Top with whipped cream just before serving.

Kentucky Pecan Pie

4	tablespoons butter, softened	¼	teaspoon salt
1	cup sugar	½	cup chopped pecans
3	eggs, beaten	½	cup chocolate chips
¾	cup light corn syrup	1	(9 inch) pie crust, unbaked

Preheat oven to 375 degrees. Cream butter and sugar. Add eggs, corn syrup and salt. Stir in pecans and chocolate chips. Pour into pie crust. Bake 40 to 50 minutes.

Chocolate Silk Pie

Pie

⅔	cup butter, softened	⅓	cup semisweet chocolate chips
1	cup sugar		
3	eggs, well beaten	1	(9 inch) graham cracker pie crust, baked and chilled
2	(1 ounce) squares bittersweet chocolate		

Topping

1	cup heavy cream		Chocolate shavings for garnish
¼	cup sugar		
1	teaspoon vanilla		

Cream butter and sugar with an electric mixer until light. Beat in eggs. Melt chocolate and chocolate chips and blend into creamed mixture. Pour mixture into pie crust and freeze for 2 to 3 hours or overnight.

To make topping, whip cream until thickened. Whip in sugar and vanilla. Spread topping over pie just before serving. Garnish with chocolate shavings.

Hershey Pie

2 cups crushed vanilla wafers	20 marshmallows
4-8 tablespoons butter, melted	1 cup heavy cream
1 (9 ounce) Hershey chocolate bar with almonds	Chocolate or white chocolate shavings for garnish
½ cup milk	

Preheat oven to 350 degrees. Combine wafers and butter in a 9 inch pie pan. Press into a crust and bake 10 minutes. Cool.

In a double boiler, melt chocolate bar, milk and marshmallows together. Cool. Whip cream and fold into chocolate mixture. Pour chocolate filling into crust. Refrigerate at least 2 hours. Serve garnished with chocolate or white chocolate shavings.

Apple Strudel

5 Granny Smith apples, peeled and sliced	½ cup sugar
¼ cup golden raisins	10 layers phyllo dough
1 tablespoon cinnamon	½ cup butter, melted
1½ tablespoons unsalted butter, softened	Sugar for topping

Preheat oven to 325 degrees. Combine apples, raisins, cinnamon, unsalted butter and sugar in a bowl. Brush each layer of phyllo dough with melted butter and stack layers.

Place apple mixture across the center of the stack and roll up dough. Place on a baking sheet and brush top with butter. Sprinkle with sugar. Bake 25 minutes. Serve mit schlag (fresh whipped cream).

Peter's Steak House
3200 N.E. Maple Ave.
Jensen Beach, Florida

Fruit Cobbler

Topping

½ cup butter, softened	1 teaspoon cream of tartar
¾ cup sugar	½ teaspoon salt
1½ cups cake flour	½ cup buttermilk
2 teaspoons baking soda	1 egg

Filling

5 cups fruit of choice	4 teaspoons flour
1 cup sugar	

Preheat oven to 350 degrees. Cream butter and sugar until fluffy. Sift together flour, baking soda, cream of tartar and salt. Add dry ingredients alternately with buttermilk to creamed mixture. Stir in egg.

Combine filling ingredients and place in a ramekin or casserole dish. Dollop topping over fruit. Bake until topping is puffed and brown and a knife inserted in the topping comes out clean.

Cherry Cobbler

Filling

1 (16 ounce) can pitted cherries	3 tablespoons tapioca
½ cup sugar	2 teaspoons lemon juice

Topping

1 cup flour	1 egg
¾ cup sugar	⅔ cup butter, melted
1 teaspoon baking powder	Whipped cream
½ teaspoon salt	

Preheat oven to 350 degrees. Combine all filling ingredients and place in a greased square baking dish.

To make topping, mix together flour, sugar, baking powder and salt. Stir in egg until crumbly. Sprinkle mixture over filling. Drizzle butter on top. Bake 45 minutes. Serve warm with whipped cream.

Neiman Marcus'
$250 Chocolate Chip Cookies

2	cups butter, softened	2	teaspoons baking powder
2	cups sugar	2	teaspoons baking soda
2	cups brown sugar	1	(24 ounce) package chocolate chips
4	eggs		
2	teaspoons vanilla	1	(8 ounce) Hershey chocolate bar, grated
4	cups flour		
5	cups oatmeal	3	cups chopped nuts
1	teaspoon salt		

Preheat oven to 375 degrees. Cream butter and sugars. Beat in eggs and vanilla. Put oatmeal in a food processor and blend until powdery.

In a separate bowl, mix together flour, oatmeal, salt, baking powder and baking soda. Blend dry ingredients into creamed mixture. Stir in chocolate chips, grated chocolate and nuts. Roll into balls and place 2 inches apart on baking sheets. Bake 6 to 10 minutes.

Yield: about 9½ dozen

Everyday Cookies

1	cup butter	3½	cups flour
1	cup oil	1	teaspoon salt
1	cup sugar	1	teaspoon baking soda
1	cup brown sugar	1	teaspoon cream of tartar
1	egg	1	teaspoon vanilla
1	cup Rice Krispies cereal	½	cup walnuts
1	cup dry oatmeal		

Preheat oven to 350 degrees. Cream butter, oil and sugars. Beat in egg. Mix in cereal, oatmeal, flour, salt, baking soda, cream of tartar, vanilla and walnuts. Form into balls and place on ungreased baking sheets. Flatten with a fork. Bake 10 minutes.

Special Chocolate Chip Cookies

2¼ cups all-purpose flour
1 teaspoon baking soda
Dash of salt
1¾ sticks butter, softened
¾ cup sugar
½ cup brown sugar
2 eggs
2 teaspoons vanilla
1 (3 ounce) package instant vanilla pudding mix

1 cup chopped pecans, toasted
1 (12 ounce) package chocolate chips
1 (4 ounce) baking or eating chocolate bar (not squares), broken into pieces

Preheat oven to 375 degrees. Stir together flour, baking soda and salt. Set aside. In a large mixing bowl of an electric mixer, cream butter and sugars. Beat in eggs, one at a time. Add vanilla.

By hand, gradually blend dry ingredients into creamed mixture. Stir in pudding mix. Add pecans, chocolate chips and chocolate bar. Drop by rounded tablespoons onto an ungreased baking sheet. Bake 9 minutes, being careful to not overbake.

Potato Chip Cookies

1 cup butter or margarine, softened
1 cup powdered sugar
1 egg yolk

1 teaspoon vanilla
1½ cups flour
½ cup chopped nuts
¾ cup crushed potato chips

Preheat oven to 350 degrees. Cream butter and sugar. Beat in egg yolk and vanilla. Stir in flour, then nuts and potato chips. Drop by spoonfuls onto a baking sheet; flatten. Bake 15 minutes.

Peanut Butter Cookies

Flourless and fabulous!

1 cup peanut butter	1 egg
1 cup sugar	½ cup chocolate chips

Preheat oven to 350 degrees. Combine all ingredients and drop by spoonfuls onto a baking sheet. Bake 10 to 12 minutes.

Coconut-Almond Macaroons

1½ cups sweetened flaked coconut	½ teaspoon almond extract
1 cup sliced almonds	2 egg whites
2 cups sweetened flaked coconut	1 tablespoon sugar
½ cup sweetened condensed milk	Pinch of salt
	Bittersweet chocolate

Preheat oven to 350 degrees. Grease 2 large baking sheets with shortening. Combine 1½ cups coconut and almonds in a baking pan. Bake, stirring occasionally for 12 minutes or until golden. Cool and place in a large mixing bowl. Add 2 cups coconut, milk and almond extract to the bowl.

In a separate bowl with an electric mixer on high speed, beat egg whites, sugar and salt until soft peaks form. Using a rubber spatula, gently fold egg whites into the coconut mixture.

Using a large spoon, form mounds 2 inches apart on prepared baking sheets. If desired, form smaller mounds for bite-sized cookies. Bake at 350 degrees for 10 minutes or until golden brown. Transfer cookies to wire racks to cool completely.

Meanwhile, place chocolate in a double boiler over barely simmering water. Take care that the pan does not touch the water and that the water does not create steam. Stir gently until chocolate melts. Line 2 baking sheets with wax paper. Dip the bottoms of the cookies in melted chocolate or spread on chocolate with a knife. Place cookies, chocolate-side down, on wax paper. Refrigerate until chocolate is set. Store in an airtight container at room temperature for up to 4 days or refrigerate for longer storage.

Yield: 18 cookies

Butter Snowballs

Also called Russian Tea Cakes.
Very popular for Christmas cookies.

1	cup butter	½	teaspoon salt
½	cup sugar	2	cups finely chopped pecans
2	teaspoons vanilla		Powdered sugar
2	cups sifted flour		

Preheat oven to 325 degrees. Cream butter, sugar and vanilla until fluffy. Sift together flour and salt. Add to creamed mixture and blend thoroughly. Mix in pecans.

Form into 1 inch balls and place on a baking sheet. Bake 20 minutes. Do not allow cookies to brown. Cool. Roll cooled cookies in powdered sugar.

Yield: 6 dozen

Coconut Macaroons Claudet

⅓	cup plus 2 tablespoons unbleached all-purpose flour	⅔	cup fat-free sweetened condensed milk
2½	cups shredded coconut	½	teaspoon vanilla
⅛	teaspoon salt	½	teaspoon almond extract

Preheat oven to 250 degrees. Combine flour, coconut and salt in a bowl. Pour in milk, vanilla and almond extract. Stir well until a thick batter forms. Drop by tablespoons onto a well greased baking sheet, allowing an inch of space between cookies.

Bake 10 minutes. Remove from oven and reshape; they will look like fried eggs, reshape them to look round again. Bake 10 minutes longer or until light golden brown. Remove from baking sheet immediately and cool on wire racks.

Bumblebee Cookies

¾ cup shortening	1 teaspoon ground ginger
1 cup sugar	½ teaspoon cinnamon
¼ cup molasses	½ teaspoon ground cloves
1 egg, lightly beaten	½ teaspoon salt
1½ cups flour	⅓ cup sugar
1 teaspoon baking soda	

Preheat oven to 325 degrees. Cream shortening. Add 1 cup sugar, a little at a time, and beat until light and fluffy. Stir in molasses and egg.

Sift together flour, baking soda, ginger, cinnamon, cloves and salt. Gradually add dry ingredients to creamed mixture. Chill dough until firm enough to handle.

Form dough into ¾ inch balls. Roll in ⅓ cup sugar. Place balls 2 inches apart on a baking sheet. Bake 10 to 12 minutes or until cookies are set but still soft in the center. Cool on wire racks.

Yield: about 4 dozen

Sue's Hermit Cookies

1 cup butter, softened	1 teaspoon cinnamon
3 cups brown sugar	¼ cup milk
4 eggs	Zest of 1 orange
6 cups unsifted flour	2 cups raisins
2 teaspoons baking soda	2 cups chopped currants
1 teaspoon nutmeg	1 cup chopped walnuts

Preheat oven to 350 degrees. Cream butter and sugar in a mixing bowl. Beat in eggs. Sift together flour, baking soda, nutmeg and cinnamon. Blend dry ingredients, alternating with milk, into creamed mixture. Stir in zest, raisins, currants and walnuts. Drop by tablespoons onto a baking sheet. Bake 8 to 10 minutes.

Holiday Fruit Drops

1 cup margarine	½ cup buttermilk
2 cups light brown sugar	1 teaspoon vanilla
2 eggs	1½ cups chopped walnuts or pecans
3½ cups flour	
1 teaspoon baking soda	2 cups halved candied cherries
½ teaspoon salt	2 cups pitted dates

Preheat oven to 350 degrees. Cream margarine and sugar. Beat in eggs. Mix in flour, baking soda and salt. Add buttermilk, vanilla, walnuts, cherries and dates. Stir until mixed. Drop by teaspoons onto a lightly greased baking sheet. Bake 12 to 15 minutes.

Yield: about 8 dozen

Overnight Meringues

2 egg whites, room temperature	¼ teaspoon orange extract
Pinch of salt	½ teaspoon vanilla extract
⅔ cup sugar	1 cup coarsely chopped walnuts
¼ teaspoon almond extract	

Preheat oven to 350 degrees. Beat egg whites and salt until foamy. Gradually add sugar and beat until stiff peaks form. Fold in extracts by hand. Fold in walnuts. Drop by teaspoons onto parchment-lined baking sheets. Mounds can be placed close together as they will not spread while baking.

Place in oven and immediately turn off heat. Leave meringues in oven overnight; do not open oven door to check them until morning.

Yield: 36 meringues

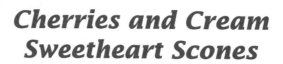

Cherries and Cream
Sweetheart Scones

2 cups all-purpose flour	⅔ cup dried pitted sour cherries
⅓ cup sugar	
1 tablespoon baking powder	1 cup heavy cream
½ teaspoon salt	2 tablespoons all-purpose flour
6 tablespoons unsalted butter, cold, cut into 12 pieces	
	2 tablespoons sugar

Preheat oven to 400 degrees. Combine 2 cups flour, ⅓ cup sugar, baking powder and salt in a large bowl. Blend in butter with a pastry blender or your fingertips until mixture resembles coarse meal. Using a fork, stir in cherries and then cream to form a soft dough. Let stand 2 minutes.

Transfer dough to a lightly floured surface. Sprinkle top of dough with 2 tablespoons flour. Gently press out dough with fingertips into a ½ inch thick round. Cut out scones using a floured heart-shaped cookie cutter and place on baking sheets. Gather dough scraps and repeat to cut out as many scones as possible. Sprinkle scones with 2 tablespoons sugar. Bake 15 minutes or until golden brown. Serve warm or cool on a wire rack and serve at room temperature; best if eaten the same day.

Yield: about 12 scones

Chocolate Raspberry Bars

Crust
1 cup all-purpose flour	½ cup butter or margarine
¼ cup powdered sugar	

Filling
½ cup seedless raspberry jam	2 tablespoons milk
½ (8 ounce) package cream cheese	1 cup vanilla-flavored baking chips, melted

Glaze
¾ cup semisweet chocolate chips	2 tablespoons shortening

Preheat oven to 375 degrees. Combine flour and sugar in a bowl. Cut in butter until crumbly. Press into an ungreased 9 inch square baking pan. Bake 15 to 18 minutes or until browned.

To prepare filling, spread jam over crust while crust is still warm. Beat cream cheese and milk in a small bowl until smooth. Beat in melted baking chips until smooth. Carefully spread over jam. Cool completely, then refrigerate 1 hour or until set.

For glaze, melt chocolate and shortening together and spread over filling. Chill 10 minutes. Cut into bars and chill 1 hour longer. Store in refrigerator.

Yield: 3 dozen

Macadamia Nut Bars

Crust

½ cup butter, softened	1 cup flour
¼ cup sugar	

Filling

2 eggs, lightly beaten	2 tablespoons flour
½ cup flaked coconut	1½ teaspoons vanilla
1½ cups light brown sugar	1 teaspoon baking powder
1½ cups chopped macadamia nuts	

Preheat oven to 350 degrees. Blend crust ingredients and press into the bottom of a 9 inch square baking pan. Bake 20 minutes.

Stir together all filling ingredients and pour over crust while crust is still hot. Bake 20 minutes longer. Cut into bars when cool.

Magnificent Brownies

1 cup sugar	1 tablespoon vanilla
½ cup semisweet or chocolate amaretto cocoa powder	½ cup flour
½ cup butter	Pinch of baking powder
2 eggs	1 cup chopped nuts

Preheat oven to 350 degrees. Combine sugar, cocoa powder and butter in a saucepan. Heat until butter melts.

In a mixing bowl, beat eggs. Add vanilla and beat. Stir in cocoa mixture. Add flour, baking powder and nuts and mix. Place batter in a parchment-lined 8 inch square baking pan. Bake 25 to 40 minutes or until done.

Lemon Bars Deluxe

Crust

2   cups sifted all-purpose flour   1   cup margarine or butter
½   cup sifted powdered sugar

Filling

4   eggs, beaten   ¼   cup all-purpose flour
2   cups granulated sugar   ½   teaspoon baking powder
⅓   cup lemon juice   Powdered sugar for topping

Preheat oven to 350 degrees. Prepare crust by sifting together flour and sugar. Cut in margarine until mixture clings together. Press into a 9x13 inch baking pan. Bake 20 to 25 minutes or until lightly browned.

To make filling, beat eggs, granulated sugar and lemon juice. Sift flour and baking powder together. Add dry ingredients to lemon juice mixture and stir until mixed. Pour over baked crust. Bake 25 minutes. Sprinkle with powdered sugar. Cool before cutting into bars.

Yield: 25 to 30 bars

Julie's Killer Brownies

1   cup butter   4   eggs
4   (1 ounce) squares   1   cup sifted flour
       unsweetened chocolate   ½   teaspoon salt
2   cups sugar   1   cup chopped nuts

Preheat oven to 350 degrees. Melt butter and chocolate in a saucepan over low heat. Add sugar and blend. Beat in eggs, one at a time. Mix in flour, salt and nuts.

Pour batter into a greased 9x13 inch baking pan. Bake 30 minutes or until a toothpick inserted in the center comes out clean.

Caroline's Brownies

Brownies
1	cup butter		1	cup flour
1	cup cocoa		1	cup chopped walnuts, toasted
2	cups sugar			
4	eggs		1	teaspoon vanilla

Glaze
6	tablespoons butter		¼	cup strong brewed coffee
½	cup cocoa powder		2	cups powdered sugar

Preheat oven to 350 degrees. Melt butter in a double boiler. Stir in cocoa and sugar. Beat in eggs, one at a time. Stir in flour, walnuts and vanilla. Pour batter into a 9x13 baking pan. Bake 25 to 30 minutes. Do not overbake. Cool.

To prepare glaze, melt butter in a saucepan. Stir in cocoa and coffee. Mix in powdered sugar. Spread glaze over cooled brownies.

Peanut Butter Bars

1½	cups creamy peanut butter		3	cups powdered sugar
¾	cup butter		1	(6 ounce) package chocolate chips
1½	cups graham cracker crumbs		4	tablespoons butter

In a glass bowl, melt peanut butter and butter together in the microwave. Mix in cracker crumbs and sugar. Press into a greased 11x7 inch pan.

Melt chocolate chips and 4 tablespoons butter together and pour over bars. Freeze 15 to 20 minutes. Store bars in refrigerator.

Texas Sheet Cake

Cake

2	cups sugar
2	cups flour
	Pinch of salt
½	cup butter
½	cup shortening
¼	cup cocoa powder
1	cup water

½ cup buttermilk or ½ cup milk plus 2 tablespoons vinegar
2 eggs
1 teaspoon baking soda
1 teaspoon cinnamon
1 teaspoon vanilla

Topping

½	cup butter
¼	cup cocoa powder
6	tablespoons milk

1 (16 ounce) package powdered sugar
1 teaspoon vanilla
1 cup chopped pecans

Preheat oven to 400 degrees. Combine sugar, flour and salt in a large bowl. In a saucepan, bring butter, shortening, cocoa powder and 1 cup water to a boil. Pour into dry ingredients and mix well. Mix in buttermilk, eggs, baking soda, cinnamon and vanilla. Pour batter into a 12x17x1 inch sheet pan. Bake 12 to 15 minutes.

While cake bakes, prepare topping by combining butter, cocoa and milk in a saucepan. Heat until melted. Bring to a boil. Combine powdered sugar, vanilla and pecans in a bowl. Add cocoa mixture to bowl and mix. Spread over cake while cake is still warm. Cut into squares when cool.

Pecan Dainties

1 egg white
1 cup brown sugar

1½ cups pecan halves

Preheat oven to 350 degrees. Beat egg white until stiff peaks form. Gradually beat in sugar. Fold in pecans. Drop by teaspoons onto a greased baking sheet. Bake about 30 minutes. Remove from baking sheet immediately and cool.

Yield: 3 dozen

Peanut Butter Fudge

My grandmother taught me to make this as a young girl.

2	cups sugar	1	teaspoon vanilla
2	(1 ounce) squares baking chocolate	⅔	cup milk
2	tablespoons butter	2	heaping tablespoons peanut butter

Combine all ingredients except peanut butter in a medium saucepan and bring to a boil. Boil until a small amount of mixture forms a firm ball when dropped into cold water. Remove from heat and add peanut butter. Beat by hand until fudge pulls away from the sides of the pan. Pour onto a baking sheet and spread to even. Cool and cut into bite-size pieces.

Butter Crunch Candy

2	cups sugar	1	(5 ounce) Hershey chocolate bar, grated
½	cup water	1¾	cups finely chopped pecans
¼	cup light corn syrup		
1	cup margarine		

Combine sugar, water, corn syrup and margarine in a heavy skillet. Cook over medium heat, stirring constantly, until a small amount of mixture forms a brittle ball when dropped into cold water. The mixture will be thick and amber colored. Pour immediately onto an ungreased baking sheet and spread to even.

Cool 5 minutes. Sprinkle chocolate over top. Allow to melt, then spread chocolate. Sprinkle with nuts. When completely cooled, break into pieces. Store in an airtight container.

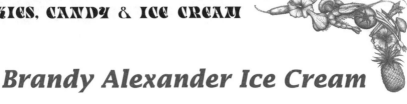

Brandy Alexander Ice Cream

½ gallon vanilla ice cream, softened

½ cup crème de cacao
½ cup brandy

Blend all ingredients and freeze until firm. To serve, scoop into individual serving dishes.

Speedy Peach Ice Cream

1 (16 to 20 ounce) package frozen unsweetened peaches
½ cup sugar

2 teaspoons lemon juice
½ teaspoon vanilla
¾ cup heavy cream

Blend peaches, sugar, lemon juice and vanilla in a blender or food processor. Add cream and process 2 minutes or until smooth. Serve immediately or place processor bowl in freezer. Before serving, scrape sides and process again until smooth.

The World's Best By Far Lime Ice Cream

1 pint heavy cream
1 cup sugar

⅓ cup fresh lime juice or to taste
2-3 tablespoons lime zest

Combine all ingredients in a bowl. Stir well. Freeze at least 5 hours. Serve with fruit, brownies, gingerbread or as desired.

Piña Colada Fruit Dip

1 (8 ounce) can crushed pineapple in own juice, undrained	1 (3½ ounce) package instant coconut pudding
	¾ cup milk
	½ cup sour cream

Combine all ingredients in a blender. Process 30 to 45 seconds. Refrigerate several hours or overnight. Serve with fresh fruit.

Grand Marnier Sauce

2 egg yolks	2 tablespoons Grand Marnier
¼ cup sugar	½ cup heavy cream

Select a 1 quart mixing bowl that will rest snugly on top of a slightly larger saucepan. Add about 2 inches of water to the saucepan and bring to a boil. Add egg yolks and sugar to the mixing bowl. Beat vigorously with a wire whisk, being sure to scrape off the bottom of the bowl. Set bowl in saucepan over but not in the water. Continue beating constantly and vigorously for 10 minutes or until yolks are thick and pale yellow. Remove from heat. Stir in Grand Marnier. Refrigerate until chilled.

Whip cream until stiff and fold into chilled sauce. Serve with poached or fresh fruit; especially good over a mixture of fresh berries.

Raspberry Chocolate Sauce

1 (12 ounce) package frozen raspberries, thawed	4 tablespoons unsalted butter, softened
¾ cup Dutch cocoa powder	1½ cups sugar
¾ cup heavy cream	⅓ cup light corn syrup

Puree raspberries in a food processor. Press through a fine strainer to remove seeds. Set aside.

Whisk together coca powder and cream in a heavy medium saucepan. Add butter, sugar, corn syrup and raspberries. Stir until blended. Bring to a boil over medium heat, stirring often. Boil slowly for 8 minutes without stirring. Remove from heat and pour into a container. Cool 15 minutes before serving, or cover and refrigerate until ready to use. Reheat slowly. Serve over ice cream or cake.

Yield: 2½ cups

Black Cherry Sauce

1 (16 ounce) can pitted dark cherries, drained, juice reserved	1 (12 ounce) jar red currant jelly
	1½ tablespoons kirsch
	Few drops brandy

Pour cherry juice into a saucepan and reduce over medium heat to ⅓ cup. Add jelly and cook until melted. Cool. Stir in kirsch, brandy and cherries. Serve over ice cream, cake or custard.

Marinades, Sauces and Salsas

DAN MALLARDI
Sunset on St. Lucie River
Watercolor, 1999

Marinades, Sauces and Salsas

Marinades

Jane's Marinade
for Chicken, Pork or Shrimp 245
Ruth Ann's Walkers
Cay Fish Marinade 245
Smoked Turkey Marinade 246
Turkey Injection Marinade 246

Sauces and Spreads

Horseradish Sauce 247
Horseradish Mold 247
Horseradish Mustard Sauce 247
Baltimore Tartar Sauce 248
Mustard Sauce 248
Mint Onion Sauce for Lamb 248

Mustard Sauce for
Crab Claws 249
Gus' BarBQ Sauce 249
Sherry Mayonnaise 250
Chipotle Butter 250
Lemon Aïoli for Crab Cakes 250
Marchands De Vin 251
Cheech's Basil Pesto 251
Blender Pesto Sauce 252

Salsas

Mexican-Style Fresh Salsa 252
Jane's Corn Salsa 253
Pam's Black Bean and Mango Salsa ... 253
Judie's "Potpourri" 254

Jane's Marinade
for Chicken, Pork or Shrimp

5	cloves garlic		Juice of 1 lime
1	large bunch fresh cilantro	1	jalapeño, seeded, or
2	teaspoons coriander		chipotle pepper, or ½
1	teaspoon ground cumin		teaspoon cayenne pepper
2	teaspoons salt	½	cup olive oil
1	teaspoon black pepper		

Blend all ingredients in a food processor. Add meat to marinade in a zip-top bag, turning occasionally. Marinate at least 1 hour.

Grill chicken breasts or pork chops 5 minutes on each side. Grill pork tenderloin a total of 15 minutes, turning often. For jumbo shrimp, grill about 2 minutes on each side.

Ruth Ann's Walkers
Cay Fish Marinade

4	tablespoons butter	1	teaspoon dried cilantro
1	teaspoon garlic powder	½	teaspoon Worcestershire
¼	teaspoon dried tarragon		sauce
1	teaspoon Pinch of Herbs		Jarred salsa
	(Lawry's)		

Melt butter in a saucepan or the microwave. Add garlic powder, tarragon, herbs, cilantro and Worcestershire sauce. Mix well. Add salsa, a little at a time, until a paste is formed. Spread on fish before grilling.

Smoked Turkey Marinade

2	cups brown sugar	2	teaspoons peppercorns
2	cups water	5	bay leaves
1½	cups coarse salt	3	cloves garlic
2½	quarts cold water		

Combine sugar, 2 cups water and salt in a saucepan. Heat until mixture dissolves. Combine dissolved mixture with 2½ quarts cold water, peppercorns, bay leaves and garlic in a container large enough to hold a turkey. Add turkey and marinate overnight in the refrigerator.

Turkey Injection Marinade

3	tablespoons salt	1	tablespoon garlic powder
2	tablespoons Creole seasoning	1	tablespoon onion powder
2	tablespoons yellow mustard	1	tablespoon lemon pepper
1	tablespoon celery salt	1	(12 to 13 pound) turkey, thawed and rinsed well
2	tablespoons cayenne pepper		

Combine all ingredients except turkey in a 1 pint mason jar. Add boiling water until jar is three-fourths full. Let stand 1 hour. Strain mixture through cheesecloth, reserving solids.

Use a syringe with a 16 gauge needle or larger to inject marinade into turkey in as many places as possible. Rub reserved marinade solids on the inside cavity and the outside of the turkey. Refrigerate turkey 48 hours before cooking.

Horseradish Sauce

1 tablespoon unsalted butter
1 cup heavy cream
2 tablespoons sherry vinegar
3 tablespoons horseradish,
    prepared or freshly grated

1 drop Tabasco sauce
  Salt and freshly ground
    black pepper to taste

Combine butter, cream and vinegar in a small saucepan. Cook over high heat, stirring constantly 2 to 3 minutes. Remove from heat. Add horseradish and Tabasco sauce. Season with salt and pepper. Serve over grilled tuna or swordfish.

Horseradish Mold

**Looks lovely on a buffet —
unusual. Serve with beef, ham or corned beef.**

1 (3 ounce) package lemon
    jello
½ cup hot water
1 cup cold water

1 tablespoon vinegar
¾ teaspoon salt
¾ cup drained horseradish
1 cup whipped cream

Dissolve jello in hot water. Stir in cold water. Add vinegar and salt. Chill until mixture starts to thicken. Fold in horseradish and cream.

Horseradish Mustard Sauce

½ cup light mayonnaise
½ cup low-fat sour cream
3 tablespoons Dijon mustard

2 tablespoons snipped fresh
    chives
1 tablespoon horseradish
¼ teaspoon black pepper

Combine all ingredients.

Baltimore Tartar Sauce

1	cup mayonnaise	1	tablespoon minced jarred jalapeño pepper
1	tablespoon capers, drained and chopped	1	tablespoon fresh lemon juice
1	tablespoon snipped fresh chives	1	tablespoon chopped fresh tarragon
1	tablespoon minced cornichons	2	tablespoons Dijon mustard
		1	teaspoon Old Bay seasoning
			Salt and pepper to taste

Combine all ingredients. Serve with fish.

Mustard Sauce

Great on flank steak.

2	tablespoons butter	6	tablespoons dry vermouth
2	tablespoons vegetable oil	3	tablespoons capers
6	tablespoons butter	½	teaspoon Worcestershire sauce
2	tablespoons Dijon mustard		

Melt 2 tablespoons butter and oil together in a saucepan over medium heat. Reduce heat to low and stir in 6 tablespoons butter until melted. Mix in mustard, vermouth, capers and Worcestershire sauce.

Mint Onion Sauce for Lamb

¼	cup olive oil	½	bottle Fischer and Wieser 1015 onion glaze
10	medium shallots, diced	1	bunch fresh mint, stemmed

Heat oil in a skillet over medium heat. Add shallots and sauté until golden brown. Add onion glaze and heat. When hot, add mint and remove from heat immediately. Let sauce stand at room temperature for 1 hour before serving over sliced lamb.

Mustard Sauce for Crab Claws

½ cup sour cream
1½ tablespoons prepared
    mustard

2 teaspoons butter or
    margarine, melted
½ teaspoon dried parsley flakes
⅛ teaspoon salt

Combine all ingredients in a nonreactive saucepan. Heat over very low heat until warm, stirring occasionally. Do not bring to a boil. Serve with chilled or warmed crab claws.

Gus' BarBQ Sauce

Braise
⅓ cup lemon juice
5 tablespoons butter

⅓ cup soy sauce

Sauce
1 (32 ounce) bottle ketchup
½ cup brown sugar
¼ cup dry mustard
¼ cup lemon juice
2 cloves garlic, minced
¼ cup Worcestershire sauce

3 tablespoons liquid smoke
¼ cup minced dehydrated
    onion
¼ cup molasses
1 teaspoon Tabasco sauce
½ (12 ounce) can beer

Combine all braise ingredients in a saucepan and heat to melt butter.

To make sauce, combine ingredients in a saucepan and heat until blended.

Spoon braise mixture over meat while cooking. About 30 minutes before meat is done, dip meat in sauce mixture. Continue grilling on both sides until done. Serve extra sauce on the side.

Sherry Mayonnaise

1	egg	¼	cup sherry vinegar
2	egg yolks		Salt and pepper to taste
1	tablespoon Dijon mustard	2	cups corn oil

Combine egg, yolks, mustard, vinegar, salt and pepper in a food processor. With motor running, add oil in a slow, steady stream, blending until thoroughly mixed. Adjust seasoning as needed.

Refrigerate in an airtight container until needed. Use in turkey salad, as a dip for vegetables or cold seafood or on sandwiches.

Chipotle Butter

½	cup unsalted butter, softened	2	tablespoons chopped red
2	canned chipotle peppers		onion
1	clove garlic		Salt and pepper to taste

Process all ingredients in a food processor until completely mixed. Refrigerate at least 30 minutes or up to 3 days. Use as a topping for grilled steaks or seafood, or grilled corn on the cob.

Lemon Aïoli for Crab Cakes

½	cup mayonnaise	2	tablespoons cream
1	clove garlic, minced		Salt and pepper to taste
1	tablespoon lemon juice	¼	teaspoon cayenne pepper

Combine all ingredients in a bowl and whisk until blended. Spoon mixture into a squeeze bottle. Squeeze onto serving plate before adding crab cakes. Serve extra on the side.

Marchands De Vin

¾	cup butter	2	tablespoons flour
⅓	cup minced mushrooms		Dash of cayenne pepper
½	cup minced onion	⅛	teaspoon black pepper
⅓	cup minced green onion	¾	cup beef broth
⅓	cup minced ham	½	cup red wine
2	tablespoons minced garlic		

Melt butter in a skillet. Add mushrooms, onions, ham and garlic, sauté until onions are golden brown. Stir in flour, cayenne and black pepper. Cook 7 to 10 minutes or until well browned. Blend in broth and wine. Simmer on low heat for 35 to 45 minutes.

Yield: 2 cups

Cheech's Basil Pesto

1	stalk celery	1	(5 pound) container walnuts or pine nuts
1	(10 ounce) package fresh spinach leaves	2	cups minced garlic
4	bunches fresh Italian parsley	2	cups extra virgin olive oil
12	bunches fresh basil		Salt and pepper to taste

Run celery, spinach, parsley, basil, nuts and garlic through the fine setting of a meat grinder. Whisk in oil, salt and pepper.

Yield: 1 gallon

This pesto can be divided into small containers and frozen.

Franco's Italian Restaurant and Lounge
1840 N.E. Jensen Beach Blvd.
Jensen Beach, Florida

Blender Pesto Sauce

¼ cup olive oil
1 cup fresh basil leaves
¼ cup fresh parsley leaves
2 cloves garlic, peeled

2 tablespoons Parmesan cheese
2 tablespoons pine nuts or walnuts

Combine all ingredients in a blender. Process until smooth. Use as a sauce for cooked pasta.

Yield: 4 servings

Add milk or warm water for a lighter consistency.

Mexican-Style Fresh Salsa

4 medium tomatoes, diced
1 (28 ounce) can diced tomatoes with juice
1 (4 ounce) can chopped green chiles
1 bunch green onions, chopped
1 medium bunch cilantro, chopped

1 tablespoon salt
1 tablespoon black pepper
2 teaspoons sugar
¼ cup oil
½ teaspoon lemon juice
2 teaspoons soy sauce
2 tablespoons vinegar
1 teaspoon oregano

Combine all ingredients in a large bowl and mix well. Cover and refrigerate overnight to allow flavors to blend. Serve with corn chips, hamburgers, eggs, etc.

Jane's Corn Salsa

2 cups fresh or frozen corn	2 tablespoons seeded and
2 tablespoons minced red bell	minced jalapeño pepper
pepper	¼ cup fresh lime juice
2 tablespoons minced tomato,	2 tablespoons olive oil
seeded	Salt and pepper to taste
3 tablespoons minced red	
onion	

If using frozen corn, rinse under hot water to thaw. Combine all ingredients in a bowl. Refrigerate if making ahead. Serve at room temperature.

Pam's Black Bean and Mango Salsa

1 (16 ounce) can black beans,	½ cup coarsely chopped fresh
drained	cilantro
1 medium mango, peeled and	½ cup fresh lime juice
coarsely chopped	1 tablespoon olive oil
½ cup chopped red onion	Salt and pepper to taste
1 jalapeño pepper, seeded and	
chopped	

Combine all ingredients. If making ahead, refrigerate for up to 24 hours. Serve at room temperature.

For a different taste, a can of drained corn can be substituted for the mango.

Yield: 2½ cups

Judie's "Potpourri"

⅓ cup olive oil
4-5 tablespoons balsamic vinegar
Juice of ½ lime
2 tablespoons sugar
2 tablespoons minced onion
4 ears fresh corn

1 large red bell pepper, chopped
1 stalk celery, chopped
½ bunch fresh parsley, chopped
2 (16 ounce) cans black beans, drained
Gorgonzola cheese (optional)

Combine oil, vinegar, lime juice and sugar in a large mixing bowl. Add onion and let stand to marinate while preparing other ingredients.

Boil corn 3 minutes. Cut kernels from cob. Add corn kernels, bell pepper, celery and parsley to oil mixture. Toss well and let stand at least 5 minutes. Add beans and mix well. If desired, sprinkle with cheese.

Acknowledgements and Index

JULIA KELLY
Krueger Creek Boathouse
Watercolor, 1999

Cookbook Development Committee of
Treasures of the Tropics

Cookbook Chairman: Pam Gardner
Assistant Chairman: Claudet Mitchell

Committee:

Jackie Awad-Jocom
Sharron Akers
Pat Baxter
Barbara Blews
Evelyn Braden
Pat Branning
Cheryl Cenderilli
Linda Coburn
Judy Cole
Judy Crompton
Glenna DeMichael
Mary Dorrance
Claire Downey
Kathryn Ford
Lynn Haynes
Gayle Harrell

Molly Hoffman
Pam Lambros
Emma Lennon
Suzanne Matlack
Susan McDonald
Kathlyn Maguire
Judy Mergler
Tracy Natiello
Carol Paul
Judy Rosasco
Linda Schwaderer
Jo Stevenson
Bonnie Tadross
Eileen Taronto
Nancy Whipkey
Emily Waage

Judie Wolfe

The Treasure Coast and Indian River Chapters
of the Hibiscus Children's Center Guild wish to thank
our members, families and friends for submitting their treasured
recipes, for testing the many selections and enthusiastically
supporting the development of this cookbook. We are truly grateful to
all the individuals and restaurants who contributed so generously to
Treasures of the Tropics.

Sharon Akers
Ginny Askew
Kristi Bennett Awad
Shirley Baer
Jennifer Baker
Demma Bailey
Pat Baxter
Barbara Blews
Jill Borowitz
Kathy Bozarth
Evelyn Braden
Patricia Branning
Carol Brilley
Kathleen Broaderick
Barb Brogan
Sarah Bryan
Judy Chisholm
Kathlyn Clark
Judy Cleaver
Linda Coburn
Judy Cole
Helen Cooper
Nancy Crake
Maralyn Crape
Pat DeLettre
Len Dinter
Veronica Doherty
Mary Dorrance
Claire Downey
Dareth Dunn
Kathryn Ford
Lisa Foster

Jane Fox
Pam Gardner
Frances Goode
Margaret Gray
Allison Patton Gregorczyk
Shane Gregorczyk
Susan Halliburton
Rene Hankins
Gayle Harrell
Pam Helmick
Lynne Henderson
Molly Hoffman
Joyce Humboldt
Mary Kelly
Kristen Kraunsae
Pam Lambros
Jackie Lazarus
Emma Lennon
Rosemary Lizars
Mary Ann Loveday
Wendy Lustgarten
Toni MacDonald
Mitch Malone
Julie Haynes Malone
Nicole Matlack Mader
Suzanne Matlack
Jimi McCormick
Julie Schwaderer McGrath
Barbara McKinney
Bertha McManus
Virginia Meier
Lynda Meldeau

Margaret Meldeau
Judy Mergler
Claudet Mitchell
Monica Manno
Eileen Morris
Desiree Mufson
Ruth Ann Nordgren
Gus Nordgren
Lynne Pappas
Diane Parsons
Brenda Parvus
Kelly Patton
Carol Paul
Mary Ann Plate
Linda Jo Pomerance
Bryna Potsdam
Murielle Potsdam
Mary Rappaport
Margaret Richebourg
Michele Reimer
Anne Salvatori
Linda Schwaderer
Margaret Schwaderer

Frances Shear
Jerry Sica
Diane Simpson
Mary Stanley
Jo Stevenson
Chris Sweet
Bonnie Tadross
Hayley Haynes Taylor
Jenna Nehls Taylor
Robyn Thulin
LaVaughn Tilton
Lynn Timothy
Emily Waage
Pat Weber
Mrs. L.H. Welch
Nancy Whipkey
Judy Williams
Maryann Williams
Roseann Wolcott
Judie Wolfe
Ann Young
Carol Zehfuss

Restaurant Contributors

11 Maple Street
Ballantrae Golf & Yacht Club
Black Marlin
Conchy Joe's
David's in the Courtyard
Dockside
Dolphin Bar
Fish Tails
Flagler Grill
Franco's Italian Restaurant
John's Island Country Club
Olive Garden

Orchid Island Golf & Beach
  Club
Peter's Steak House
Prawnbroker
Ruth's Chris Steak House
Sailfish Point Country Club
Seminole Inn
Sonya's - Disney's Vero
  Beach Resort
Tango's
Twisted Grille
Upton Grill
Yacht & Country Club

About the Artists

Meg Winter Carell

Tropical Daydreams, watercolor, 1999

When Meg Carell sits down at a canvas, the beauty of the tropics is just a few brush strokes away. Her art encourages the viewer to mentally escape to a Bahamian Island, feel the warm sand and gentle breezes or sail leisurely down a Florida river with the sound of the ocean a few miles away. Carell perceives her painting as a celebration of the beauty of the tropics. Her watercolors reflect the warmth and sunshine so vividly associated with the southern climates. Meg earned a BFA from Loyola University and also studied at the Accademia Bella Arti in Rome. Her work can be found in many private and corporate collections throughout the United States.

Design Showcase   Stuart, Florida   (561) 287-8666   Mcarrell@bellsouth.net

Linda Coburn

Tea By The Sea, oil, 1999

A charter member of The American Impressionist Society, Linda especially enjoys capturing the gentle wonderment of childhood...as expressed in her painting, *Tea By The Sea,* from the collection of Joan and King Durant. Originally from Baltimore, MD., Linda now splits her time between the Treasure Coast of Florida and the mountains of North Carolina. Linda has been an active Hibiscus Guild member for nine years and an ardent contributor to the Center.

Home Gallery   Palm City, Florida   (561) 286-4966   Agent: Joan Canizares   (561) 220-2337

Norma DeSantis

Summer Table, watercolor, 2000

Norma DeSantis is best known for her floral paintings and fanciful studies of children at play. She is a "wet and wet" watercolorist, a technique that involves wetting both sides of the paper. Not many people do this kind of watercolor and it is difficult to control but the results are amazing. The primary colors run together and it gives the painting a glow. As the paper dries, more color and detail are added. She is careful not to add too much detail to her paintings. Instead, she suggests images through light and color. She has studied with nationally renowned teachers and participates in many local art fairs and exhibits. She had a one-woman show at the Elliott Museum.

Home Gallery   Jensen Beach, Florida   (561) 334-5652

Margaret Gray

At Home In Paradise, watercolor, 2000

From garden scenes, to wildlife, to floral studies, Margaret plumbs the depths of nature to impart her singular viewpoint and signature style through a series of dramatic and original paintings. A former flower shop owner, she turned to painting to express her artistic visions. At her home in the midst of the South Florida landscape, Margaret is provided with an abundance of subject matter, as the intense sunlight, with it's constantly lengthening shadows, highlight the indigenous flora and fauna which come to life on Margaret's canvases. Her work was chosen as a cover for the Hibiscus Children's Center's Christmas Card and as the 1999 poster for ArtsFest. Gray is an award-winning artist and serves on the Public Art Advisory Board and Exhibition Committee in Martin County. She maintains affiliations with many organizations and galleries and has participated in juried, solo and group shows in Florida.

Home Gallery   Palm City, Florida   (561) 283-0204   margaretlgray@yahoo.com

Julia Kelly

Krueger Creek Boathouse, watercolor, 1999

A native of Provincetown, Massachusetts, Julia grew up in an environment rich in subject matter and vivid light. Enjoying an Impressionist's view of the world, she paints directly from nature and redesigns the ideas into large formats in her studio. She utilizes both watercolor and oils, where drawing, composition and color all play key roles in her works. Powerful compositions entice the viewer to linger in her Utopian vistas. It is the excitement and passion she feels for nature and for color against color that gives her paintings the lively quality they possess. She has been featured at numerous galleries throughout the United States and her work can be found in many corporate and private collections.

Home Gallery   Stuart, Florida   (561) 283-8519   kelper@bellsouth.net

Terry Madden

Magnolia & Teacup, watercolor, 1999

Terry began painting later in life and has become an award-winning watercolor artist, hosts an instructional PBS television series on painting with watercolor and teaches live workshops throughout the United States. He began learning on this own and developed a fun, casual style. His passion for art and his natural love for children inspired a program -Art for Life Excellence - that he hopes to launch in America's schools and communities to help popularize art and recognize the important role art plays in developing leadership characteristics in children and balanced lives in adults.

Madden Galleries   Stuart, Florida   (561) 287-4988   Terrymadden.com

Robin Lee Mackowski

Succulents, watercolor, 2000

Robin's work is inspired by her connection with nature and her desire to preserve the environment. She has worked with the Wild Dolphin Project for ten years, having many encounters with wild Atlantic spotted dolphins and participating in two documentaries filmed on the research vessel. She has illustrated more than 25 children's books, nine of which she also authored. Her illustrations have appeared in the National Geographic Magazine and the New York Times. She has illustrated posters for The Discovery Channel, the Wild Dolphin Project and two posters for the American Cetacean Society, which were featured in the movie Free Willy.

Ocean Imagery   Hobe Sound, Florida   (561) 287-0818   LaArtista@aol.com

Dan Mallardi

Sunset on St. Lucie River, watercolor, 1999

A graduate of the Cooper Union Art School in New York, Dan majored in architecture and continued his studies in anatomy, perspective and drawing in Paris. He began drawing at an early age and won a New York City-wide competition for school children. Painting in watercolor, oil and acrylics, he is known for his realism and eye for detail. He has taught watercolor at IRCC, Martin County Council for the Arts and Martin County Cultural Center. His paintings have been displayed in many local, as well as national, galleries and he has had a one-man show at the Elliott Museum.

Home Gallery   Stuart, Florida   (561) 335-5790   flatopdann@aol.com

Jean Sanders

Dining Room, watercolor, 1999

Jean Sanders paints her surroundings: portraits, gardens, interiors and landscapes with a whimsical style that invites you to come in and be a part of the painting. She has won numerous awards for her paintings, including the Y2K, New Media/News Genres 1999. Jean's work hangs in many corporate and private collections. Her festive and creative paintings have been chosen for two years to be one of the featured covers of the Hibiscus Children's Center's Holiday Cards.

Design Showcase   Stuart, Florida   (561) 221-9226   Sandfam@treco.net

Brian Sylvester

Yellowfins, acrylic and oil, 2000

Brian, a Stuart native, was introduced at an early age to the environment and life forms he now loves to paint. Although paying attention to the forms, patterns and colors found in nature, his paintings reflect a creative perspective of the natural world.

Believing conservation is essential to protecting our fragile ecosystem, Brian captures the beauty of nature, reminding us that it should remain unspoiled and enjoyed for many years to come. He was awarded "Best of Show" at the 1999 A.E. Backus Art Festival. His work may be seen in Florida Sportsman's 2000-2001 "Fish of the Month" series featuring larval illustrations using Brian's own unique style. He has done graphic design work and logos for many marine companies and participates in art shows and festivals. He also created the corner illustration found on each page of the cookbook.

Home Studio   Stuart, Florida   (561) 219-2768   bsylvesterart.com

A heartfelt thanks goes out to all the artists who submitted their work for consideration, for their continued support of the Hibiscus Children Center, for their commitment to fight abuse and for helping make a difference in the many lives of the children and families we serve.

A

Almond Cake with Plum
  Compote 206
Angel Hair Commotion 106
Angel Hair Pasta with Lemon
  and Pine Nuts 113
Angel Hair with
  Puttanesca Sauce 115
Angry Pork Tenderloin 161

Appetizers *(also see Dips and Spreads)*
Baked Nuts 7
Bay Scallop Ceviche 24
Cheese Wafers 9
Clams Oreganatta 26
Cocktail Meatballs 16
Conch Fritters 25
Crabmeat Quarters 27
Empanadas
  (Little Meat Pies) 18
Grilled Texas Shrimp 21
Jalapeño Cheese Squares ... 9
King Crab Puffs 27
Marinated Grilled Shrimp 20
Miami Chicken Wings 19
Mini Beef Wellingtons 17
Mont Blanc
  Chicken Spread 20
Mushrooms à la Russe 15
Mushrooms in
  Patty Shells 15
Old English Cheese
  Hors d'oeuvres 7
Olive Spread on Crostini 14
Parmesan Spinach Balls 14
Pickled Shrimp 21
Pickled Shrimp and
  Mushrooms 22
Salted Pecans 8
Shrimp Bread 23
Shrimp Pesto Canapés 24
Shrimp Snacks 22
Spicy Chicken Quesadillas 19
Temptation Appetizers 9
Thai Pot Stickers 30

Apples
Apple Ding-A-Lings 221
Apple or Pear Cake 205
Apple Pound Cake 201
Apple Strudel 226
Apple Stuffed
  Chicken Breast 132
Robin's Blue Ribbon
  Apple Pie 222
Sauerkraut and Apples 179
Sissy's Orange-Cream
  Fruit Salad 63
Sonoma Salad 73
Summer Salad 60

Artichokes
Artichoke and Mushroom
  Chicken 130
Artichoke Crab Spread 29
Baked Crock of Artichoke,
  Brie and Lump Crab 28
Chilled Artichoke Hearts
  and Peas 56
Grouper Provolone 86
Hot Crab and
  Artichoke Dip 29
Layered Greek Salad 66
Opulent Chicken 125
Paella Salad 74
Spinach Soufflé 171

Asparagus
Fresh Asparagus Salad 64
Aspirin Cake 193
Australia's Finest Sticky
  Toffee Pudding 215

Avocado
Bow Tie Pasta Salad 70
California Gazpacho 51
Chutney Chicken Salad 78
Fruit and Almond Salad
  with Curry Vinaigrette
  Dressing 61
Hearts of Palm Salad 55
Mandarin Orange Salad 60

B

Baby Carrot Soup 46
Bacon, Tomato and Fish
    Casserole 89
Bahamian Grouper 88
Bahamian Pigeon Peas
    and Rice 188
Baked Asian Fish Packets 93
Baked Crock of Artichoke,
    Brie and Lump Crab 28
Baked Nuts 7
Baked Orzo 187
Baked Squid with
    Garlic Anchovy Pasta 109
Baltimore Tartar Sauce 248
Bananas
    Banana Nut Bread 34
    Banana Split Cake 199
    Best Banana Bread Ever 34
    Caribbean Banana
        Snapper 88
    Fresh Fruit Cake 198
    Snapper Martinique 91
Basil Butter 100
Basil Marinated Fish 95
Basmati Rice with Dried
    Fruits and Nuts 189
Bay Scallop Ceviche 24
Bayou Pasta Salad 70
Beans and Peas
    Bahamian Pigeon Peas
        and Rice 188
    Baked Lima Beans 171
    Black Bean Soup 47
    Chilled Artichoke Hearts
        and Peas 56
    Dolphin Safe Pasta 71
    Don's Slow Cooked
        Baked Beans 183
    Green Bean and
        Mozzarella Salad 64
    Green Beans
        with Pecans 172

Hearty Tortilla Soup 53
Judie's "Potpourri" 254
Layered Greek Salad 66
Lentil-Rice Burgers 113
Mike Szary's Black Beans
    and Rice 133
Minted Pea Soup 46
Nantucket Cassoulet 127
New Year's Day Caviar 8
Pam's Black Bean and
    Mango Salsa 253
Quick Cassoulet 128
Sabana (Beef
    Tenderloin Mexicana) 145
Savory Cream Peas 184
Texas Stir-Fry 130
Vegetable Casserole 176
Béchamel Sauce 164
Beef
    Fillet
        Beef Wellington 144
        Steak Diane 147
    Ground Beef
        Beef Bar-B-Que 153
        Cocktail Meatballs 16
        Don's Slow Cooked
            Baked Beans 183
        Fred's Meatloaf 154
        Horseradish Meatloaf 152
        Mexican Lasagna 150
        Picadillo 153
        Texas Five Alarm Chili 55
    Roast
        Prime Rib with Roasted Garlic
            and Horseradish Crust 146
    Steak
        Steak Fajitas 148
        Top Round Steak with
            Jalapeño Marinade 147
    Stew Beef
        Beef Bourguignonne 149
        Burgundy Stew 150

The Best Chicken
  Fried Steak 152

Tenderloin
Beef Tenderloin 143
Grilled Fillet of Beef 142
Mini Beef Wellingtons 17
Sabana (Beef Tenderloin
  Mexicana) 145
Savory Roast
  Fillet of Beef 142
Steak Salad 72
Tournedos of Beef
  Tenderloin Roquefort 143
Beer Bread 36

Bell Peppers
Bayou Pasta Salad 70
Fred's Meatloaf 154
Grilled Chicken Breast
  with Pineapple Salsa 134
Mike Szary's Black Beans
  and Rice 133
Steak Fajitas 148
Best Banana Bread Ever 34
Best Ever Cornbread 32
Black Bean Soup 47
Black Cherry Sauce 243
Blender Pesto Sauce 252
Blue Cheese Dressing 82

Blueberries
Key Lime Bread
  with Blueberries 36
Bow Tie Pasta Salad 70
Braised Veal Shanks (Osso Buco) with
  White Wine, Butter
  and Lemon Sauce 158
Brandy Alexander
  Ice Cream 241
Bread and Butter Pudding 214
Bread Pudding 213

Breads
Banana Nut Bread 34
Beer Bread 36
Best Banana Bread Ever 34

Best Ever Cornbread 32
Easy Living Coffee Cake 37
Jalapeño Cornbread 32
Jordan Pond
  House Popovers 31
Key Lime Bread
  with Blueberries 36
Oatmeal Sunflower
  Seed Bread 35
Peppery Cheese Bread 33
Pumpkin Coffee Cake 39
Pumpkin Ring 40
Raisin Bread 33
Robert Frost Popovers 31
Sour Cream Coffee Cake 38
Zucchini
  Pineapple Bread 35

Breakfast and Brunch
Crustless Spinach Quiche 44
Dixie's "Leekless" Quiche 43
Easy Living Coffee Cake 37
Eggs Hussarde 39
Mexican Breakfast Casserole . . . 41
Overnight Egg and Sausage
  Casserole 42
Pumpkin Coffee Cake 39
Scrambled Egg Casserole 41
Sour Cream Coffee Cake 38
Southern Cheese Grits 40
Brie with Sun-Dried Tomatoes . . . 12

Broccoli
Broccoli and Rice
  Casserole 170
Broccoli Salad 67
Broccoli Soufflé with
  Almonds 170
Broccoli with Deviled
  Cream Sauce 169
Cheesy Broccoli Bisque 45
Cheesy Broccoli-
  Corn Strudel 112
Chicken Stir-Fry 131
Fusilli with Broccoli,
  Sicilian Style 119

Sweet-and-Sour
 Broccoli 169
Swiss Vegetable
 Medley 174
Broque Potatoes 186
Bumblebee Cookies 232
Burgundy Stew 150
Butter Crunch Candy 240
Butter Snowballs 231

C

Cabbage
Chinese Chicken Salad
 with Noodles 75
Napa Salad 69
Stuffed Cabbage 151

Cakes *(also see Candy, Chocolate, Cookies and Bars, Desserts, and Pies)*
Almond Cake with
 Plum Compote 206
Apple or Pear Cake 205
Apple Pound Cake 201
Aspirin Cake 193
Banana Split Cake 199
Chocolate, Chocolate
 Chip Cake with
 Powdered Sugar 197
Fresh Fruit Cake 198
Frosting Cake 206

Frostings and Icings
 Cream Cheese Frosting 202
 Frosting 193
 Glaze 40
Granny Shear's
 1-2-3-4 Pound Cake 203
Lite Angel Food Torte 201
Low-Fat Chocolate Torte 197
Macadamia Fudge Torte 196
Mandarin Orange Cake 200
Miracle Cake 204
Old Fashion Prune Cake 205

Out Of This World
 Fruitcake 199
Popcorn Cake 203
Red Velvet Cake 193
Sinful Chocolate Cake 194
Texas Sheet Cake 239
The Best Carrot Cake 202
Winner's
 Chocolate Cake 195
Calamondin Pie 224
California Gazpacho 51

Candy *(also see Cakes, Chocolate, Cookies and Bars, Desserts, and Pies)*
Butter Crunch Candy 240
Peanut Butter Fudge 240
Capellini with Veal and
 Tomatoes 155
Caramel-Coconut Pie 216
Caribbean Banana Snapper 88
Caroline's Brownies 238

Carrots
Baby Carrot Soup 46
Lucy's Marinated Carrots 174
The Best Carrot Cake 202

Casseroles
Bacon, Tomato and Fish
 Casserole 89
Broccoli and Rice
 Casserole 170
Cheesy Broccoli-
 Corn Strudel 112
Chicken and Rice Bake 134
Chiles Rellenos Casserole 181
Corn and Cheese Pie
 with Chiles 180
Kelly's Veggie Enchilada
 Casserole 111
Mexican Breakfast
 Casserole 41
Mom's Shrimp
 Casserole Au Gratin 103
Nantucket Cassoulet 127

INDEX

North Carolina
  Tomato Pie 181
Overnight Egg and
  Sausage Casserole 42
Quick Cassoulet 128
Rice and Onion
  Casserole 191
Scrambled Egg Casserole 41
Southwest Potato
  Casserole 185
Squash Pie 175
Turkey Casserole 138
Vegetable Casserole 176
Cheech's Basil Pesto 251

Cheese
Bacon, Tomato and Fish
  Casserole 89
Baked Crock of Artichoke,
  Brie and Lump Crab 28
Brie with Sun-Dried
  Tomatoes 12
Cheese Wafers 9
Cheesey Rigatoni 192
Cheesy Broccoli Bisque 45
Cheesy Broccoli-
  Corn Strudel 112
Cheesy Summer Squash 175
Chicken Dijon Parmesan 136
Chicken Linguine with
  Sun-Dried Tomatoes
  and Olives 139
Chiles Rellenos Casserole 181
Corn and Cheese Pie
  with Chiles 180
Cottage Potatoes 185
Crabmeat Quarters 27
Crustless Spinach Quiche 44
Feta Stuffed Herbed
  Chicken Breasts 124
Fresh Tomato Pizza
  with Sausage 163
Goat Cheese Salad with
  Warm Dressing 57

Green Bean and
  Mozzarella Salad 64
Grilled Texas Shrimp 21
Hot Chili Dip 18
Jalapeño Cheese Squares 9
Jalapeño Cornbread 32
Kelly's Veggie Enchilada
  Casserole 111
Mandarin Orange Salad 60
Marinated Goat Cheese 12
Mexican Breakfast
  Casserole 41
Mexican Lasagna 150
Mom's Onion Shortcake 179
Mom's Shrimp Casserole
  Au Gratin 103
Old English Cheese
  Hors d'oeuvres 7
Olive Spread on Crostini 14
Overnight Egg and
  Sausage Casserole 42
Parmesan Spinach Balls 14
Penne with Sun-Dried
  Tomato Sauce 118
Peppery Cheese Bread 33
Pizza Bianco 114
Pork Chop Potato Bake 161
Quick and Easy Macaroni
  and Cheese 191
Rice and Onion
  Casserole 191
Roquefort Potato
  Gratin 184
Scrambled Egg Casserole 41
Shrimp and Lobster
  Linguine 102
Smoked Turkey Salad 79
Sonoma Salad 73
Southern Cheese Grits 40
Spicy Chicken
  Quesadillas 19
Swiss Chicken Bake 131

INDEX

Swiss Vegetable Medley 174
Temptation Appetizers 9
Tournedos of Beef
    Tenderloin Roquefort 143
Trio Pesto Goat Cheese
    Cake 10
Tuna Angel Hair Pasta 99
Walnut and Goat Cheese
    Salad with Raspberry
    Dressing 54
Warm Spinach Dip 13
Zucchini Stuffed with
    Corn and Cheese 172
Cheesecake 208

Cherries
Black Cherry Sauce 243
Cherries and Cream
    Sweetheart Scones 234
Cherry Cobbler 227
Holiday Fruit Drops 233

Chicken (also see Turkey)
Apple Stuffed
    Chicken Breast 132
Artichoke and Mushroom
    Chicken 130
Chicken and Dumplings 136
Chicken and Linguine 138
Chicken and Rice Bake 134
Chicken Breast with Creamy
    Mustard Sauce 137
Chicken Cacciatore 121
Chicken Dijon Parmesan 136
Chicken French
    Country Style 122
Chicken Linguine with
    Sun-Dried Tomatoes
    and Olives 139
Chicken Livers Fabuloso 140
Chicken Louisa 132
Chicken Mushroom in
    Puff Pastry Shells 135
Chicken Paprikash 125
Chicken Salad 77

Chicken Stir-Fry 131
Chicken with Fig and
    Port Sauce 135
Chinese Chicken Salad
    with Noodles 75
Chutney Chicken Salad 78
Curry Cajun Chicken 120
Dill Chicken Salad 75
Easy Chinese
    Chicken Salad 79
Feta Stuffed Herbed
    Chicken Breasts 124
Fresh Mushroom
    Chicken Soup 51
Garlicky Chicken 122
Grilled Chicken Breast
    with Pineapple Salsa 134
Lemon Chicken
    with Cashews 137
Miami Chicken Wings 19
Mike Szary's Black Beans
    and Rice 133
Mont Blanc
    Chicken Spread 20
Moroccan Chicken 129
Nantucket Cassoulet 127
North African Roast Chicken
    Thighs with Raisins,
    Almonds and Apricots 126
Opulent Chicken 125
Paella Salad 74
Pam's Oriental
    Chicken Salad 76
Perfect Roast Chicken 120
Quick Cassoulet 128
Sonoma Salad 73
Southern Pecan Encrusted
    Chicken with a Warm
    Berry Sauce 121
Spicy Chicken
    Quesadillas 19
Spinach Stuffed
    Chicken Breasts 123
Swiss Chicken Bake 131

Texas Stir-Fry 130
Thai Pot Stickers 30
Chicken Livers Fabuloso 140
Chilean Sea Bass over Portobella
    Mushroom with a Roasted
    Red Bell Pepper Sauce 94
Chiles Rellenos Casserole 181
Chili *(also see Soups, Stews and*
Chowders)
    Texas Five Alarm Chili 55
Chilled Artichoke Hearts
    and Peas · · · · · · · · · · · · · 56
Chilled Mint-Cucumber
    Yogurt Soup · · · · · · · · · · · 50
Chinese Chicken Salad with
    Noodles 75
Chipotle Butter 250
Chocolate *(also see Cakes, Candy,*
Desserts, and Pies)
    Butter Crunch Candy 240
    Caroline's Brownies 238
    Chocolate, Chocolate
        Chip Cake with
        Powdered Sugar 197
    Chocolate Fondue 210
    Chocolate Mousse 211
    Chocolate Peanut
        Butter Pie 219
    Chocolate Pecan Pie 218
    Chocolate Pudding
        or Pie Filling 210
    Chocolate
        Raspberry Bars 235
    Chocolate Silk Pie 225
    Classic Tiramisu 204
    Death By Chocolate 194
    Frozen Chocolate Crêpes
        with Vanilla Custard
        Sauce 212
    Hershey Pie 226
    Julie's Killer Brownies 237
    Macadamia Fudge Torte 196

Magnificent Brownies 236
Miracle Cake 204
Neiman Marcus' $250
    Chocolate Chip Cookies 228
Peanut Butter Bars 238
Peanut Butter Cookies 230
Peanut Butter Fudge 240
Raspberry
    Chocolate Sauce 243
Sinful Chocolate Cake 194
Special Chocolate Chip
    Cookies 229
Texas Sheet Cake 239
Turtle Pecan Cheesecake 209
Warm Chocolate Gâteau 208
White Chocolate
    Cheesecake 207
Winner's Chocolate Cake 195
Chutney Chicken Salad 78
Clams Oreganatta 26
Classic Creamy Risotto 188
Cocktail Meatballs 16
Coconut
    Caramel-Coconut Pie 216
    Coconut Macaroons
        Claudet 231
    Coconut Rice 190
    Coconut-Almond Macaroons 230
    Granola 38
    Out Of This World
        Fruitcake 199
    The Best Carrot Cake 202
Cold Cucumber Soup 50
Conch Chowder 54
Conch Fritter 25
Condiments and Relishes *(also see*
Marinades, and Sauces and Seasonings)
    Baltimore Tartar Sauce 248
    Basil Butter 100
    Cheech's Basil Pesto 251
    Chipotle Butter 250

Curry Mayonnaise 74
Horseradish Mustard
   Sauce 247
Horseradish Sauce 247
Jane's Corn Salsa 253
Lemon Aïoli
   for Crab Cakes 250
Marchands De Vin 251
Mint Onion Sauce
   for Lamb 248
Mustard Sauce 248
Mustard Sauce for
   Crab Claws 249
Pam's Black Bean and
   Mango Salsa 253
Sherry Mayonnaise 250

Cookies and Bars (also see Cakes,
Candy, Chocolate, Desserts, and Pies)
Bumblebee Cookies 232
Butter Snowballs 231
Caroline's Brownies 238
Chocolate Raspberry Bars 235
Coconut Macaroons
   Claudet 231
Coconut-Almond
   Macaroons 230
Everyday Cookies 228
Holiday Fruit Drops 233
Lemon Bars Deluxe 237
Macadamia Nut Bars 236
Magnificent Brownies 236
Neiman Marcus' $250
   Chocolate Chip Cookies 228
Overnight Meringues 233
Peanut Butter Bars 238
Peanut Butter Cookies 230
Pecan Dainties 239
Potato Chip Cookies 229
Special Chocolate
   Chip Cookies 229
Sue's Hermit Cookies 232

Corn
Cheesy Broccoli-
   Corn Strudel 112
Corn and Cheese Pie
   with Chiles 180
Dolphin Safe Pasta 71
Frogmore Stew 104
Hearty Tortilla Soup 53
Jane's Corn Salsa 253
Judie's "Potpourri" 254
Kelly's Veggie Enchilada
   Casserole 111
Mom's Onion Shortcake 179
Southern Corn Pudding 180
Southwest Potato
   Casserole 185
Texas Stir-Fry 130
Vegetable Casserole 176
Zucchini Stuffed with
   Corn and Cheese 172
Cottage Potatoes 185
Couscous
Moroccan Chicken 129
Crab Dip 26
Crabmeat Quarters 27
Cranberries
Cranberry Salad 68
Sonoma Salad 73
Creamy Five Onion Soup 49
Crustless Pear Tart 223
Crustless Spinach Quiche 44
Cucumbers
California Gazpacho 51
Chilled Mint-Cucumber
   Yogurt Soup 50
Cold Cucumber Soup 50
Cucumber Salad 65
Emerald Salad 69
Marinated
   Cucumber Salad 65
Curry Cajun Chicken 120
Curry Mayonnaise 74

INDEX

D

Dates
Australia's Finest Sticky
    Toffee Pudding 215
Holiday Fruit Drops 233
Out Of This World
    Fruitcake 199
Death By Chocolate 194

Desserts *(also see Cakes, Candy,*
Chocolate, Cookies and Bars, and Pies)
Apple Ding-A-Lings 221
Apple Strudel 226
Australia's Finest Sticky
    Toffee Pudding 215
Black Cherry Sauce 243
Brandy Alexander
    Ice Cream 241
Bread and Butter
    Pudding 214
Bread Pudding 213
Cheesecake 208
Cherry Cobbler 227
Chocolate Fondue 210
Chocolate Pudding
    or Pie Filling 210
Classic Tiramisu 204
Crustless Pear Tart 223
Frozen Chocolate Crêpes
    with Vanilla Custard
    Sauce 212
Fruit Cobbler 227
Grand Marnier Sauce 242
Key Lime Mousse Tart 220
Mexican Flan 211
Piña Colada Fruit Dip 242
Pumpkin Delight 216
Raspberry
    Chocolate Sauce 243
Speedy Peach Ice Cream 241
Summer Fruit "Tart" 217
The World's Best By Far
    Lime Ice Cream 241

Three-Ginger
    Gingerbread 200
Turtle Pecan
    Cheesecake 209
Warm Chocolate Gâteau 208
White Chocolate
    Cheesecake 207
Dijon Veal 156
Dill Chicken Salad 75

Dips and Spreads *(also see Appetizers)*
Artichoke Crab Spread 29
Brie with Sun-Dried
    Tomatoes 12
Crab Dip 26
Hot Chili Dip 18
Hot Crab and Artichoke Dip . . . 29
Hot Pecan Spread 16
Marinated Goat Cheese 12
New Year's Day Caviar 8
Party Salmon Ball 25
Pat's Pâté 17
Pesto and Sun-Dried
    Tomato Torte 11
Shrimp Mould 23
Shrimp Spread 24
Trio Pesto Goat Cheese
    Cake 10
Warm Spinach Dip 13
Dixie's "Leekless" Quiche 43
Dolphin Grand Cay 84
Dolphin Safe Pasta 71
Don's Slow Cooked
    Baked Beans 183

E

Easy Chinese Chicken Salad 79
Easy Living Coffee Cake 37
Eggplant
Eggplant with
    Kalamata Olives 177
Whole Baked Eggplant 178

Eggs

Bread and Butter Pudding 214
Chocolate Mousse 211
Eggs Hussarde 39
Frozen Chocolate Crêpes
    with Vanilla Custard
    Sauce 212
Mexican Breakfast
    Casserole 41
Mexican Flan 211
Overnight Egg and
    Sausage Casserole 42
Scrambled Egg Casserole 41
Southern Corn Pudding 180
Emerald Salad 69
Emily's Italian
    Salad Dressing 81
Empanadas
    (Little Meat Pies) 18
Everyday Cookies 228

Fabulous Pecan Pie 217
Feta Stuffed Herbed
    Chicken Breasts 124
Feta-Pesto Stuffed
    Pork Chops 160
Fiesta Tortilla Soup 52
Fish *(also see Shellfish)*
Bacon, Tomato and
    Fish Casserole 89
Baked Asian Fish Packets 93
Basil Marinated Fish 95
White Fish Epicurean 93

  Crawfish
    Bayou Pasta Salad 70

  Dolphin
    Dolphin Grand Cay 84

  Grouper
    Bahamian Grouper 88

Fresh Grilled Grouper Topped
    with a Roma Tomato-Fresh
    Mint Salsa 85
Grouper Chowder 53
Grouper Provolone 86
Pan Seared Grouper,
    Blackening Rub 87
Pecan Grouper 86
Mahi Mahi
Mahi Mahi with Spicy Mango
    Cilantro Sauce 83
Marinated Mahi Mahi 83
Pompano
Nutty Pompano,
    Orange-Passion Fruit Menuière
    92
Salmon
Grilled Salmon with Honey-
    Mustard Sauce 96
Guilt Free Salmon 96
Party Salmon Ball 25
Salmon Fillets Aloha 95
Susie's Scrumptious
    Gingery Grilled
    Salmon Salad 80
Sea Bass
Chilean Sea Bass over Portobello
    Mushroom with a Roasted Red
    Bell Pepper Sauce 94
Snapper
Caribbean Banana
    Snapper 88
Heavenly Fillets 89
Herb Crusted Snapper
    with Roasted Plum
    Tomato Vina 90
Snapper Martinique 91
Tuna
Dolphin Safe Pasta 71
Grilled Tuna with
    Arugula Tomato Salad
    and Garlic 97

Peppercorn Crusted Tuna
with Orange BBQ Glaze
with Jerked Shallots and
Jicama Cake 98
Tuna Angel Hair Pasta 99
Fred's Meatloaf 154
Fresh Asparagus Salad 64
Fresh Fruit Cake 198
Fresh Grilled Grouper Topped
with a Roma Tomato-Fresh
Mint Salsa 85
Fresh Mushroom
Chicken Soup 51
Fresh Tomato Pizza
with Sausage 163
Fresh Tomato Sauce
for Pasta 117
Frogmore Stew 104
Frosting Cake 206
Frozen Chocolate Crêpes
with Vanilla Custard
Sauce 212
Frozen Key Lime Pie 220
Fruit and Almond Salad
with Curry Vinaigrette
Dressing 61
Fruit Cobbler 227
Fusilli with Broccoli,
Sicilian Style 119

G

Game Hens
Grilled Raspberry
Game Hens 141
Garlicky Chicken 122
Goat Cheese Salad
with Warm Dressing 57
Grains and Cereals
Everyday Cookies 228
Granola 38
Moroccan Chicken 129
Neiman Marcus' $250
Chocolate Chip Cookies 228

Oatmeal Sunflower
Seed Bread 35
Southern Cheese Grits 40
Granny Shear's
1-2-3-4 Pound Cake 203
Granola 38
Grapes
Chicken Salad 77
Fruit and Almond Salad
with Curry Vinaigrette
Dressing 61
Smoked Turkey Salad 79
Summer Salad 60
Gratin of
Cherry Tomatoes 182
Greek Salad,
Layered 66
Green Bean and
Mozzarella Salad 64
Grilled Chicken Breast
with Pineapple Salsa 134
Grilled Fillet of Beef 142
Grilled Portobello
Mushrooms 183
Grilled Raspberry
Game Hens 141
Grilled Salmon with
Honey-Mustard Sauce 96
Grilled Shrimp Salad with
Balsamic Vinaigrette
and Corn Salsa 81
Grilled Texas Shrimp 21
Grilled Tuna with
Arugula Tomato Salad
and Garlic 97
Grits
Pan Seared Jumbo BBQ Shrimp,
Country Style Grits and
Pineapple Salsa 105
Southern Cheese Grits 40
Grouper Chowder 53
Grouper Provolone 86
Guilt Free Salmon 96
Gus' BarBQ Sauce 249

H

Hearts of Palm Salad 55
Hearty Tortilla Soup 53
Heavenly Fillets 89
Herb Crusted Snapper
   with Roasted Plum
   Tomato Vinaigrette 90
Herbed Pork Roast 163
Hershey Pie 226
Holiday Fruit Drops 233
Holiday Sweet Potatoes 186
Horseradish Meatloaf 152
Horseradish Mold 247
Horseradish
   Mustard Sauce 247
Horseradish Sauce 247
Hot Chili Dip 18
Hot Crab and
   Artichoke Dip 29
Hot or Cold Spinach Soup 45
Hot Pecan Spread 16

I

Italian Scallops 102

J

Jake's Blackened Lobster Tails
   with Spinach Fettuccine
   with Tomato-Basil Cream
   Sauce 108
Jalapeño Cheese Squares 9
Jalapeño Cornbread 32
Jambalaya 162
Jane's Balsamic Vinaigrette 80
Jane's Corn Salsa 253
Jane's Marinade for Chicken,
   Pork or Shrimp 245
Jicama Cakes 98
Jordan Pond House Popovers 31

Judie's "Potpourri" 254
Julie's Killer Brownies 237

K

Kelly's Veggie
   Enchilada Casserole 111
Kentucky Pecan Pie 225
Key Limes
   Frozen Key Lime Pie 220
   Key Lime Bread
      with Blueberries 36
   Key Lime Mousse Tart 220
   Pat's Florida
      Key Lime Pie 222
   Sasha's Key Lime Pie 221
King Crab Puffs 27

L

Lamb
   Curried Lamb with Cashews . . . 168
   Fred's Meatloaf 154
   Lamb Chops with
      Caper Sauce 167
   Leg of Lamb 166
   Perfect Roast Leg of Lamb 167
Layered Greek Salad 66
Leeks
   Cheesy Broccoli Bisque 45
   Fusilli with Broccoli,
      Sicilian Style 119
Lemon Aïoli for Crab Cakes 250
Lemon Bars Deluxe 237
Lemon Chicken
   with Cashews 137
Lentil-Rice Burgers 113
Lite Angel Food Torte 201
Low-Fat Chocolate Torte 197
Lucy's Marinated Carrots 174

M

Macadamia Fudge Torte 196
Macadamia Nut Bars 236
Mahi Mahi with Spicy Mango Cilantro
    Sauce 83
Mandarin Orange Cake 200
Mandarin Orange Salad 60

Mango
  Pam's Black Bean and
    Mango Salsa 253
Marchands De Vin 251

Marinades
  Jane's Marinade for Chicken,
    Pork or Shrimp 245
  Marinades 76, 141
  Ruth Ann's Walkers Cay
    Fish Marinade 245
  Smoked Turkey
    Marinade 246
  Turkey Injection
    Marinade 246
Marinated Goat Cheese 12
Marinated Grilled Shrimp 20
Marinated Mahi Mahi 83
Martha's Vineyard Salad 71
Maryland Jumbo Lump
    Crab Cakes 110
Mexican Breakfast
    Casserole 41
Mexican Flan 211
Mexican Lasagna 150
Mexican-Style Fresh Salsa 252
Miami Chicken Wings 19

Microwave Recipes
  Dill Chicken Salad 75
  Fresh Asparagus Salad 64
  Hot Chili Dip 18
Mike Szary's Black Beans
    and Rice 133
Minced Lobster 106
Mini Beef Wellingtons 17
Mint Onion Sauce for Lamb 248
Minted Pea Soup 46

Miracle Cake 204
Mom's Onion Shortcake 179
Mom's Shrimp Casserole
    Au Gratin 103
Mont Blanc Chicken Spread 20
Moroccan Chicken 129
Moroccan Orange Salad 59

Mushrooms
  Artichoke and Mushroom
    Chicken 130
  Beef Bourguignonne 149
  Bow Tie Pasta Salad 70
  Broccoli Soufflé
    with Almonds 170
  Burgundy Stew 150
  Cheesy Broccoli Bisque 45
  Chicken and Linguine 138
  Chicken and Rice Bake 134
  Chicken Livers Fabuloso 140
  Chicken Mushroom
    in Puff Pastry Shells 135
  Chilean Sea Bass over
    Portobella Mushroom
    with a Roasted Red Bell
    Pepper Sauce 94
  Grilled
    Portobello Mushrooms 183
  Grouper Provolone 86
  Italian Scallops 102
  Layered Greek Salad 66
  Mushrooms à la Russe 15
  Mushrooms in Patty Shells 15
  Opulent Chicken 125
  Pickled Shrimp
    and Mushrooms 22
  Portobello Mushroom Salad . . . 67
  Rigatoni con Zucchini 116
  Shrimp Victoria 104
  Spaghetti Carbonara 164
  Spinach Stuffed
    Chicken Breasts 123

Straw and Hay Pasta 166
Turkey Casserole 138
Veal Escalopes
 with Spinach 156
Mustard Sauce 248
Mustard Sauce
 for Crab Claws 249

N

Nantucket Cassoulet 127
Napa Salad 69
Neiman Marcus' $250
 Chocolate Chip Cookies 228
New Year's Day Caviar 8
Noodles and Sauerkraut 192
North African Roast Chicken
 Thighs with Raisins, Almonds and
 Apricots 126
North Carolina Tomato Pie 181

Nuts
Granola 38
Julie's Killer Brownies 237
Magnificent Brownies 236
Neiman Marcus' $250
 Chocolate Chip Cookies 228
Nutty Pompano, Orange-
 Passion Fruit Menuière 92
Old Fashion Prune Cake 205

Almonds
Apple Stuffed
 Chicken Breast 132
Broccoli Soufflé
 with Almonds 170
Chicken Salad 77
Chinese Chicken Salad
 with Noodles 75
Chutney Chicken Salad 78
Coconut-Almond
 Macaroons 230
Crustless Pear Tart 223

Fruit and Almond Salad
 with Curry Vinaigrette
 Dressing 61
Mandarin Orange Salad 60
North African Roast Chicken
 Thighs with Raisins,
 Almonds and Apricots 126
Picadillo 153
Warm Spinach-Orange
 Salad 58

Cashews
Curried Lamb
 with Cashews 168
Lemon Chicken
 with Cashews 137

Hazelnuts
Sonoma Salad 73

Macadamia Nuts
Macadamia Fudge Torte ... 196
Macadamia Nut Bars 236
Mahi Mahi with Spicy
 Mango Cilantro Sauce 83

Peanuts
Popcorn Cake 203

Pecans
Baked Nuts 7
Banana Nut Bread 34
Butter Crunch Candy 240
Butter Snowballs 231
Chocolate Pecan Pie 218
Cranberry Salad 68
Fabulous Pecan Pie 217
Frosting Cake 206
Green Beans
 with Pecans 172
Holiday Sweet Potatoes 186
Hot Pecan Spread 16
Kentucky Pecan Pie 225
Orange Salad Bowl 59
Pecan Dainties 239
Pecan Grouper 86
Red Velvet Cake 193

Salted Pecans 8
Sour Cream Coffee Cake 38
Southern Pecan Encrusted
   Chicken with a Warm
   Berry Sauce 121
Special Chocolate Chip
   Cookies 229
St. Bart's Salad 56
Summer Salad 60
Texas Sheet Cake 239
Turtle Pecan
   Cheesecake 209
Zucchini Pineapple Bread 35

Pine Nuts
Angel Hair Pasta with
   Lemon and Pine Nuts 113
Classic Creamy Risotto 188
Goat Cheese Salad with
   Warm Dressing 57
Martha's Vineyard Salad 71
Trio Pesto Goat
   Cheese Cake 10

Walnuts
Baked Nuts 7
Caroline's Brownies 238
Cheech's Basil Pesto 251
Fresh Fruit Cake 198
Holiday Fruit Drops 233
Mont Blanc
   Chicken Spread 20
Moroccan Orange Salad 59
Out Of This World
   Fruitcake 199
Overnight Meringues 233
Sue's Hermit Cookies 232
Walnut and Goat Cheese
   Salad with Raspberry
   Dressing 54

O

Oatmeal Sunflower
   Seed Bread 35

Old English Cheese
   Hors d'oeuvres 7
Olive Spread on Crostini 14
Onions
Creamy Five Onion Soup 49
Mint Onion Sauce
   for Lamb 248
Mom's Onion Shortcake 179
Onion Rings 177
Rice and Onion Casserole 191
Opulent Chicken 125
Oranges
Fresh Fruit Cake 198
Fruit and Almond Salad
   with Curry Vinaigrette
   Dressing 61
Lite Angel Food Torte 201
Mandarin Orange Cake 200
Mandarin Orange Salad 60
Moroccan Orange Salad 59
Orange BBQ Glaze 98
Orange Salad Bowl 59
Sissy's Orange-Cream
   Fruit Salad 63
Warm Spinach-Orange
   Salad 58
Oriental Rice 189
Overnight Egg
   and Sausage Casserole 42
Overnight Meringues 233

P

Paella Salad 74
Pam's Black Bean and
   Mango Salsa 253
Pam's Oriental Chicken Salad 76
Pan Seared Grouper,
   Blackening Rub 87
Pan Seared Jumbo BBQ
   Shrimp, Country Style
   Grits and Pineapple Salsa . . . 105
Parmesan Spinach Balls 14

INDEX

Parslied Cherry Tomatoes
    with Garlic 66
Party Salmon Ball 25
Pasta
  Angel Hair Commotion 106
  Angel Hair Pasta with
    Lemon and Pine Nuts 113
  Angel Hair with
    Puttanesca Sauce 115
  Baked Orzo 187
  Baked Squid with
    Garlic Anchovy Pasta 109
  Bayou Pasta Salad 70
  Bow Tie Pasta Salad 70
  Capellini with Veal
    and Tomatoes 155
  Cheesey Rigatoni 192
  Chicken and Linguine 138
  Chicken Linguine with
    Sun-Dried Tomatoes
    and Olives 139
  Dolphin Safe Pasta 71
  Fresh Mushroom
    Chicken Soup 51
    Fresh Tomato Sauce
      for Pasta 117
  Hearty Tortilla Soup 53
  Jake's Blackened Lobster Tails with
    Spinach Fettuccine
    with Tomato-Basil
    Cream Sauce 108
  Noodles and Sauerkraut 192
  Pam's Oriental
    Chicken Salad 76
  Penne with Sun-Dried
    Tomato Sauce 118
  Quick and Easy Macaroni
    and Cheese 191
  Rigatoni à la Vodka 117
  Rigatoni con Zucchini 116
  Rigatoni with Lemon
    Cream Sauce 115
  Shrimp and Lobster
    Linguine 102

  Shrimp Cristoforo 100
  Shrimp Scampi 101
  Spaghetti Carbonara 164
  Straw and Hay Pasta 166
  Tuna Angel Hair Pasta 99
Pat's Florida Key Lime Pie 222
Pat's Pâté 17
Peaches
  Sissy's Orange-Cream
    Fruit Salad 63
  Speedy Peach Ice Cream 241
  Summer Fruit "Tart" 217
Peanut Butter Bars 238
Peanut Butter Cookies 230
Peanut Butter Fudge 240
Pears
  Crustless Pear Tart 223
Pecan Dainties 239
Pecan Grouper 86
Penne with Sun-Dried
    Tomato Sauce 118
Peppercorn Crusted Tuna
    with Orange BBQ Glaze
    with Jerked Shallots and
    Jicama Cake 98
Peppery Cheese Bread 33
Perfect Roast Chicken 120
Pesto and Sun-Dried
    Tomato Torte 11
Picadillo 153
Pickled Shrimp 21
Pickled Shrimp
    and Mushrooms 22
Pies *(also see Cakes, Candy, Chocolate, Cookies and Bars, and Desserts)*
  Calamondin Pie 224
  Caramel-Coconut Pie 216
  Chocolate Peanut Butter Pie . . . 219
  Chocolate Pecan Pie 218
  Chocolate Silk Pie 225
  Fabulous Pecan Pie 217
  Frozen Key Lime Pie 220

Hershey Pie 226
Kentucky Pecan Pie 225
Pat's Florida Key Lime Pie 222
Pumpkin Ice Cream Pie 218
Robin's Blue Ribbon
    Apple Pie 222
Sasha's Key Lime Pie 221
Strawberry Pie 224
Piña Colada Fruit Dip 242

Pineapple
Banana Split Cake 199
Chicken Salad 77
Grilled Chicken Breast with
    Pineapple Salsa 134
Lite Angel Food Torte 201
Mandarin Orange Cake 200
Pan Seared Jumbo BBQ Shrimp,
    Country Style Grits and
    Pineapple Salsa 105
Piña Colada Fruit Dip 242
Salmon Fillets Aloha 95
Sissy's Orange-Cream
    Fruit Salad 63
Snapper Martinique 91
The Best Carrot Cake 202
Zucchini Pineapple Bread 35

Pizza
Fresh Tomato Pizza
    with Sausage 163
Pizza Bianco 114

Plums
Almond Cake with
    Plum Compote 206
Popcorn Cake 203
Poppy Seed Dressing 82

Pork

Bacon
Bacon, Tomato and Fish
    Casserole 89
Broccoli Salad 67
Chicken Livers Fabuloso . . . 140
Chutney Chicken Salad 78

Don's Slow Cooked
    Baked Beans 183
Scrambled Egg Casserole 41
Spaghetti Carbonara 164
Spinach Salad with
    Mimosa Dressing 58
Texas Potato Salad 61
Zucchini with Bacon 173

Ground Pork
Thai Pot Stickers 30

Loin
Angry Pork Tenderloin 161
Herbed Pork Roast 163
Pork St. Hubert 162

Pork Chops
Feta-Pesto Stuffed
    Pork Chops 160
Pork Chop Potato Bake 161

Roast
Herbed Pork Roast 163

Sausage
Bayou Pasta Salad 70
Black Bean Soup 47
Chicken French
    Country Style 122

Empanadas
    (Little Meat Pies) 18
Fresh Tomato Pizza
    with Sausage 163
Frogmore Stew 104
Jambalaya 162
Mexican Breakfast
    Casserole 41
Nantucket Cassoulet 127
Overnight Egg and
    Sausage Casserole 42
Pat's Pâté 17
Quick Cassoulet 128
Sausage-Spinach Soufflé 165
Portobello Mushroom Salad 67

Potato Chip Cookies 229

Potatoes
Beef Bourguignonne 149
Broque Potatoes 186
Conch Chowder 54
Cottage Potatoes 185
Frogmore Stew 104
Grouper Chowder 53
Pork Chop Potato Bake 161
Potato Salad 62
Roquefort Potato Gratin 184
Southwest Potato
    Casserole 185
Texas Potato Salad 61
Virginia's Holiday
    Mashed Potatoes 187
Prime Rib with Roasted Garlic
    and Horseradish Crust 146

Prunes
Old Fashion Prune Cake 205

Pumpkin
Pumpkin Coffee Cake 39
Pumpkin Delight 216
Pumpkin Ice Cream Pie 218
Pumpkin Ring 40

Q

Quiches
Crustless Spinach Quiche 44
Dixie's "Leekless" Quiche 43
Quick and Easy Macaroni
    and Cheese 191
Quick Cassoulet 128

R

Radishes
Moroccan Orange Salad 59

Raisins
Bread Pudding 213
Fresh Fruit Cake 198

Raisin Bread 33
Sue's Hermit Cookies 232
Summer Salad 60

Raspberries
Grilled Raspberry
    Game Hens 141
Martha's Vineyard Salad 71
Raspberry
    Chocolate Sauce 243

Recipes for Large Groups
Banana Nut Bread 34
Bayou Pasta Salad 70
Cocktail Meatballs 16
Creamy Five Onion Soup 49
Fred's Meatloaf 154
New Year's Day Caviar 8
Pat's Pâté 17
Shrimp Pesto Canapés 24
Texas Five Alarm Chili 55
Tomato Basil Soup 48
Red Velvet Cake 193
Ribbon Jello Mold 68

Rice
Bahamian Pigeon Peas
    and Rice 188
Basmati Rice with Dried
    Fruits and Nuts 189
Broccoli and Rice Casserole 170
Chicken and Rice Bake 134
Chicken Stir-Fry 131
Classic Creamy Risotto 188
Coconut Rice 190
Lentil-Rice Burgers 113
Mike Szary's Black Beans
    and Rice 133
Mom's Shrimp Casserole
    Au Gratin 103
Oriental Rice 189
Rice and Onion Casserole 191
Shrimp Victoria 104
Spiced Rice 190
Stuffed Cabbage 151
Swiss Chicken Bake 131

Rigatoni à la Vodka 117
Rigatoni con Zucchini 116
Rigatoni with
  Lemon Cream Sauce 115
Roasted Tomatoes 182
Robert Frost Popovers 31
Robin's Blue Ribbon
  Apple Pie 222
Roquefort Potato Gratin 184
Ruth Ann's Walkers Cay Fish
  Marinade 245

S

Sabana (Beef
  Tenderloin Mexicana) 145
Salads
Broccoli Salad 67
Chilled Artichoke Hearts
  and Peas 56

Congealed Salads
  Cranberry Salad 68
  Emerald Salad 69
  Horseradish Mold 247
  Ribbon Jello Mold 68
Cucumber Salad 65
Fresh Asparagus Salad 64
Fruit and Almond Salad
  with Curry Vinaigrette
  Dressing 61

Fruit Salads
  Sissy's Orange-Cream Fruit Salad
  63
  Summer Salad 60
  Goat Cheese Salad with
  Warm Dressing 57
Green Bean and
  Mozzarella Salad 64
Grilled Tuna with Arugula
  Tomato Salad and Garlic . . . 97
Hearts of Palm Salad 55
Layered Greek Salad 66

Main Course Salads
Chicken Salad 77
Chinese Chicken Salad
  with Noodles 75
Chutney Chicken Salad 78
Dill Chicken Salad 75
Easy Chinese
  Chicken Salad 79
Grilled Shrimp Salad with
  Balsamic Vinaigrette and Corn
  Salsa 81
Smoked Turkey Salad 79
Susie's Scrumptious Gingery
  Grilled Salmon Salad 80
Mandarin Orange Salad 60
Marinated Cucumber Salad 65
Martha's Vineyard Salad 71
Moroccan Orange Salad 59
Napa Salad 69
Orange Salad Bowl 59
Paella Salad 74
Pam's Oriental
  Chicken Salad 76
Parslied Cherry Tomatoes
  with Garlic 66

Pasta Salads
  Bayou Pasta Salad 70
  Bow Tie Pasta Salad 70
Portobello Mushroom Salad 67
Potato Salad 62

Salad Dressings
  Blue Cheese Dressing 82
  Celery Seed Dressing 59
  Dressings 60, 61, 63, 65,
            66, 69, 75, 77, 78
  Emily's Italian
  Salad Dressing 81
  Jane's Balsamic
  Vinaigrette 80
  Lemon-Scented
  Vinaigrette 72
  Mimosa Dressing 58
  Poppy Seed Dressing 82

Raspberry Vinegar 71
Raspberry-Maple
    Dressing 71
Sauerkraut Salad 62
Sonoma Salad 73
Spinach Salad with Mimosa
    Dressing 58
Spinach-Strawberry Salad 57
St. Bart's Salad 56
Steak Salad 72
Strawberry Salad 63
Texas Potato Salad 61
Walnut and Goat Cheese Salad
    with Raspberry Dressing 54
Warm Spinach-Orange Salad 58
Watercress and
    Pickled Ginger Salad 80
Salmon Fillets Aloha 95
Salted Pecans 8
San Francisco Scampi 99
Sasha's Key Lime Pie 221

Sauces and Seasonings (also see
Condiments and Relishes, and Marinades)
Baltimore Tartar Sauce 248
Béchamel Sauce 164
Black Cherry Sauce 243
Blackening Rub 87
Blender Pesto Sauce 252
Creamy Peanut Sauce 76
Fresh Tomato Sauce
    for Pasta 117
Grand Marnier Sauce 242
Gus' BarBQ Sauce 249
Horseradish
    Mustard Sauce 247
Horseradish Sauce 247
Mint Onion Sauce for Lamb 248
Mustard Sauce 248
Mustard Sauce
    for Crab Claws 249
Orange Basting Sauce 167
Orange BBQ Glaze 98

Pineapple Salsa 105
Raspberry
    Chocolate Sauce 243
Rub 160
Sauerkraut
Noodles and Sauerkraut 192
Sauerkraut and Apples 179
Sauerkraut Salad 62
Sausage-Spinach Soufflé 165
Savory Roast Fillet of Beef 142
Scrambled Egg Casserole 41
Shellfish (also see Fish)
    Clams
    Clams Oreganatta 26
    Conch
    Conch Chowder 54
    Conch Fritter 25
    Crabmeat
    Angel Hair Commotion 106
    Artichoke Crab Spread 29
    Baked Crock of Artichoke, Brie
        and Lump Crab 28
    Bayou Pasta Salad 70
    Chilean Sea Bass over Portobella
        Mushroom with a Roasted Red
        Bell Pepper Sauce 94
    Crab Dip 26
    Crabmeat Quarters 27
    Hot Crab and
        Artichoke Dip 29
    King Crab Puffs 27
    Maryland Jumbo Lump
        Crab Cakes 110
    Paella Salad 74
    Twisted Crab Cakes 110
    Lobster
    Florida Lobster Pot Pie 107
    Jake's Blackened Lobster
        Tails with Spinach
        Fettuccine with Tomato-
        Basil Cream Sauce 108

Minced Lobster 106
Shrimp and
    Lobster Linguine 102

Mussels
Paella Salad 74

Scallops
Bay Scallop Ceviche 24
Italian Scallops 102

Shrimp
Frogmore Stew 104
Grilled Shrimp Salad with
    Balsamic Vinaigrette and Corn
    Salsa 81
Grilled Texas Shrimp 21
Jambalaya 162
Marinated Grilled Shrimp 20
Mom's Shrimp Casserole
    Au Gratin 103
Paella Salad 74
Pan Seared Jumbo BBQ
    Shrimp, Country Style
    Grits and Pineapple
    Salsa 105
Pickled Shrimp 21
Pickled Shrimp and
    Mushrooms 22
San Francisco Scampi 99
Shrimp and Lobster
    Linguine 102
Shrimp Bread 23
Shrimp Cristoforo 100
Shrimp Mould 23
Shrimp Pesto Canapés 24
Shrimp Scampi 101
Shrimp Snacks 22
Shrimp Spread 24
Shrimp Victoria 104

Squid
Baked Squid with Garlic Anchovy
    Pasta 109
Sherry Mayonnaise 250

Shrimp and Lobster
    Linguine 102
Shrimp Bread 23
Shrimp Cristoforo 100
Shrimp Mould 23
Shrimp Pesto Canapés 24
Shrimp Scampi 101
Shrimp Snacks 22
Shrimp Spread 24
Shrimp Victoria 104
Sinful Chocolate Cake 194
Sissy's Orange-Cream
    Fruit Salad 63
Smoked Turkey Marinade 246
Smoked Turkey Salad 79
Snapper Martinique 91

Snow Peas
Lemon Chicken
    with Cashews 137
Pam's Oriental
    Chicken Salad 76
Sonoma Salad 73

Soups, Stews and Chowders
(also see Chili)
Baby Carrot Soup 46
Black Bean Soup 47
Burgundy Stew 150
California Gazpacho 51
Cheesy Broccoli Bisque 45
Chilled Mint-Cucumber
    Yogurt Soup 50
Cold Cucumber Soup 50
Conch Chowder 54
Creamy Five Onion Soup 49
Fiesta Tortilla Soup 52
Fresh Mushroom
    Chicken Soup 51
Frogmore Stew 104
Grouper Chowder 53
Hearty Tortilla Soup 53
Hot or Cold
    Spinach Soup 45

Minted Pea Soup 46
So Easy Tomato Soup 48
Strawberry Soup 49
Texas Five Alarm Chili 55
Tomato Basil Soup 48
Sour Cream Coffee Cake 38
Southern Cheese Grits 40
Southern Corn Pudding 180
Southern Pecan Encrusted
    Chicken with a Warm
    Berry Sauce 121
Southwest Potato Casserole 185
Spaghetti Carbonara 164
Spaghetti Squash Florentine 173
Spiced Rice 190
Spicy Chicken Quesadillas 19

Spinach
Cheech's Basil Pesto 251
Crustless Spinach Quiche 44
Fruit and Almond Salad
    with Curry
    Vinaigrette Dressing 61
Hot or Cold Spinach Soup 45
Jake's Blackened Lobster
    Tails with Spinach
    Fettuccine with Tomato-
    Basil Cream Sauce 108
Moroccan Orange Salad 59
Parmesan Spinach Balls 14
Sausage-Spinach Soufflé 165
Spaghetti Squash
    Florentine 173
Spinach Salad with Mimosa
    Dressing 58
Spinach Soufflé 171
Spinach Stuffed
    Chicken Breasts 123
Spinach-Strawberry Salad 57
Veal Escalopes
    with Spinach 156
Warm Spinach Dip 13
Warm Spinach-
    Orange Salad 58

Squash *(also see Zucchini)*
Cheesy Summer Squash 175
Posh Squash 176
Spaghetti Squash
    Florentine 173
Squash Pie 175
St. Bart's Salad 56
Steak Diane 147
Steak Fajitas 148
Steak Salad 72
Straw and Hay Pasta 166

Strawberries
Banana Split Cake 199
Spinach-Strawberry Salad 57
Strawberry Pie 224
Strawberry Salad 63
Strawberry Soup 49
Stuffed Cabbage 151
Sue's Hermit Cookies 232
Summer Fruit "Tart" 217
Summer Salad 60
Susie's Scrumptious Gingery
    Grilled Salmon Salad 80

Sweet Potatoes
Holiday Sweet Potatoes 186
North African Roast Chicken Thighs
    with Raisins, Almonds and
    Apricots 126
Swiss Chicken Bake 131
Swiss Vegetable Medley 174

T

Temptation Appetizers 9
Texas Five Alarm Chili 55
Texas Potato Salad 61
Texas Sheet Cake 239
Texas Stir-Fry 130
Thai Pot Stickers 30
Three-Ginger Gingerbread 200

Tomatoes
Angel Hair with
 Puttanesca Sauce 115
Bacon, Tomato and Fish
 Casserole 89
Bow Tie Pasta Salad 70
Brie with Sun-Dried
 Tomatoes 12
Burgundy Stew 150
Capellini with Veal
 and Tomatoes 155
Chicken Cacciatore 121
Chicken Linguine with
 Sun-Dried Tomatoes
 and Olives 139
Chicken Louisa 132
Conch Chowder 54
Dolphin Safe Pasta 71
Fiesta Tortilla Soup 52
Fresh Grilled Grouper
 Topped with a Roma
 Tomato-Fresh Mint Salsa 85
Fresh Tomato Pizza
 with Sausage 163
Fresh Tomato Sauce
 for Pasta 117
Fusilli with Broccoli,
 Sicilian Style 119
Gratin of
 Cherry Tomatoes 182
Green Bean and
 Mozzarella Salad 64
Grilled Tuna with Arugula
 Tomato Salad and Garlic 97
Hearty Tortilla Soup 53
Herb Crusted Snapper
 with Roasted Plum Tomato
 Vinaigrette 90

Jake's Blackened Lobster
 Tails with Spinach
 Fettuccine with Tomato-
 Basil Cream Sauce 108
Jambalaya 162
Mexican-Style Fresh Salsa 252
Nantucket Cassoulet 127
North Carolina Tomato Pie 181
Parslied Cherry Tomatoes
 with Garlic 66
Penne with Sun-Dried
 Tomato Sauce 118
Pesto and Sun-Dried
 Tomato Torte 11
Quick Cassoulet 128
Rigatoni à la Vodka 117
Roasted Tomatoes 182
Shrimp Scampi 101
Texas Five Alarm Chili 55
Texas Stir-Fry 130
Tomato Basil Soup 48
Veal Escalopes with
 Tomato Basil Sauce 157
Top Round Steak with
 Jalapeño Marinade 147
Tournedos of Beef
 Tenderloin Roquefort 143
Trio Pesto Goat Cheese Cake 10
Tuna Angel Hair Pasta 99
Turkey (also see Chicken)
Smoked Turkey Salad 79
Turkey Casserole 138
Turkey Injection Marinade 246
Turkey Meatloaf 139
Turtle Pecan Cheesecake 209

V

Veal
Beef Wellington 144

INDEX

Braised Veal Shanks (Osso Buco)
with White Wine, Butter and
Lemon Sauce 158
Capellini with Veal
and Tomatoes 155
Dijon Veal 156
Fred's Meatloaf 154
Thai Pot Stickers 30
Veal Chop Sicilian 159
Veal Escalopes
with Spinach 156
Veal Escalopes with
Tomato Basil Sauce 157
Veal Piccata 157
Veal Stew 159
Vegetable Casserole 176
Virginia's Holiday
Mashed Potatoes 187

W

Walnut and Goat Cheese Salad
with Raspberry Dressing 54
Warm Spinach Dip 13
Watercress and Pickled
Ginger Salad 80
White Chocolate Cheesecake 207
White Fish Epicurean 93
Winner's Chocolate Cake 195

Z

Zucchini *(also see Squash)*
Hearty Tortilla Soup 53
Rigatoni con Zucchini 116
Zucchini Pineapple Bread 35
Zucchini Stuffed with
Corn and Cheese 172
Zucchini with Bacon 173

Hibiscus Children's Center

P.O. Box 305
Jensen Beach, Florida 34958
(561) 334-9311 Office
(561) 334-1991 Fax

Please send me _____ copies of
Treasures of the Tropics   @ $19.95 each $ _____

    Florida residents add sales tax   @   1.40 each $ _____

    Postage and handling $ 4.00 ($2.00 each additional book) $ _____

                                   Total: $ _____

Name _____

Address _____

City _____ State _____ Zip _____

Make checks payable to: **Hibiscus Children's Center**

Or include your credit card information as follows: (Circle one) VISA   MasterCard

Card Number _____ Expiration Date _____

Signature of Authorization _____

Hibiscus Children's Center

P.O. Box 305
Jensen Beach, Florida 34958
(561) 334-9311 Office
(561) 334-1991 Fax

Please send me _____ copies of
Treasures of the Tropics   @ $19.95 each $ _____

    Florida residents add sales tax   @   1.40 each $ _____

    Postage and handling $ 4.00 ($2.00 each additional book) $ _____

                                   Total: $ _____

Name _____

Address _____

City _____ State _____ Zip _____

Make checks payable to: **Hibiscus Children's Center**

Or include your credit card information as follows: (Circle one) VISA   MasterCard

Card Number _____ Expiration Date _____

Signature of Authorization _____